DATE DUE

DE ~~6 00~~			
JE ~~6~~ '05			

DEMCO 38-296

Free Trade?

Informal Economies at the U.S.–Mexico Border

Free Trade?

Informal Economies
at the U.S.–Mexico Border

KATHLEEN STAUDT

Temple University Press
Philadelphia

Temple University Press, Philadelphia 19122
Copyright © 1998 by Temple University. All rights reserved
Published 1998
Printed in the United States of America

♾ The paper used in this book meets the requirements of the
American National Standard for Information Sciences—
Permanence of Paper for Printed Library Materials, ANSI
Z39.48-1984

Text design by Erin Kirk New

Library of Congress Cataloging-in-Publication Data

Staudt, Kathleen A.
    Free trade? : informal economies at the U.S.-Mexico border /
Kathleen Staudt.
        p.   cm.
    Includes bibliographical references and index.
    ISBN 1-56639-567-4 (cl : alk. paper). — ISBN 1-56639-568-2
(pb : alk. paper)
    1. Informal sector (Economics)—Mexican-American Border
Region.   2. Industries—Mexico, North.   3. Industries—Texas.
I. Title.
HD2346.U52M497   1998
338.0972'1—DC21   97-12414

Contents

Illustrations

Tables

Photographs follow page 90
Neighborhood businesses on a paved street just outside an
    unpaved *colonia* (Juárez)
Political identifications on Juárez homes
A home-based business in Juárez
Home building, *poco a poco* in El Paso County
A vegetable vendor in El Paso County
Semifixed stalls in a public market in Juárez
The NSF-supported researchers in the Franklin Mountains
An *FBI* ("Fun But Illegal") tag on a campaign sign (El Paso)
Sex-typing in some maquiladora job recruitment advertisements
Prominent officials at Seeds Across the Border conference, Juárez,
    October 1995

Preface and Acknowledgments

Acknowledgments usually begin with people and institutions. This one is different. I feel a profound sense of gratitude and satisfaction about a *place*. That place is the international border that joins Mexico and the United States.

Shall I start with the stark beauty of the place? The landscape is open, high desert with breathtaking mountains, horizons, and sunshine. My t-shirt from the Juárez astronomical society says on the sleeve: "Escuchando la voz del infinito": "listening for the voice of infinity." Does the high desert bring out this quest?

More than the aesthetic quality of the place is the everyday opportunity for insight that comes with borders. Borderlands are the frontlines of global change. I have become convinced that the U.S.–Mexico border foreshadows the future in the heartlands.

Although trained as a political scientist, I have more than once declared myself to be a closet anthropologist. Fortunately for me, during the 1970s the University of Wisconsin offered its graduate students a critical mass of specialists in comparative politics (and many comparativists are anthropologists in disguise). Comparativists believe in immersive field research, wherein the study of politics is augmented with language, literature, and sustained contact with people.

Nearly two decades of life and work at the border have given me ample opportunity to be "in the field," to observe and collect data at some analytic distance, *and* to experience some of what was studied as well. My family and I live in an unplanned settlement, and the big black dots of the U.S. General Accounting Office map (see Map 3) identify the neighborhood as a *colonia*. My husband, Robert Dane'el, designed and built this home with his own artistic, design, and construction skills.

Each day, on my way to and from work, I pass through this unincorporated town that embraces my post office and school district, a place where many migrants have settled. On one side I see a drive-through store named Zacatecas, after a state to the south from which many residents have come. The vegetable vendor has a big painted sign on his semifixed street location: "Acepta aqui la tarjeta Lone Star," proclaiming the acceptability of the Texas Lone Star food stamp cards. The man who weighs aluminum cans confides his vigilance: "Tiene tierra," he says about the cans with an inch of dirt in them to add weight. Each Saturday, a vacant lot swells into a giant flea market. Presenting myself to the owners as a possible vendor, I ask if I need a permit; they reassure me, "Don't worry; no one asks." Where my children, Mosi and Asha, go to elementary school, *las paletas con chile y limón* (suckers with chile and lemon) are among the hottest items sold to kids; those who cross to Juárez resell them to friends.

Borders here cut across lots of space: international, state, city, county, school district. People get upset about those who "prove" a New Mexico residence to avoid the extra cost of Texas license plates. They get even angrier about New Mexican nonresident and Mexican resident kids who attend schools in this property-tax-driven school district, but at least the Mexican residents pay property tax, either directly or through their rent.

But so much for life and work. It takes lots more—especially time, commitment, and resources—to transform observation and experience into field research. I have many to thank for assistance on that score. In 1991 the Center for Inter-American and Border Studies at the University of Texas at El Paso supported a conference that officially initiated this work; we brought together scholars from the University of California at San Diego, Carleton University, the University of Iowa, and the Universidad Autónoma de Ciudad Juárez: Maxwell Cameron, Florence Babb, and Rubén Lau Rojo. Back then, my good friend and colleague Beatriz Vera began hauling over large bags of newspapers from Juárez, including *Diario de Juárez* and, later, *Norte de Ciudad Juárez*, which I perused daily for the next five years, tracking the changing political climate in Juárez and the city's high-visibility issues: housing, popular/partisan organizations, and jobs.

In 1991, the Ford Foundation, through PROFMEX, provided small but flexible sums to generate data from samples of specific "informal" workers. Equally important, Ford's vision brought together researchers and practitioners to discuss the policy implications of these data. Later that year, with assistance from sociologist Cheryl Howard, a proposal was made to the National Science Foundation

(NSF), primarily to fund students to assist with a labor-intensive effort to generate data from a large, random sample of households on both sides of the border.

Thanks to the NSF (HRD #9253027), several colleagues collaborated in data collection and processing: Cheryl Howard, who managed interviewer training, mapping, and sample selection; political scientist Gregory Rocha, who managed the coding activities; and anthropologist Alejandro Lugo, who helped us all acquire an ethnographic eye. Twelve students, all of them Spanish-speaking, assisted in the sometimes grueling work of tracking down respondents in the hot desert summer of 1992: Luis Aguirre, Magda Alarcón, Irma Carrillo, John Fong, David Garza, Claudia Hernández, Angélica Holguín, Patricia Molina, Margaret Nogales, Lorena Orozco, Sylvia Peregrino, and Jessica Santascoy. Anthropologist Beatriz Vera conducted a number of in-depth interviews with Juárez municipal officials and leaders.

Other colleagues provided advice, inspiration, sample questionnaires, good conversation, and other assistance: Sylvia Chant, Gordon Cook, Sandra McGee-Deutsch, Alonso Pelayo, Bryan Roberts, Richard Simpson, David Spener, Carlos Vélez-Ibañez, Otto Verkoren, Pablo Vila, and William Weaver. Mike Cabral helped me with some of the graphics. Veronica Martínez and Eva Zapata helped with other interviews as well. Peter Ward, keen analyst of Mexican political economy, reminded me that purposive sampling of informals would reap at least as much data as random sampling of households. Conversations with Timothy Shaw elevated my thinking at a crucial juncture in the analysis.

Applying research to practice is a challenge that some comparativists actually avoid. Although we can hardly address all the global forces that help structure reality, to do nothing would be irresponsible. I thank my colleagues at the Mexican Federation of Private Associations for Community Development and Health (FEMAP), for the opportunity to work together and discuss cross-border efforts through Seeds Across the Border. On the Mexico side they are la Presidenta (of FEMAP) Guadalupe de la Vega, Dr. Enrique Suárez, Graciela de la Rosa, and Eduardo González; on the U.S. side they are Helenmarie Zachritz, Kym Hemley, Adair Margo, and Margaret Schellenberg.

Comparativists frequently go half- or one-quarter-way around the world to do research in a specific, limited timeframe. This comparative research was done while I lived at home, for my home is the international border. Physical closeness to, or embeddedness within, the research site creates a kind of immersion and accountability that few comparativists seek or desire. Ultimately, though, that closeness has allowed me to pursue a variety of research methods that build on, validate, and complement one another in comprehensive ways. Readers, enjoy and share in this quest!

CHAPTER I

Introduction
Culture, Politics, and Informal Economies at the U.S.–Mexico Border

The U.S.–Mexico border, once considered the periphery of both countries, is now at the center of global economic change in the late capitalist period. Mexico's Border Industrialization Program of 1965 helped initiate this shift, and the North American Free Trade Agreement (NAFTA) consolidated it. Despite these ostensibly promising formal policy changes, the heart of life at the borderlands involves people in transition: migrant people who, seeking a better life, move toward and across borderlines, as well as people who live within a transition zone.

The Meaning of Borders

We who live at the border have long been inspired by the work of border scholars in core disciplines like history and sociology and in interdisciplinary fields such as environmental studies.[1] Those who founded the Association of Borderlands Scholars (ABS) and the *Journal of Borderlands Studies* have valiantly mined not only the rich U.S.–Mexico border locale, but binational borders elsewhere in the world. Yet their work has not been as visible as it should be: to national heartlands; to the global political economy; and to critics of modern paradigms in anthropology, geography, literature and other

This book could not have been written without research assistance from the following borderlanders and border-crossers: anthropologist Alejandro Lugo, sociologist/demographer Cheryl Howard, political scientist Gregory Rocha, and the social science students named in the Preface, who, thanks to the National Science Foundation, were supported with stipends to conduct interviews and to code the data. They labored outdoors in 100-degree temperatures, usually dry heat, except when rain made mobility virtually impossible over the unpaved neighborhood streets. About half of these Spanish-speaking students resided or studied on both sides of the border for significant parts of their lives.

fields. While borders might be viewed as special and unique, border-land experiences have lots to say to the mainstream and heartlands.

Borders are not just elegant literary metaphors; nor are they merely the territorial lines that separate countries. In this book I conceive of borderlands in ways that speak to a much wider audience. This audience sees borders as new spaces of transformation and reflection, not lines that separate or mark difference. It sees borders in many places, even inside a country's heartland. This audience wonders about ambitious state-driven modernization projects, plans sometimes undone by poverty, by people's resistance, by skewed political participation, or by the planners' own inadequate vision. This audience understands the importance of the everyday lives of people making work and homes for themselves. This audience, further, listens for people's voices through methodical and transparent samples, rather than through official numbers and high-level abstractions about global capital and industrial forces. The highly contentious concept around which this understanding has evolved is *informality,* a concept born in economics but gradually rescued therefrom by a highly eclectic literature.[2] Yet this audience appreciates that informal work and self-help housing occur in context, including contexts of public policies and politics that steer reality in more or less significant ways.

Renato Rosaldo challenges classic definitions of culture and makes central the "zones of difference within and between cultures," at borderlands of all kinds: "sites of creative cultural production that require investigation."[3] Why, he asks, are those with full citizenship deemed uninteresting in cultural terms? What better place to examine criss-crossing borderlands than at an international border, where the lines drawn by nation, gender, ethnicity, formal employment, immigration, citizenship, neighborhood, community, and by public regulations for each nation and for border crossing itself are enforced by multilevel hierarchical bureaucracies?

The pages that follow present the U.S.–Mexico borderlands as counterhegemonic sites. Beneath the veneer of formal rules, political machinery, immigration laws, and gender constructions, people move, work, shelter themselves, and otherwise engage in creative cultural production. But it is a counterhegemony with little *political* recourse—though it has more recourse in Mexico than in the United States. Civil society is much more than that which the state authorizes, but the terms of people's engagement with government set boundaries around policy agendas. Modern government in the United States, along with the aspirant modernism of northern Mexico's opposition party, now in government, uses policy rhetoric that strips informality of its public legitimacy. Organizing around informality is difficult, given people's extensive noncompliance with petty regulations. However, just beneath the surface of state-authorized political engagement and regulation is a complex and rich mosaic. It has the potential, if people operate with openness and trust, to transform political communities.

Research in a Border Economy

This book begins with the working hypothesis that people generate income and develop their housing informally on *both* sides of the U.S.–Mexico border, in sizable, perhaps comparable, numbers. It also assumes that differences of gender, spatial location, and income exist, both across and within social, political, and geographic borderlines. Certainly, we would not be surprised to find sizable amounts of informality for Mexico; its presence has been documented in a rich academic and official literature. But comparable informality would be surprising for the United States. Literature on informality in the United States is narrow and sparse, based on the assumption that informality is either minimal, criminal, or segregated within immigrant and poverty enclaves. I challenge these assumptions.

To measure and document these expectations, I look at three matched neighborhoods in Ciudad Juárez and in El Paso, a combined metropolitan area of two million people. This area is the largest urban area joining the so-called first and third worlds, north and south, or rich and poor countries. As later chapters show, the El Paso–Juárez region has undergone massive economic restructuring. It is also an area of rapid growth, a result of migration from Mexico's interior to its frontier, from the U.S. heartland to its sunbelt, and from Mexico to the United States. It is, finally, an area that shares a Mexican heritage, for 70 percent of El Paso residents are census-defined Hispanics but self-defined largely as Mexican Americans and Mexicanos.

Of the neighborhoods I examine, two are in the core (near the downtown); two are in the old periphery; and two in the new periphery. The neighborhoods also vary in terms of their economic prosperity, with the old peripheries exhibiting middle-income characteristics based on loosely comparable data from the 1990 censuses of both countries. The neighborhood units allow comparisons on the basis of poverty, space, and organization. Map 1 shows the rough location of these neighborhoods in Juárez–El Paso, in the river valley between two mountain ranges that once was called the Paso del Norte ("Pass of the North"), a region examined in Chapter 3.

Where does the information in the following chapters come from? A random sample of 100 households in each neighborhood was chosen, for a total of 600 households. Using a sixteen-page questionnaire (and a four-page supplement for self-employment), interviewers spent approximately an hour and a half talking face to face with members of each household. With a response rate of 77 percent, we in the NSF team collected information on 2,031 individuals in 465 households with 131 informal businesses. I refer to these results as the "householders" or the "household sample."

To comprehend informality more fully, we talked to more than sixty government officials and political leaders; in the text and notes, I refer to them by position. Second, I analyzed census data from both countries, although it should be noted that this "formal" source describes only a veneer of reality. Third, I reviewed newspapers from both cities (*Diario de Juárez*, *Norte de Ciudad Juárez* [Juárez], El Paso *Times*) every day from 1991 through 1995. Fourth, we collected information from particular informal workers, or "informals," such as street vendors and cross-border traders, in smaller, nonrandom samples numbering a hundred or fewer each. These samples are referred to specifically in the text and notes. Finally, I drew on participant observation, from unobtrusive immersion in city council and planning meetings and on streets to active years of service in Seeds Across the Border, a nongovernment cross-border organization that put some of the research findings to use.

This design allowed me to use comparative analysis to explain the extensiveness of informality, the spaces in which it flourishes, its viability, and its connection to various aspects of people's lives. I was particularly interested in the comparative political laboratories: Mexico and the United States, the states of Texas and Chihuahua, and local governments in El Paso City/County and in the Juárez Municipality. The comparative lens provoked several questions. What different macro- and micro-level policies are pursued? How are policies put into practice? How do enforcement strategies touch people in their everyday lives? Can ideologies and policy rhetoric

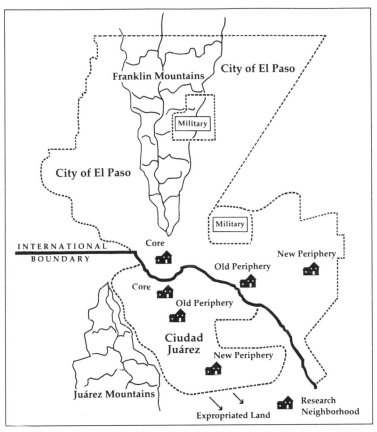

Map 1   El Paso–Juárez (the New Paso del Norte)

legitimize informality and its collective political voice—and, if so, where and for whom? And what consequences does this legitimacy have for informals' work and housing?

Culture is also of interest in this comparative analysis. To borrow Rosaldo's fine metaphors, though, neither Mexican nor U.S. culture is a well-preserved museum; rather, both are more like garage sales.[4] And garage sales are more than an apt metaphor, for some informals make a business out of buying and reselling used goods, even going to *al otro lado* ("the other side," i.e., crossing an international border) to do so. Although Mexican heritage transcends the border, residents on either side exhibit a mixture of cultural characteristics associated with short- versus long-time border residency and with assimilating, resisting, and/or negotiating with the regional and institutional cues that come to be associated with "American" or "Mexican." Subsequent chapters focus more extensively on the recent crossers, particularly those born outside the United States. How much cultural "baggage" is associated with informal labor, self-help housing, negotiated policy enforcement, and collective political voices? Is the real motor for informality the lack of housing and of (formal) jobs paying a realistic wage?

Invariably, people are anxious about the methods used in studies of informality. We collected information from multiple sources through purposive and random samples. In purposefully sampling informals, we talked to people who do not fully comply with regulations, and thus appear on no lists from which to draw random samples. We cast wider, more representative nets with random samples of households, including many households with no obvious informal practices.

But even complementary methods like these do not allow us to generalize about everyone, as the censuses in both countries pretend to do. This book focuses on neighborhoods as units of analysis in both cities, rather than the cities themselves. The neighborhoods represent low- and middle-income residents, rather than wealthy ones; thus the study neither generalizes patterns to whole cities nor includes their minorities of privileged residents.[5]

Concerns about studies like this include the extent to which people will respond honestly to queries if they perceive risk. We in the research team gave considerable attention to questionnaire wording and translation, and tried to get at the different ways people conceive of "informality." There were no questions about drugs, sex, gambling, or other illegal goods and services. Besides the respected guarantees of anonymity, including the decision to keep neighborhood locations anonymous, Spanish-speaking student interviewers—wearing visible identification—distanced this research from the surveillance various government agents sporadically exercise over people at the border (and elsewhere). Our face-to-face interviews probably increased validity, compared with the use of mail-in questionnaires or phone queries.

Interviewers encountered surprising frankness, particularly about documents and income-generation. Invariably, they heard and recorded "don't know" and "hard to say" responses. Prior to the large-scale 1992 sampling, I directed a pilot test on income-generation in every other unit in two U.S. subsidized housing projects. The numbers reported there (in the context of greater risk, given needs-based rental subsidies) convinced me that this study errs on the side of conservatism in documenting informality in one out of every three sampled households.[6]

Deepening Meanings and Explanations

In this book I depart from other border scholars, narrow studies of informality, and traditional ways to interpret information about informals in order to stretch and transform existing explanations of borders and their meaning for the heartlands. I also challenge some comfortable conclusions that are long overdue for contestation. Above all, I focus on people located in the bottom half of the income scale.

Alejandro Portes and others have challenged the formal versus informal dualism of the literature on informality.[7] But border people's actions also raise questions about the narrow economic measures of informal studies. These questions dovetail with an approach that analyzes connections with housing, culture, and politics, as well as how people avoid, ignore, resist, and sporadically comply with the hegemonic institutions that aim to govern their lives. Informality is as much about power and control as about economics.

I challenge the narrow focus of an individualized civic culture that reduces political participation to voting and occasional group formation. I further question the blanket of surveillance that shrouds some people's lives in a land that prides itself on freedom. The conception of participation in this book includes political community, along with what James Scott calls everyday resistance and hidden transcripts that depart from official ones.[8] Informals resist hegemonic laws and regulations, but what new world are they building (or undermining) in place of the old? In certain ways, informals counter transnational hegemony, but are their modest everyday victories feeding transnational hegemony at another level by supplying cheap labor without social safeguards? And are transformative political coalitions being built? Collective action is a special focus in subsequent chapters, allowing answers to the question of why public services reach Mexican residents at the new periphery faster than those at the U.S. periphery, in *colonias* outside the city limits under atomized, fragmented federalism. But political communities can and should operate at more than neighborhood levels, for people share common interests that cross borderlines.

I also question the modern control schemes described in the planning and policy literature. Subsequent chapters examine an enforcement process with negotiations, cracks, holes, and logical inconsistencies. Surveillance and enforcement strategies touch people in forms that range from minimal to brutal; the strategies have "costs." In that touch, the everyday experiences of those in the bottom half may foster political engagement, avoidance, and/or deceit. Yet I acknowledge aspiring modernist policy grids, along with their ability to structure politics, reactions, and resistance. I take up the task of policy recommendations, but in unusual and comprehensive ways, including analysis of a nongovernment organization in Mexico that provides technical assistance to U.S. residents.

Like others who study informality, I see the participation of women and men as almost evenly balanced, albeit in ways that reflect gendered constructions of tasks and their value. However, I move beyond celebrating women's entrepreneurialism or decrying their exploitation to look instead at the strategic decisions men and women make that maximize border opportunities. Intriguingly, male and female informal border-crossers generate earnings that (however meager) reduce globally ubiquitous and deep gender inequities. But U.S. resident men still enjoy advantages. I also look at gendered leadership in neighborhoods, asking if these newly visible people and agendas can help restore the loss of political community so many observers now bemoan.

Many in political studies recognize how local politics and policies mediate the effects of national and international policies on people's lives. Comparative urban studies often analyze global cities and cities within national borders or across borders of industrialized market economies. In subsequent chapters, however, I compare two cities in an urban region—an aspiring global city—divided by a borderline. Each city potentially offers a mirrorlike reflection of the other.[9] People's interests transcend those borders, and we must consider new ways to make political institutions responsive and accountable to those people.

Despite increased attention to local politics and policies, many Mexicanists have chosen until recently to focus on *national* politics and elections, busily reporting official vote counts down to fractions of a percent. At the outset of this project, some colleagues doubted the significance of Mexican *municipal* politics and policies, assuming that Mexico City determines almost everything. Fortunately, my orientation was soon validated by the important work of Victoria Rodríguez and Peter Ward, who compare opposition party rule at state and local levels; Vivienne Bennett, who analyzes gender in Monterrey's politics of water; and Diane Davis, who draws distinctions between local Mexico City politics and that of the central government.[10] As subsequent chapters show, however, I part ways from these scholars both in the focus on informality and in the interpretation of transition to conservative opposition party control in Juárez, with its emphasis on individualized citizens and its applause for modernity.

An analytic picture of Ciudad Juárez under conservative party control provides a deeper understanding of the political transitions that Mexico is undergoing as a conservative opposition pursues a populist agenda and clientelist political strategies. Painting this picture also allows me to reflect more on U.S. local politics and technical administration, often stripped of partisanship and hostile to low-income outcasts. Paradoxically, the land of individualism and freedom, through its modern surveillance and threats of surveillance, inhibits residents' ability to pursue self-sufficient work and shelter in visible ways.

I move from border to mainstream in the closing chapter. While international borders are not the only borderlines that divide people, the combination of globalization and counterhegemonic practices is a lens that offers insight into the late capitalist global economy. As Chapter 8 shows, official efforts to "hold the line" at borders are probably ill-considered. Relatively open borders provide opportunities for people to work, enhance their earnings, and reduce poverty. The petty regulations that serve hegemonic interests may render such activity "illegal," but those regulations are often made and enforced without political accountability to those affected and without reasoned judgment. Under such conditions, legitimacy is threatened; uneven compliance—the counter to hegemony—is inevitable. As the cost of enforcement increases, along with the level of surveillance, people's abilities to build transformative coalitions are also threatened. Questions, therefore, can and should be raised about the meaning of democracy in the borderlands and, subsequently, in the heartlands.

CHAPTER 2

Gazing at Space

Borders, Institutions, Informality,
and Political Community

> Borders are in-between places.
>   Homi Bhabha, "Narrating the Nation"

From a flat, horizontal perspective, borders may be viewed as the margins, the frontlines, or the centers of change. From a hierarchical, vertical perspective, one can gaze from the top down or from the bottom up. By conventional wisdom, the U.S.–Mexico border is positioned at the margins—the edge. But it may also be viewed as a center of global political-economic change.

We will also position ourselves at the bottom looking up, focusing on the seeming "noninfluentials in two border cities":[1] low- and middle-income people, many of whom have at least one foot in the informal economy. These people represent important social forces for two reasons. First, the experiences of this critical mass of people correspond to those of a majority of border residents. Second, as they ignore, negotiate with, resist, or comply with ideas and institutions that aim to control or assimilate them, they call into question what Gramscian theorists have called hegemonic control.

In this chapter, we gaze at border space through four lenses: international borders, comparative institutions, informal economies, and political communities. Combined, those lenses form a Gramscian theoretical prism, allowing us to understand and interpret the voices and behavior recorded in subsequent chapters.

The International Border

International borders evoke images of containment lines that divide opposing sides. One might predict a different political economy on either side of a borderline. Yet, as Homi Bhabha's eloquent definition suggests, border regions are an odd sort of integral space with characteristics shared by both sides. Can a single discipline address this reality?

Compartmentalized Knowledge, Compartmentalized States

Many disciplines rest upon state-nation models within which data are collected and compared. Disciplinarians study the United States, Britain, and/or Mexico, or compare groupings of states in regions, or in the south and north, east and west. The word *discipline* itself is double-edged; besides a field of knowledge, it suggests rigidity and control.[2]

Discipline extends to those summary symbols on which we all depend: numbers. The state organizes and reports these data collections through censuses and other means. According to Theodore Lowi, former president of the American Political Science Association, the term *statistics* "takes its name from *state* and *statist*."[3] Census-takers gather numbers for the state, using national boundaries and the territorial units therein to organize the data used, in turn, to inform public policies, taxing and spending calculations, and regulatory controls. Labor statistics count mostly "authorized" jobs. At borders, the way official data are sorted out between national censuses is also problematic.

When gazing at north–south borders from an interdisciplinary, international-development perspective, reasonable analysts bring healthy skepticism about official figures, whether invented by the bureaucratic hand or imperfectly collected from people wary of the state or working in ways that do not fit state census categories. Much of the early literature on women (later gender) and development exposed the mismatch between categories and realities.[4] Analysts focused on apparent marginals, in this case women, to lay bare the delusions upon which official numerical edifices rest. Multiple sources of knowledge are necessary to understand spaces of uncertain state control.

The movement of capital, people, and goods across borders, from one nation-state to another, is only partially captured in official numerical claims about international trade and migration. The official counts and claims pretend that unauthorized work does not exist. To "discipline" the border in these ways is to do understanding an injustice.

Yet another aspect of state-centric lenses distorts our understanding of society and economy at international borders. Borders are among the first spaces where global forces permeate people's everyday experiences, from job loss/generation and multiple currency use to ordinary shopping as a form of export-import trade and the exploitation of comparative advantages in wages and prices. But a purely global framework *over*states borders and integral regions, distorting reality as well with high-level abstract macro-structures that seem uninformed by the voices and everyday practices of real people. Still, state-centricity *under*states the global and transnational forces that shape states. Both statist and global-determinist terminology have the further drawback of *under*stating social forces that contradict, resist, or remain oblivious to those systems. Border lenses readjust state and global blinders to comprehend a region.

Gramsci at the Border: Hegemonic and Counterhegemonic Forces

Thanks to voices who speak from the margins of the field of international relations, we can better understand the hegemony of transnational capital, along with the social forces that counter that hegemony. By *hegemony*, Antonio Gramsci referred to the broad range of forces that ruling groups use, from state institutions to ideologies, to govern with seeming consent rather than coercion.[5] We can think of counterhegemony as resisting, avoiding, maneuvering, and/or negotiating with those institutional and ideological forces, in informal or organized ways. Counterhegemonic practices at one level increase the use of coercion, but at another create conditions that challenge the dominant hegemony.

In this so-called Gramscian approach to global political economy,[6] the dominant hegemony also dominates the literature; the research on counterhegemonic forces seems dormant. It is high time that research focus upon—even privilege—counterhegemonic forces, whether organized or unorganized. Such a focus would bring real people's experiences and voices into the analysis, not simply the larger structures and systems that (try to) embrace them.

Borderlines complicate the necessarily multiple hegemonic forces that people counter. We can count Gramsci's original writings among state-centric analyses, after all. What hegemonies do people counter, at what level? States, unpacked across their agencies, at all their levels within a federal system, including local government, which touches people quite directly? Civil society and acculturation ideologies, probably weak at the borders? Linguistic (English- or

Spanish-language) hegemony? Naturalization in national citizenship terms? Or do people counter transcendent global hegemony? Institutions claiming transcendent hegemony use the ideologies, regulations, and labor standards and values of *different* states to sustain their mission, but in border-straddling contexts, control is inherently imperfect. In their unfailing ingenuity, people use those differences or identify uncontrolled spaces that they use for their own benefit.

Observers tend to assume—within an approach that uses state lenses—that state control is more or less effective inside territorial boundaries. For Max Weber, modern authority legitimizes itself through rational-legal bureaucracy. Ominously, he referred to the "iron cage of bureaucracy." The hallmark of the modern state rests on an administrative system "with coordinated control over delimited territorial arenas, [a control which] depends upon the development of *surveillance* capacities."[7] Surveillance, says Anthony Giddens, "refers to the supervision of the activities of subject populations in the political sphere. Supervision may be direct . . . , but more characteristically it is indirect and based on the control of information."[8]

In contemporary terms, immigration surveillance is pervasive, especially at the frontlines of borders. Yet large numbers of people get around the guards and technology, especially in the great deserts that characterize the western half of the 2,000-mile U.S.–Mexico border. Surveillance is maintained in border cities and on interstate highways, but the more subtle surveillance is found in the banal collection and cross-checking of completed forms in public agencies.

Public administrators supervise the extension of rational planning across the landscape. Planning emerged in response to the conflicts associated with unbridled industrial and urban growth more than a century ago. Through zoning, technicians and professional planners authorize land use for residential, industrial, and commercial purposes. Administrators design rules and standards for uniform public services.

Planning is generally a top-down rather than bottom-up activity. As Oren Yiftachel argues, "urban and regional planning . . . [is] an integral part of what is often termed 'the modernist project.'"[9] With planner-classified and -mapped land use, states use space politically, to build homogeneity and to reduce conflict, all with the armor of scientific legitimacy, according to Sidney Plotkin. Planners are "like Gramscian 'organic intellectuals,'" he continues, "experts who help in organizing the general system of relationships external to the [production system] itself."[10]

From a Gramscian perspective, rational, comprehensive planning and practice contribute to hegemony, no matter how reasonable or benevolent they are. An all-pervasive hegemonic power uses institutions and ideologies to permeate various aspects of civil society from schools to churches and the media. These institutions shape expectations and behavior.

In subsequent chapters, I call into question such hegemonic forces at international borders, including the one between the United States and Mexico. Borders are good places to look for counterhegemonic forces that have the potential to change power relations or increase the cost of maintaining hegemony through force, regulation, and surveillance. The counterhegemonic activities on which I focus are migration and informality in both labor and housing.

Counterhegemony in Migration
Historically, the border tended to be viewed as the periphery, a marginal space. State-centered hegemony was probably weak at the frontier, even though the trappings of power might be most visible, as in a military or border-control apparatus. To the extent that the apparatus is leaky—for the trappings of physical control are always costly—borders become gateways for, and homes to, migrant populations. Do migrants shed, or unevenly pack, the baggage of national-origin hegemony?

Once migrants reach their destination, they are subject to assimilationist experiences. First, migrants themselves seek to differentiate themselves from the people and places they come from.[11] Second, migrants are exposed to multiple institutions of hegemony, from schools and the media to civic participation. The legal naturalization process in the United States involves more than a loyalty oath; it involves the demonstration of new language capabilities and civic information. But some migrants distance themselves from such institutions, in part to avoid implicit and inevitable surveillance, particularly if they cannot opt or have not opted for naturalized citizenship. Even without such a distancing, full assimilation and citizenship are lengthy processes, sometimes extending into subsequent generations.

Counterhegemony in Informality

Informality, however we define it, is at bottom an escape from routine surveillance. A widely used definition for the informal economy comes from Alejandro Portes: "the sum total of income-producing activities in which members of a household engage, excluding income from contractual and legally regulated employment."[12] Expanded conceptions embrace income-stretching activities like self-help housing, discussed in subsequent chapters.

At borders, hegemonic forces are inconsistent, contradictory, and therefore somewhat weak. In subsequent chapters, looking from the bottom up, I use sources that are fuller and more comprehensive than official statistics to document extensive informal income-generation, self-help housing, and cross-border movement. We will answer questions like the following: Why is informality so extensive? Does it emerge under certain spatial, institutional, immigration, or poverty conditions? And what does that underbelly of informality mean for the formal, hegemonic forces that aim to prevail both transnationally and in Mexico and the United States? People use this incomplete control, these in-between spaces, to earn money and to construct shelter. In later chapters, we will analyze the contexts in which people act. Gramscians wonder whether people act against states, or against global economic forces, and whether they act in individual or collective ways. Part of that wonder may become worry about whether in-between space leaves room for relatively more powerful forces, even informal ones, to exploit the less powerful.

Ultimately, though, we must ask if this counterhegemony is simply the other side of dominance relations, which inevitably invoke relations of resistance.[13] James Scott develops the question: "In as much as [domination] involves the use of power to extract work, products, services, taxes against the will of the dominated, it generates considerable friction and can be sustained only by continuous efforts at reinforcement, maintenance, and adjustment."[14]

Gramsci hoped that relations of resistance could transform relations between the governed and those who govern. During and after transformation, those who govern would be a different cast of characters, governing on different terms. But collective organization is necessary for resistance and counterhegemony to prevail through such a transformation. We must ask, therefore, under what conditions do people raise their voices, organize, and become politically engaged over a legitimate public agenda? And where are the lines drawn around political engagement and political community? The answers to those questions become complicated at borders.

While borderlands have many things in common, they are also blessed (and cursed) with different political institutional and policy baggage. Let us move to that theme.

Comparative Institutions

Although international borders have special characteristics derived from their "in-between" status, they are lines that divide two or more political jurisdictions, each with their own institutions that authorize civic participation for particular people around policy agendas beset with historical baggage. The borderline both creates spatial commonality and divides contrasting politics and policies. Efforts to "bring the state back in" have involved increasingly nuanced attention to states, neither monolithic nor uniformly strong; to states' uneven engagement with social forces; and to states *in* societies.[15]

Institutions have been "rediscovered" in various disciplines over the last decades. One working definition sees institutions both as "formal organizations and informal rules and procedures that structure conduct."[16] Institutions *shape* the relations of power; within those relations, institutions shape the ways people define their interests.

In this book, we consider such institutions as formal entities of government, public agencies, and public rules and policies. Policy enforcement occurs at the frontlines of bureaucratic interaction between official agents and residents; invariably, this interaction is an imperfect expression of those formalities. Michael Lipsky calls these agents "street-level bureaucrats" (SLBs), who operate with considerable discretion.[17] SLBs include inspectors, police officers, teachers, social workers, and border patrol agents, among others. The image of modern, technical agencies of impersonal control is transformed at the street level: street-level bureaucrats "rule" in more or less flexible ways. They put the policy into practice, representing real policies from the bottom up. Their subjects comply, ignore, negotiate, and/or resist those rules. International borders allow comparative analysis of these agencies along with their personal enforcers.

Behind Institutional Curtains: Transcripts

James Scott's discussion of the discrepancies between "public transcripts" and "hidden transcripts" seems particularly apt for explaining the institutional components of dominance/resistance relations at borders. Public transcripts comprise officials' language, policies, and symbols, which, in keeping with the metaphor of drama, are the stages to which audiences direct (or pretend to direct) their attention. The hidden transcript "takes place 'off-stage,' beyond direct observation by powerholders, with a history that rarely gets written."[18]

At international borders, the public transcripts are multiple, even spoken in different languages. People may present themselves in alternative ways, depending on the context. Is "Batista"—street vendor and six-time repeat offender—a Cuban, Peruvian, or Mexican (Chapter 4)? Policy cracks are easier to identify among border-crossers, experienced in negotiating both sides. The promise, possibility, or curse of different policy language[19] finds its mirror at the border.

Institutions in Border Places

Urban geographers have also called attention to institutions that shape place. For Anne Shlay, institutions are "organized systems that are regular and established parts of the metropolitan scene,"[20] examples of which include government, business, and finance organizations. She privileges the everyday banal routines that are conventionally taken for granted. Like hegemony, those routines seem natural ("naturalized"—also a term for citizenship acquisition), and they come to be viewed as such by those they envelop. Because institutions create and maintain space-based inequality, Shlay pointedly asks "how space gets its victims."[21] But space can both victimize and privilege people, who are in part agents of their histories and destinies. At borders, we must also ask how space gets its opportunists.

Aspiring global cities[22] at the international border are a perfect site in which to compare institutions as shapers of behavior. One urban space sits next door to another, with interdependent economies[23] but different institutions. Borders contradict powerholders' comfortable assumption that everyday, banal routines are "natural." Different practices do not pass unnoticed; they create pockets of uncontrolled space in which people act. At borders, these mirrorlike reflections operate "something like counter-sites . . . in which the real sites . . . are simultaneously represented, contested, and inverted."[24]

Clearly, then, border officials must grapple with "governmentality—that is, with coordinating social exchanges among selves constituted so as to ensure the stability of the order."[25] Modernity is also an issue. As Sanford Schram continues, "modernity's initial dilemma" is similar to that of its postindustrial variant: it requires people to prove they are autonomous, rational, economically self-sufficient, and productive, in a context wherein worth, even self-worth, is determined in economic terms.[26] Notions of modernity are bound to clash at the border, given a globalized economy that induces people to make do through informal means, and starkly unequal conditions on either side.

The struggle for economic self-worth is particularly acute amid structural economic adjustment, wherein a sufficient number of formal jobs or wages of sufficient value are not available. Herein lies the significance of informal economies, income-stretching behavior, and self-help housing—all prevalent at the border.

Informal Economies: Society, Space, and Policies

Informal economies have spawned a research cottage industry. Much ink has been spilled defining, redefining, and/or attacking alternative concepts of informal economies. Writers conjure up different images of informal workers, depending on when they write and where they are situated in the conceptual debates. In the early stages, writers evoked low-capitalized, small-scale, low-tech businesses, problematizing informals' lack of resources and skills. In the middle stages, writers evoked subcontractor labor in homes and in sweatshops, problematizing corporate labor-cheapening strategies. In some Mexican studies, researchers queried workers about social security payments, congruent with the middle approach. Meanwhile, from the margins, analysts argued that labor-intensive self-help, an income-substituting activity, ought to be included in studies of informality.

In subsequent chapters, informality is defined and measured more *inclusively*. "Informals" range from self-sufficient home- and street-based workers to employees of companies that cut costs below the basement of state-imposed protections and benefits to people engaged in labor-intensive, income-substituting activities.

The literature has evolved from a narrow focus on a seemingly isolated sector toward one connected to national and global economies as well as to society, family, and gender.[27] In subsequent chapters, I contextualize informality in individual, gendered, and household terms. Some analysts find that women make up almost half of informals,[28] but that their labor reaps less value within the diverse but monotonous global gender hierarchy.[29] At the border, could such hierarchies be flattened, exaggerated, or upset?

If we follow Portes' basic definition, informality involves income-generating activities outside contractual law and regulation. For reasons of focus and safety, our study differentiated informal work from crime that harms people directly, such as the drug trade: while the *means* of informality do not comply with all regulations, its *ends* (goods and services) are legitimate.

Cash is generally the medium of exchange in informality, but it would be remiss to exclude other activities that a broader conception of informality embraces. The housing analyst Alan Gilbert cautions about the exclusion of self-help housing.[30] Self-help housing construction and improvement occur outside contractual relationships with formal builders, bankers, and public inspectors in order to stretch incomes. Members of our research team queried residents about the labor-intensive, income-substituting activities that supplement informal work, like self-help housing. People also stretch incomes through cross-border shopping, looking for comparative price advantages. Border locales open up space for such broadened conceptions of work that is time-consuming, strategic, and risky.

The concept of informal labor was born in the early 1970s in Africa, where a modern industrial economy had yet to cast its net of formal wage-paying jobs over large numbers of people.[31] Census categories, developed in industrialized economies, offer a clumsy framework for the income-generating work of the majority of the world's population. But whether an economy is modern and industrial or not, women's work tends to be undercounted or warped by cultural ideologies that devalue it.[32] We must take special care to avoid reproducing these problems in studies of informality.

Initially, analysts established a connection between expanding economic modernization and a shrinking informal domain. Subsequently, they focused on the way late twentieth-century capitalism fostered a flexible workforce, thus stimulating informality.[33] No longer do analysts separate dual *sectors*, formal and informal.[34] Although some threw up their analytic hands at this seemingly "fuzzy" concept, it continues to be used to represent significant and important activity unaddressed through other means.[35] Economic determinism has driven important parts of this literature, but it is high time to situate informality in *space*.

Geographers remind us that power and resistance are embedded in space,[36] as well as historical time and vertical top-down structures. *Space matters* in Bryan Roberts' identification of five state-centric contexts:[37]

- Transition toward market economy (postcommunist states)
- Welfare-state economy (Britain)
- Community dependence, amid poverty, partial welfare, and widespread immigration (United States)
- Uneven regional development, amid partial welfare (Italy, Spain)
- Uneven regional development, without welfare (Mexico)

Roberts' categories also suggest that *policies matter*, especially those relating to welfare and immigration. But where does the U.S.–Mexico border fit in Roberts' analysis and for our use here? Borders themselves are conceptualized in this book as counterhegemonic sites and spaces. Still, the side of the borderline on or over which informality occurs has a policy framework. Does the U.S.–Mexico border lean more toward Mexico or the United States? Public policy differences provide the kind of official transcripts Scott describes, but economy and society provide settings and scripts as well, even if they are hidden from the official gaze.

Analysts of informality rarely integrate policies and politics,[38] except for the antiregulation bent of many writers. Most such writers are economists or staff members of international development organizations, promoting state downsizing during an era of "structural adjustment" and market-driven development.[39] Curiously, studies of informality come from every social science except political science. No wonder politics and policies are *under*stated in such studies. The Gramscian perspective is thoroughly political. And people's evasive practices and selective compliance with regulations of surveillance and control are just as important as official policies and implementation.

To draw boundaries around the burgeoning literature on informality, I focus in the following subsections on Mexico and the United States. Both countries have pursued fiscal austerity in the 1980s and beyond with the sort of moves that have been associated with "structural adjustment." Of course, the United States usually disassociates itself from this terminology, reserving it for countries of the south that do business with the international banks.

The Mexican Policy Lens

Mexico legitimizes informality as policy-relevant in its official transcripts. It has sponsored studies, from as early as 1977, on informal labor.[40] Its quarterly employment surveys show that a quarter to a third of the economically active population works informally.[11]

Informal workers in Mexico are a heterogeneous group.[42] Small business owners earn more than their employees. Men earn more than women (who have joined the ranks of the "economically active" in larger numbers since the Mexican economic crisis of 1980).[43] Through industrial subcontracting, home-based workers seek the meager opportunities available to them.[44] And informals' earnings are nearly comparable to other workers'[45] or higher at the northern border.[46] Many employees at the northern frontier work in export-processing factories, earning official minimum wages that are below market value, if we take informal earnings to be one indicator of market value.

Some Mexican studies define informality in regulatory and size terms (five or fewer workers). This definition meshes with the early approach to informal studies. Informal businesses do not comply fully with license, tax, and labor regulations. And these regulations are Byzantine. Nestor Elizondo outlines them for industrial, commercial, and service enterprises: "There are eleven procedures that must be followed when setting up a business: ten authorities are involved, thirteen forms have to be filled out, and between 83 and 240 days are needed to complete the formalities."[47] Drawing on a sample of 22 enterprises in Mexico City, he finds that legal compliance increases as work moves from the home to public settings. A legacy of Spanish colonialism, rules are so elaborate that few follow the letter of the law. The negotiability of enforcement (see Chapter 7) rewards those with resources, including organizational resources.

Studies of informality in the United States are few and far between. Official studies view informality in terms of tax evasion or criminal activity,[48] and informals rarely organize groups, whether unions or lobbies, around work that authorities render invisible or criminal. Consequently, informality appears to be absent or illegitimate. A conservative think tank, the Heritage Foundation, ranks countries globally according to ten criteria, one of them called "Black Market." On a scale of 1 to 5, Mexico gets a score of 3, while the United States gets a 1: "confined to the sale of goods and services—narcotics, prostitution, guns, and stolen goods—that are considered harmful to public safety."[49] Ironically, the antiregulation rhetoric of conservatives like these fueled the supply-side economics of the 1980s.[50]

Informal earnings have consequences for modern agencies and their data-generation agendas. The U.S. Internal Revenue Service treats informality as a way of avoiding tax compliance.[51] For residents near the poverty line, tax payment is often irrelevant, but they may be compelled to file tax returns even without financial obligation. Besides revenue generation, information is important for modern surveillance, including assessments of voluntary compliance and audit targets. Social programs base eligibility for aid on full knowledge of cash earnings, assets, and even social capital like gifts and help (see Chapter 4). Incorrect reporting can have severe consequences (including termination and criminal charges) for need-based welfare benefits such as food stamps and housing subsidies.

The Census Bureau counts self-employed workers, a group that has hovered between 9 and 11 percent of the workforce since 1950. Its Current Population Survey (CPS) counts each person once, classifying dual jobholders according to their primary job.[52] Drawing on a 1985 CPS, a study of home-based workers found that 3 percent of employed women work entirely at home, and 13.5 percent work partially at home; 90 percent are "white-non-Hispanic."[53] CPS data do not allow us to judge the effects of space and economy in these numbers; [54] it will, however, be possible for us to do so in subsequent chapters.

Ethnic enclaves and ethnic economies offer considerable self-employment and contracted labor opportunities, for better or worse. Pioneering analysts like Ivan Light critique census documents for their inability to capture this reality.[55] Research on immigrant populations in large cities, especially those involved in subcontracting relationships in homes and sweatshops, suggests a need for regulation to reduce exploitation.[56]

The focus on ethnics and immigrants, whether residing in enclaves or not, separates the study of informal economies from the study of the mainstream economy and society. Immigrants are, of course, a diverse group, ranging from the undocumented to legal residents and to those undergoing the naturalization process, with or without citizen children. Few studies attend to autonomous self-employment and multiple-income-generating strategies within the mainstream, whether second- or nth-generation immigrants are concerned. As Joan Moore and Raquel Pinderhughes point out, informal work is stigmatized, and so is its study.[57]

Domestic servants, a key female occupational group that spans the Americas,[58] are quintessential informal workers. Curiously, some call for redefining informality to exclude most paid domestic labor,[59] to avoid "feminizing" informality or rendering its study more complex through the inclusion of women. Maids symbolize the complexities and contradictions of surveillance, particularly for employers. The enforcement of labor and immigration regulations became a public issue only after President Clinton nominated Zoë Baird for attorney general and it was revealed that she herself was not in compliance with those rules, crushing her prospects for approval. Mayan immigrant maids' home-based work in Houston is shielded from labor laws and immigration surveillance alike; the employer sanctions of the 1986 Immigration Control and Reform Act ignore such domestic labor.[60]

Historically, migrants have used self-employment and unpaid family labor as stepping stones toward economic security. Today, migrants with small businesses use kinship and ethnic connections to secure loans and customers.[61] Apart from immigration-driven research rationales, the globalization of the U.S. economy makes it imperative that we conceive of informality in broad self-employment terms, as has been common in international development studies of southern countries.[62] Of course, this is not how people usually think of the modern, even postindustrial, U.S. economy.

The state-specific orientation to informality described above brings much-needed attention to public policies. Yet it would be a mistake to privilege public policies alone, for popular organization also matters. Are informals organized to protect, advance, or defend their interests? Moreover, does policy rhetoric incorporate informality as legitimate work? If so, does that offer a basis for political engagement between informals and their government? Does organization have a community or spatial basis? To political community we now turn.

Political Communities

Conventional studies of politics in the United States have reduced and fragmented discrete acts of individual participation in order to measure behavior and opinions more easily. Overall patterns of voter turnout have declined since the 1960s, until a half or fewer of those eligible vote. The same downturn is apparent in people's trust in politicians, political institutions, and deliverable policy agendas. Public opinion polls, whether research- or candidate-driven, measure sometimes stable, sometimes shifting, reactions to sophisticated political marketing and stimuli. For some, public opinion polls represent their only voice in the political process.[63]

One strand of Mexican studies exhibits such trends. Mexicanists with a numerical bias have analyzed voter turnout figures down to tenths or hundredths of a percentage point, even during elections widely viewed as fraudulent. Surveys and public opinion polling have become more widely used in Mexico during the 1990s.[64]

The Civility of "Civic Culture"

Conventional voting studies risk losing sight of organization and political community. More than thirty years ago, Gabriel Almond and Sidney Verba celebrated the idea of "civic culture" in a five-country study that included the United States and Mexico. In a civic culture, citizens view *institutions and policies as legitimate;* they *tolerate plural interests,* and they feel *politically competent.*[65] Political competence is measured and exercised in political participation, such as voting, contacting officials, and joining organizations and political parties.

Perhaps unsurprisingly, Almond and Verba concluded that the United States exemplified civic culture. During the 1960s, the United States was, for academics, the model of political modernity. Yet the strength of U.S. independent organizations had acquired fame as far back as the mid-nineteenth century, through the writings of French observer Alexis de Tocqueville. Mexico, on the other hand, acquired the derogatory label "parochial culture," for the ties between citizens and officials reeked of personalism and clientelism: a system of machine-style, vertically organized party organizations where patrons seek and deliver goods for their clients in nonideological relationships.[66] Citizens exercised participatory rituals but expected little fair play.

Recent observers have bemoaned the loss of community in the United States. Once vibrant and vigorous community life has given way to occasional participation and a proliferation of self-help groups. Individualism flourishes at the expense of communitarianism. Robert Putnam, titling his work with a mostly male sports metaphor, worries that Americans are "bowling alone," no longer joining traditional civic groups.[67] Uniting political study and market discourse, he establishes the importance of social capital: "features of social organizations such as networks, norms, and social trust that facilitate coordination and cooperation for mutual benefit."[68] He thereby broadens notions of civic culture, but it is important to place those notions in space, introducing dimensions such as neighborhoods and political communities, the boundaries of which are not necessary imposed from above.

Anthropologists have long appreciated the importance of social capital. Through the study of culture, they document how people communicate information, spread resources, and provide support through social networks and shared values. Curiously, though, analysts tend to focus on those at the margins of mainstream society: low-income, "minority," or power elites (however privileged this margin may be).[69] Rosaldo calls our attention to the seemingly inverse relationship between culture and citizenship. Citizens seem to lack culture (one of those exotic "museums" anthropologists once fashioned for the "garage sales" of shared values), but people with culture lack full citizenship.[70]

Conventional U.S. political scientists, who disdain cultural analysis,[71] frequently treat low or sporadic voter participation as a sign of overall public satisfaction. And conventional public administration treats public service delivery and policy enforcement as problems that universalistic, rational management will solve, optimally outside the political process. In many modern societies, says Ayşe Güneş-Ayata, the individual is the political unit, and seemingly equal individuals become atomized in impersonal relations. But in situations of scarcity, individual needs go unrecognized: "bureaucratic universalism boils down to indifference and gives rise to feelings of impotence and helplessness. When tested against the hard realities of life, then, modern concepts of equality and universalism tend merely to demonstrate the nonegalitarian nature of the society."[72] Although some analysts perceive clientelism as denoting the transition to modernity, it rarely disappeared in modern societies. Rather, it joined other strategies that people use to gain influence and share power. And economic clout matters in a political process that depends heavily on campaign contributions.

In a hierarchical, clientelist political system like Mexico's, few operate under the delusion that all parts of the public will be fairly served. Rather, people, organizational, and partisan connections make the system work for parts of the public. Neither officials nor conventional political analysts treat lightly voters' "abstentionism" (labeled "low voter turnout" in the United States). In the 1994 presidential election, three-fourths of the Mexican electorate cast ballots;[73] in general, more than half of the electorate votes, a rate that surpasses U.S. participation statistics. To abstain is to refuse cooptation and fraud.

Political discourse in Mexico uses an ideological rhetoric tied to the country's revolutionary heritages. Mexico's dominant political party incorporates revolution in its name: the Institutional Revolutionary Party/Partido Revolucionario Institucional (PRI) has a corporatist structure that formalizes representation for peasants, workers, and popular organizations. But PRI has proved unable to represent its constituents, and a stronger civil society has begun to emerge outside the confines of party control. Mexico has therefore been lumped together with other countries in the Americas undergoing "transition to democracy." This association is not a "comfortable fit," says Judith Hellman, for in fact the country limps along, neither repressive nor democratic, but "more Mexican than ever," with a "manipulative interplay of persuasion and coercion."[74]

Mexico's transition, however manipulative, is also associated with the rise of multiparty competition for control of municipal, state, and national government. Rampant voter abstentionism during the 1980s led to a 1986 electoral reform that enlarged the national Chamber of Deputies; along with 300 single-member seats, 200 more deputies were seated through proportional representation, a system wherein ideological opposition parties flourished in permanent minority status until 1997.[75]

An even smaller female minority is seated at the national level. Men monopolize nine of ten representation and appointment slots, a proportion roughly similar in the United States and Mexico.[76] Women's citizenship deserves special comment, for it was only in 1953 that they acquired the voting franchise in Mexico. Thereafter, political parties mobilized women through "feminine sectors." Many neighborhood organizations are built upon a female foundation. As household managers, women have perhaps the largest stakes in access to water, electricity, sewer, and other services. Alejandra Massolo puts it this way: "Urban politics are women's politics."[77] Although women's involvement tends to address practical community needs, rather than their subordination to men, that very involvement creates a sense of citizenship.[78]

A spatial focus on the border and on neighborhoods allows us to analyze how Mexico reflects on the United States and vice versa. U.S. civic culture seems less civil than this lofty phrase suggests. Both Juárez and El Paso share globalization, economic restructuring (including informality), and poverty, as subsequent chapters discuss, but their institutional heritages differ markedly, as do the numbers of those authorized to be civic.

Civic Culture at the Border?

Borders seem like dividing lines. Social-psychological studies have neatly differentiated between "individualist" cultures north of the U.S.–Mexico border and "communalist" cultures south of it.[79]

Almond and Verba's sharply distinguished civic and parochial cultures are actually quite blurred at that border, for several reasons. First, on the U.S. side the border is a magnet for migrants; the tolerance of plural interests that supposedly characterizes U.S. civic culture frequently stops at the line of citizenship. Second, as we will analyze in Chapter 3, globalization (for which the the border is a frontline location) has fostered a cheapened and destabilized workforce, highlighting the nonegalitarian nature of borderzone society. And third, as we will see in Chapters 4–7, counterhegemonic practices call into question the extent to which citizens view official transcripts (regulations) as legitimate. People's hidden transcripts are voices of political competence, a thorn in the side of rational bureaucracy.

Regulations governing housing, work, and trade are generally decided behind the closed doors of bureaucracy. These doors are frequently local ones, less amenable to partisan and ordinary people's influence in professionalized government. Immigration laws are formulated in capital cities, but enforcement decisions are made behind bureaucratic doors as well. Citizens are authorized to influence those decisions.

Yet, contrary to equalizing and universalistic notions in the public transcript, some citizens are more equal than others. Judith Shklar says we cannot discuss citizenship

> as if it existed in an institutional deep freeze. . . . It is in the marketplace, in production and consumption, in the world of work in all its forms, and in voluntary associations that the American citizen finds his social place, [her] standing, the approbation of his fellows, possible, some of [her] self-respect. . . . We are citizens only if we 'earn.'"[80]

Shklar's remarks call attention to those who earn nothing or little and to those whose earnings are less visible—that is, acquired through informal means. She also calls into question the notion of citizenship as entitlement to social programs. If low-income women's engagement with politics occurs primarily through social entitlement programs, as Barbara Nelson once warned, it is an engagement of dependency that reinforces gendered social constructions.[81] Among migrants, however legal their residency, such engagement over entitlements also incurs risks. The rules of entitlement are not transparent. Rules change in response to forces that rarely include the voices of migrants or entitlees.

Lawrence Fuchs, immigration scholar and member of the Commission on Immigration Reform (CIR), frames his analysis in civic culture terms. Drawing on Tocqueville, like the others quoted above, Fuchs argues that the nationality of immigrants is constructed through the "exercise of civil rights."[82] The CIR's 1994 report to Congress proposes strategies to close the border further to undocumented movement, to deter employers from hiring the undocumented, and to encourage legal immigrants to become citizens.[83] To enforce employer sanctions is to focus on the formal workplace, for immigration control is frustrated by a flourishing informal economy, particularly if home-based. But home- and street-based work can also frustrate people's efforts to organize for power and political community, as we discover in later chapters.

The 1986 Immigration Reform and Control Act granted amnesty and the opportunity for naturalized citizenship to undocumented migrants with evidence of residence in 1982 and before. The vast majority of amnesties went to migrants of Mexican heritage.[84] Yet Latinos of Mexican heritage never received the sort of subsidies that Cuban migrants gained after they fled the Cuban revolution, permitting them to turn legal citizenship into economic citizenship of the kind Shklar outlines. Under Cold War conditions, Cuban Americans acquired public investments that strengthened the economic stakes of their citizenship. An unprecedented $1 billion in assistance was associated with the Cuban Refugee Program from 1965 to 1976, including small business loans.[85]

The relatively undersubsidized Mexican American population, in contrast, consists of both citizens and residents who opt to maintain their Mexican citizenship or seek naturalization after longer periods than other nationalities. (Alejandro Portes and Rubén Rumbaut discuss the "notorious resistance among Mexican and Canadian immigrants to change flags.")[86] For those at the border, proximity to the homeland undoubtedly figures into these decisions. Jorge Castañeda warns that "Mexican immigration is contributing to the 'dedemocratization' of California society."[87]

Castañeda passes on the opportunity to discuss what sort of democratic heritage immigrants bring from the homeland. A "communal" one, to use the terminology of social psychology? A cynical one, derived from a tradition of cooptative and fraudulent partisanship? A clientelist one, with populist overtones? Clientelism, however flawed, involves political engagement, both between individual clients and patrons and between patrons and groups. In northern Mexico, group-based clientelism occurs in the context of multiparty competition, wherein opposition party victories have been recognized. As pioneering studies of opposition rule document, the conservative National Action Party/Partido Acción Nacional (PAN) emphasizes efficiency and streamlined management.[88]

Ideological organizations have the potential to transform, rather than merely to reinforce, the existing political structure. Northern Mexico is home to a variety of these organizations, including the Popular Defense Committee/Comité de Defensa Popular (CDP) and Land and Liberty/Tierra y Libertad in northern states. These organizations settle residents on public and private land through "invasions," autonomously and in alliance with other political parties.

Seemingly ideological organizations, however, may reproduce conventional, clientelist politics. In many, leaders are not accountable to members; furthermore, men monopolize leadership. But members also calculate their own interests. In the Durango-based CDP, members were "more concerned with the organization's ability to deliver goods and extract concessions from the state."[89] Do concessions come through politically negotiated connections or as a matter of right?

As part of its modernization project, the PAN seeks to individualize the relationship between individual and government. This modern relationship occurs on the U.S. side, although its benefits for low-income, informally employed residents are uncertain. Instead, residents patch together livelihood strategies, relatively self-sufficient but noncompliant—strategies that counter hegemonic institutions.

Conclusions

A Gramscian framework brings perspectives on borders, comparative institutions, informality, and political community to bear on the U.S.–Mexico border in the late capitalist era. This chapter has introduced the conceptual tools and insights I have used to organize the multifaceted field research that is the heart of this book. In this chapter, I challenged disciplinary boundaries and the use of numbers from a single source as ways to comprehend border realities. Multiple validations are key in this analysis.

Multiple hegemonies operate at the border: local, national, and transnational; petty and grand. To pretend they cohere is to engage in the sort of fiction that public transcripts hope to convey. Through informal means, people resist, ignore, and negotiate in this drama, as we will see in subsequent chapters. Taken together, people's hidden transcripts offer little collective challenge to national hegemonies, let alone any chance of achieving national policy reform. But the challenges have the potential to alter the balance of consent and coercion in governance. They send a mixture of complex signals to transnational hegemony. To the contexts and people we now turn.

CHAPTER 3

Contextualizing
a Border Global City

Juárez–El Paso

> The environment does not need a passport.
> Juárez official, 1993

At the frontlines of global economic restructuring stand the workers of Ciudad Juárez and El Paso. Over the last three decades the border labor pool has swollen to create the largest urban area joining the so-called first and third worlds. The magnet is perceived economic opportunity. Multinational export-processing factories in Juárez offer employment; El Paso represents a gateway to the north, where some crossers stay and which others pass through. Given the internationalization of its economy and social structure, this border urban sprawl could be called an *aspiring* "global city."[1]

Saskia Sassen offers the definitive analysis of late twentieth-century global cities. Here, since the 1960s, the "expansion of a downgraded manufacturing sector" has taken the place of once-numerous organized and reasonably well paid jobs.[2] What is special about the *border* global city is the way such expansion and contraction cross legal territorial lines in a contiguous and coherent spatial zone. In the Juárez–El Paso borderzone, many people work in subcontractor firms, or in subsidiaries of multinational firms, which fragment labor production through partial processing. These people belong to labor pools that are valued quite differently, depending primarily on their spatial location (north or south of the border) and secondarily on their gender construction. On one side of the international boundary line, modern factories mushroom, clones of those once located in the north except for the more relaxed regulatory environment and wages that are a fraction of those formerly paid. On the other side, garment factories emerged and died, ranging from modern workplaces to the grimmest of sweatshops.

El Paso–Juárez is currently home to approximately two million people. A century ago, the border frontier of each country was its margin, in economic, population, and figurative terms. The story of the move away from the margin to the mainstream parallels global economic restructuring and the ensuing changes in the demand for low-cost labor.

But it would be a mistake to look solely from the top down, focusing on the regional economic overlay of modern formal employment and administrative structures within these two political economies, with their different layers of federal authority and cross-border administration—however fascinating that study would be. Underneath this shell, people recreate another, informal layer of economic activity and social and kinship relationships, all of which allow them to use the border in strategic ways. A mostly unofficial minifree trade zone has long been in place.

In this chapter, I focus on El Paso and Juárez in the context of this border global city status. I begin a historical perspective on the ways that people, capital, and labor cross the border. Contemporary portraits of El Paso and Juárez follow, drawn from official figures, neighborhood narratives from interviews and surveys, and the discourse of the popular media, all focused on a border region poised for the anticlimax of the North American Free Trade Agreement (NAFTA).

Historical Perspectives

Situated in the Rio Grande/Río Bravo Valley between two mountain ranges is the region once known as the Pass of the North: El Paso del Norte. The river now seems neither grand nor brave. People easily wade the seam that joins El Paso and Juárez, and before the 1993 Border Blockade, *lancheros* carried shoppers and workers across on their backs so that the latter would look dry upon arrival.

During the nineteenth century, the Pass of the North was a major gateway for crossers from east to west, south to north, and vice versa. El Paso became a county in 1850; city incorporation followed in 1873. Railroad construction and smelting operations facilitated even more movement, both to and through the area. Asian and Mexican male migrant labor built railroad tracks for what was soon to become a regional transport hub. Female labor served men's and households' needs. Women laundered, cleaned, and cooked, on both paid and unpaid bases.[3] On women's literal backs, the city generated revenue; prostitutes paid "fines," perhaps more like informal licenses, for their work.[4]

When Mexico lost half of its territory after the 1848 Treaty of Guadalupe Hidalgo, the part of Paso del Norte south of the international border became known as Ciudad Juárez, named after the Mexican patriot Benito Juárez. Mexico's elementary school textbooks graphically illustrate this loss through maps as (as one was titled) "Invasion from the North."[5]

With a stagnant economy and an underpopulated northern frontier, Mexico welcomed immigration. Mexicans who lived north of the new border became U.S. citizens.[6] The first U.S. exclusionary immigration law, enacted in 1882, aimed to control Chinese, not Mexican, migrants. To elude these restrictions, some Chinese migrants went to Mexico, obtained citizenship, and renamed themselves while learning English in order to migrate northward. Turn-of-the-century U.S. immigration inspectors, a mere sixty to cover a 2,000-mile border, "were commonly known as 'Chinese Inspectors.'"[7] (Contrast these figures with the 550 positions at the current El Paso sector, one of five enforcing unauthorized-entry laws against largely Mexican migrants at the U.S.–Mexico border.)[8]

Before 1917, U.S. immigration control was lax, with few restrictions against Mexican crossers.[9] In his authoritative *Foreigners in Their Native Land*, David Weber cites a Mexican immigrant who said that all he needed to do to pass through was tell the officer, "I am a Mexican," in Spanish.[10] The eminent historians Oscar Martínez and Mario García estimate that thousands crossed monthly, depending on economic demand.[11] Between 1900 and the Great Depression of the 1930s, one million Mexicans crossed, of whom half remained in Texas.[12] In 1924 the U.S. Congress created the Border Patrol. By the time of the 1929 world depression, Mexicans faced what James Cockroft calls a "revolving door" immigration policy, facing deportation, expulsion, and/or intimidation.[13]

Rail construction helped stimulate growth in late nineteenth-century Juárez. Mexico's Free Trade Zone (Zona Libre), in place through 1898, made the city a contrast to sleepy El Paso. Northerners regularly crossed the border for price advantages, including imported goods.[14] Yet Mexico's considerable growth in the late nineteenth century brought no benefits for the majority under the dictator Porfirio Díaz. The Mexican Revolution of 1910, in the name

Table 1   Urban Population Growth, El Paso
             and Juárez, 1900–1995

Year	El Paso	Juárez
1900	15,906	8,212
1910	32,279	10,621
1920	77,560	19,457
1930	102,421	39,669
1940	96,810	48,881
1950	130,485	122,566
1960	276,687	262,119
1970	322,261	407,370
1980	425,829	649,275
1990	515,342 (city)	798,522
	591,610 (county)	
1995		1,011,000

Sources: City of El Paso Department of Planning, Research, and Development (packet, 1992); 1995 mid-decade census count, reported in *Norte de Ciudad Juárez,* April 26, 1996.

of land and liberty, spawned a decade of economic instability and regional rebellions within the Revolution. It pushed vast numbers of crossers northward. Pancho Villa, hero to some, bandit to others, had his base of operations in the border State of Chihuahua. The people who sought refuge on the U.S. side congregated between El Paso's downtown and the border in an area called Chihuahuita (Little Chihuahua). Economically privileged Mexicans also fled. Through a higher-elevation area with grand homes runs a once major thoroughfare named Porfirio Díaz Street, now a startling freeway exit.

Juárez itself, labeled a boom town for considerable periods of the twentieth century, drew migrants from the interior of Mexico for what remained a tourist economy for several decades. The U.S. liquor-prohibition period cultivated the seamy side of the service economy. Both cities mushroomed in the twentieth century, quadrupling their populations in the postwar period (Table 1).

In the United States, ethnic census categories have shifted with the prevailing political winds. Total figures are also hotly contested, as discussed below for Juárez. García says that only in the 1930s did the U.S. census include a category for Mexicans, and "these figures did not include 'illegals' or those counted as whites."[15] Richard Bath and Roberto Villarreal note that "the Texas Attorney General officially classified Mexicans as "'black,' then 'brown,' and even later 'nonwhite.'"[16] Regardless of the official shifts in categories, people of Mexican heritage have made up a majority of El Paso residents throughout the twentieth century.

The 1990 census counts El Pasoans as 70 percent "Hispanic." El Paso's official representatives present a very different profile. From 1881 to 1951, no Mexican American served on City Council; El Paso has had just two Mexican American mayors in its history. In their historical analysis of the local power elite, Bath and Villarreal conclude that Anglo (European American) men dominated until the late 1980s.[17] Only in 1996 did El Paso select its first Mexican American congressional representative: Silvestre Reyes, the former director of the Border Patrol who earned high name recognition when he installed the Border Blockade, subsequently renamed Operation Hold the Line.

On both sides of the border, sizable numbers of residents come from outside the country (especially in El Paso) or the municipality (especially in Juárez). Mexico's 1990 census found that fully half of Juárez residents had been born outside the city, mostly in the states of Zacatecas, Coahuila, and Durango. El Paso counts a quarter of its population as "foreign born."[18] While the economic depression of the 1930s repatriated people of Mexican heritage southward, the Bracero Program, which lasted from the second World War until 1964, attracted unskilled workers northward. Later, profound changes in the structure of manufacturing would lead migrants to settle more permanently in the El Paso region.

In the postwar period, U.S. capital moved southward in search of lower-cost labor, first to the southern states, including those at the border, and then beyond the border. Some writers refer to this as "offshore" investment—hardly an appropriate metaphor in the middle of the Chihuahuan desert, eight hundred miles from either shore. A change in the U.S. Customs Code reduced customs fees to the mere value added in export-processing assembly plants known as both *maquilas* and *maquiladoras* in northern Mexico.

A new sort of economic transformation had begun in this border global city, nourished with low-cost labor. In the 1960s, El Paso's per capita income diminished as a percentage of U.S. per capita income. We can appreciate the depth of this decline if we look at the figures on a decade-by-decade basis, as reported by El Paso's Department of Planning, Research, and Development in 1992 (based on figures from the U.S. Department of Commerce). From 102 percent of the national income in 1950, El Paso dropped to 84 percent in 1960, 72 percent in 1970, 68 percent in 1980, and finally to 59 percent in 1991. To analyze why, let us first consider the U.S. side of the border.

Structural Adjustment in El Paso

Over a forty-year period, El Paso's once high-paying manufacturing sector was transformed into a collection of low-paying plants, largely in the apparel industry. Overall trends presage those now emerging elsewhere in the United States. At the border, however, the shift is not an abstraction; people can literally *see* the other side where jobs go.

In his methodical study, George Towers groups manufacturing jobs into five categories, based on wages as a percentage of the national manufacturing average. In 1950, top-category jobs paying 115 percent of the national average represented 34 percent of El Paso manufacturing jobs, compared with 23 percent of manufacturing jobs nationally. By 1985, that category had shrunk to 11 percent of El Paso's manufacturing jobs, and 21 percent of U.S. manufacturing jobs. Meanwhile, El Paso's bottom category of manufacturing jobs (paying less than 85 percent of the national average) swelled to 57 percent of the jobs, compared with just 16 percent at the national level.[19] Most of those jobs are in apparel manufacturing, traditionally considered women's work.

Apparel manufacturers recruit a substantial number of first-generation immigrant women into their fold. In a 1994 study of 300 randomly selected women garment workers in El Paso, the median pay was slightly more than the minimum wage, or $196 weekly. Seventy-eight percent were born in Mexico, although most of them were long-term residents of El Paso. Citizens represented nearly half the sample, but the majority were legal residents.[20] Some workers organize collectively through La Mujer Obrera/The Woman Worker, an advocacy organization that responds to abuse in the workplace, particularly nonpayment of wages and payment of sub-minimum wages.[21]

El Paso's border location offered investors the attraction of a labor pool for whom minimum-wage jobs provided opportunities for upward mobility. Immigration law set the stage for these opportunities. Enforcers cannot monitor all crossings in an urban space in which innumerable social and commercial transactions are embedded. First, various legal documents permit crossing, ranging from authorization to work (temporary and permanent) and family unification for citizens and permanent residents to Border Crossing Cards and visas for university enrollment.[22] Pedestrian and automobile crossings number in the millions each year at official crossing points.[23]

On the whole, border enforcement has been leaky and uneven. Until 1993, the Border Patrol invested considerable agent time in street surveillance of people who "looked" Mexican or had the "Mexican look,"[24] and were therefore assumed to be undocumented. At the official bridges today, scrutiny is stricter for people with that look. For those without it, the prompt "Citizenship?" with the unaccented response "U.S." or "American," usually merits a nod to pass. Before the 1986 Immigration Reform and Control Act, employers who hired undocumented workers faced no official penalties; even after the act, enforcement was lax.[25]

Immigration policies have been selectively enforced to facilitate crossing, to stimulate commerce, and to meet employers' needs. Border Crossing Cards, which border residents call *pasaportes locales* ("local passports"), allow formally employed border residents and members of their households to visit and to shop in El Paso for a period of up to seventy-two hours.[26] Commuters also cross in both directions. In the 1970s, 14,794 Juarenses commuted to work legally in El Paso, where they represented 9 percent of the workforce; 36 percent of total wages in Juárez came from work in El Paso. Benjamin Márquez, who cites both figures, concludes that "this is not a good situation for working people in El Paso."[27] U.S. managers, who number around 1,600 in the 1990s, cross daily to work in maquilas.[28]

Structural Adjustment in Juárez

The economic transformation of Juárez offers a marked contrast with that of El Paso. Throughout the twentieth century, prominent leaders in Juárez pushed for the institution of an official free trade zone. A de facto free trade zone existed, as shoppers frequently purchased goods in El Paso, despite periodic calls to "Buy Mexican" and protests from commercial establishments in Juárez.[29] National investment to industrialize the border began in 1940, but, as noted above, a significant one-third of wages were coming from El Paso in the 1970s.

Fuller industrialization occurred with the 1960 Programa Nacional Fronterizo (PRONAF), the National Border Program of the federal government. Juárez became a magnet for capital after 1965, when a group of industrialists transformed Mexico's fifth-largest urban area into a major site for the Border Industrialization Program. Antonio Bermúdez, head of PRONAF, worked with his nephew Jaime Bermúdez, founder of the Grupo Bermúdez, whose brochure states its commitment "to attracting foreign development to Mexico." Well connected to Mexico's dominant party, the PRI, each served as municipal president of Juárez.[30]

Juárez is home to the largest number of maquila workers in northern Mexico. Export-processing industries currently employ approximately 150,000, the majority of whom are women.[31] For reasons of size, employment generation, and foreign-exchange value, the importance of the maquiladora industry to Mexico cannot be overstated. Maquiladoras pay the official minimum wages, along with the legally required fringe benefits to the Instituto Mexicano del Seguro Social/Mexican Social Security Institute (IMSS), which provides public health, and the Instituto de Fomento Nacional de Vivienda de Trabajadores/National Institute to Promote Worker Housing (INFONAVIT). In 1992, the time of our household interviews, the minimum wage was approximately thirty dollars a week, although employers' total costs included the fringe benefits and, for some, such extra benefits as cafeteria food, transportation, bonuses for punctuality and attendance, and food coupons. After the peso devaluation of 1994–95, the minimum wage dropped to fifteen dollars a week. Crises like the devaluation are generally a boom to maquiladora industries.

Worker turnover rates make U.S. managers shudder. They respond with a variety of material benefits rather than with increased wages. Municipal officials negotiated with maquila owners to pay an annual head tax for each worker, which they hoped to transform subsequently into a payroll tax, to compensate for the costs associated with extending public services to migrants swelling and expanding the municipality. No doubt exists that maquilas attract migrants; planners estimate that forty families arrive daily.[32] But the structure of opportunity in Juárez is wider than the formal grid of modern factories. It includes market niches into which informal producers, traders, and service providers situate themselves on streets and in homes.

What are the consequences of economic restructuring for the region? The answer for perhaps half its population is this: growth but not development, if by development we mean people's ability to live at higher than poverty standards. Officials treat poverty (like wages) as relative, and measure it in ways that make it difficult to compare Mexico and the United States. To the official measurement portraits we now turn.

Border City Snapshots: Official, Neighborhood, Popular

The portrait of a border global city can be constructed from official figures, neighborhood research, and the popular media. None of these sources by itself taps the full dimensions of political-economic life.

The term "official figures" has a double meaning. On the one hand, such data are collected at great cost and with the goal of generalizing to the universe of what is studied. On the other hand, the superficiality of the questions asked and the guarded responses wary people are likely to give government agencies inspire skepticism. U.S. census results for the region are based on mail-in questionnaires, with English (instead of Spanish-language) versions mailed to heavily Spanish-speaking areas, and a response rate of slightly more than two-thirds. The census also uses short and long versions, and generalizations are extended from the long form's smaller sample to the whole area. Can we trust such extensions?

Unemployment figures, official and seemingly precise, ignore (and conceal the existence of) people who are unengaged with the bureaucracy. Real unemployment is underestimated for the following uncounted groups: involuntary part-time workers, the discouraged, and the long-term unemployed. Even so, El Paso's official unemployment figures consistently report rates ranging from 10 to 14 percent over the last two decades. Yet it is meaningful to report that El Paso rates *always* surpass those of the United States and Texas.

Mexico counts as employed anyone who has worked any number of hours the week prior to enumeration, so its official unemployment figures are ludicrously low. The rate in Juárez generally hovers between 1 and 3 percent. Considering the official attention to informal work and the government's willingness to publicize the fact that a quarter to a third of the economically active are employed "informally," some view informality as disguised under- and unemployment. Priscilla Connolly says informality "mystifies poverty."[33]

Poverty rates, also official and precise, are based on questionable formulas. A reasonable calculation strategy for poverty was developed decades ago in the United States, but it was politicized once it crossed the border from academic research to policy analysis.[34] Still, El Paso counts a quarter of its households as falling below the poverty line, based on the 1990 census and the poverty borderline of that year. Examined in another way, El Paso is the fifth-poorest Metropolitan Statistical Area in the United States, measured in per capita income terms. Conservative estimates place 25 percent of El Paso's wage earners at the minimum-wage level, compared with 6 percent of wage earners at the national level (according to the annual *Statistical Abstract*). Families of four must earn one and a half times the minimum wage to rise above the official U.S. poverty level. City boosters frequently cite a lower cost of living (COL), but El Paso's COL for 1990–96 hovers around 95 percent of national COL figures, according to Chamber of Commerce sources. Mexican observers unofficially consider three times the Mexican minimum wage as a rough poverty line.[35]

Census Portraits

One picture of life emerges from official census figures of the three neighborhoods in El Paso County. In Table 2, we see a fuller picture of income and housing conditions, as well as self-employment figures that differ dramatically from those my colleagues and I uncovered.

The official picture of Juárez looks quite different (Table 3), partly because Mexico collects census data differently. Caveats must immediately be raised about some of the figures. The official 1990 population of Juárez stands at 798,522, which planners in both cities recognize as an undercount of at least a half-million people. Juárez is estimated to number 1.2 million people, but the federal government acknowledged its passage beyond the million mark only in the 1995 mid-decade count.[36] Therefore, official figures of all types are based on a pool that is probably two-thirds of the real population of Juárez.

Table 2   El Paso: Official Snapshot, 1990

Income	
Per capita income	$ 9,150
Median household income	$ 22,644
Median family income	$ 24,057
Census tract range of per Capita Income:	
Lowest	$ 2,614
Highest	$ 31,869
Education and Culture	
Aged 25+ without high school diploma	36%
Hispanic	70%
Foreign-born (141,616)	24%
Noncitizens among foreign-born	67%
Self-Employment	
Self-employed as percentage of labor force	6%
Housing	
Buying/own	64%
Renting	36%

Source: U.S. Census, 1990.

We face more difficulties comparing income and education, due to the measures used and their alternative meanings. For example, Mexico's census counts the number of minimum wages earned on per capita or household/family bases, rather than providing average incomes. The length of years associated with primary and secondary school also differs. In Mexico, primary education lasts six years, to which secondary education adds three; an additional three years is preparatory education for advanced study. In the United States, a high school diploma is generally equivalent to twelve years of schooling. But housing rental/ownership rates are comparable. Juárez counts fewer renters than El Paso.

Numbers alone rarely convey the texture of life, change, and movement. Both cities have grown in population and area: El Paso covers 247 square miles, and Juárez about half that figure (the latter is expanding with the municipality's land expropriation of 1993, still contested in the courts in 1997, as detailed in Chapter 5). In Map 2, we see a densely settled urban mass, not two entities clearly separated by an international border.

Table 3   Juárez: Official Snapshot, 1989–93

Income (in minimum wages [MWs])ª	
Jobs earning less than 3 MWs	64%
Jobs earning 3–5 MWs	15%
Jobs earning 5+ MWs	14%
Self-employed workers	
Without social security coverage	28%
In unregistered businesses	13%
Employed informally	30%
Education	
Aged 16+ with less than complete secondary education	51%
Housing	
Buying/own home	79%
Rent	21%

ª1993, MW = U.S. $30 weekly. Unemployed people and those not earning MW are not included.
Sources: Enrique Suárez and Octavio Chávez, *Profile of the United States–Mexico Border* (Juárez: FEMAP, 1996), 102; David Spener, preliminary analysis of 1989 unemployment census (N=2032): "The Mexican Border Crossing Card and US Border Patrol Policy," paper presented to the Meeting of the American Sociological Association, August 19–23, 1995, Washington, D.C., p. 9; *Chihuahua: Resultados Definitivos Datos por AGEB Urbana: XI Censo General de Población y Vivienda, 1990* (Aguascalientes: Instituto Nacional de Estadística, Geografía e Informática, 1992).

The different neighborhoods help tell the larger story of a border global city, in both population and spatial terms. In each city, we begin with the core, adjacent to the downtown area, and move eastward, first to the old periphery and then to the new periphery of urban sprawl.

Neighborhood Portraits

Residents' everyday lives and needs differ depending on their neighborhoods. Each neighborhood is bounded by the invisible lines of the census tract (El Paso) or the *colonias* (Juárez).

El Paso Neighborhoods
El Paso's core neighborhood is squeezed between the high-rise bank buildings of the old central commercial district and the international borderline. Now divided into various census tracts, the settlement

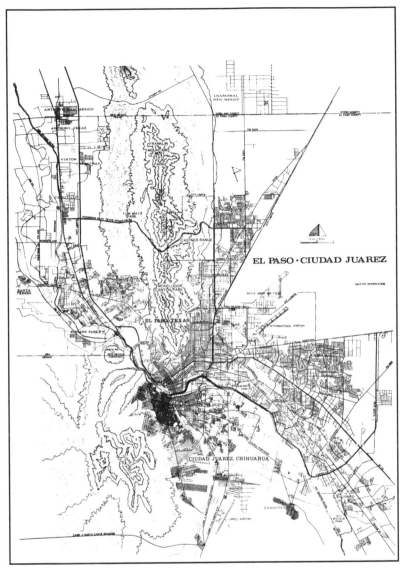

Map 2   Urban Mass: El Paso–Juárez

Source: The Plan for El Paso (El Paso: City Plan Commission, 1988), p. 14

once had a high residential density. At the turn of the century, it was home to the majority of Mexicans in El Paso.[37] The area lost half its population when the Chamizal Agreement (which returned disputed territory to Mexico) and highway construction displaced residents.[38]

In the heart of the city, small houses sit close to multi-family tenement buildings and public housing projects. Residents in tenement buildings share common toilets and faucets; some buildings violate housing codes and are long overdue for official condemnation. Some might label the continued neglect of these violations informal tolerance. The buildings go uncondemned for several reasons. First, the rent is low, and there is a two- or three-year waiting list for the city's 7,000 public housing spaces. Second, several prominent individuals own the tenements, speaking with politically persuasive voices about the high property tax, low rental income, and the insufficient return on expensive rehabilitation, given residents' inability to pay steep rents. Finally, condemnation costs public inspectors time as well as legal and political capital; their superiors choose not to act, making what political scientists call "nondecisions."

No Key to Turn, a poignant film produced by Renata Caldwell in 1983, outlined the dilemmas of core residents and community activists. In that era, members of La Campaña por la Preservación del Barrio/the Neighborhood Preservation Campaign used high-visibility tactics to protest against housing problems. They packed City Council meetings at which leaders asked sharp, shrill questions of a political system accustomed to quiescence from residents. The housing dilemmas were multiple, with spatial consequences for outlying areas to which those with resources sometimes move. Further tenement destruction would displace more residents, while construction of more public housing, which segregates low-income residents, faced opposition in outlying neighborhoods with uncertain public transportation. Not all residents sought to be uprooted from neighbors, churches, and groceries that catered to their needs—all within walking distance. Moreover, during the 1980s the federal government retreated from large-scale housing projects and moved toward rent vouchers and credit support, which spread subsidies to wider and more powerful political constituencies, including bankers and landlords.

La Campaña sought funding to rehabilitate rundown homes and multifamily dwellings rather than to stimulate commercial encroachment. Eventually, this protest organization transformed itself, with federal funds, into a nonprofit entity dedicated, in an era of declining federal support for community development, to rehabilitating homes with public funds. Residents are once again quiescent politically.

Rehabilitation has just begun, and hazards to public safety pervade the area. Interviewers' ethnographic journals provide some vivid neighborhoodwide commentary that complements household-level numeric and narrative analysis. They report that gangs congregate on corners at mid-day. One interviewer witnessed a purse-snatching; he was a block away from a shooting at the neighborhood grocery. Others noticed that residents seem to lock themselves inside small, nearly airless units, "prisoners of their surroundings."[39] Yet they comment that people pursue self-improvement strategies inside their largely rented units: one painted coat after coat on the walls, stopping presumably when the can was empty; holes are patched to keep roaches out; shiny appliances are decorated with beautiful floral arrangements.[40]

The old periphery neighborhood hugs the lower river valley. This area was once home to cotton farms and irrigation ditches that supplied cheap water to farmers until the largest city annexation in El Paso's history took place. The bulk of its ranch-style homes were built in the 1950s and thereafter. The neighborhood appears to be typically middle-class, with medium-sized houses and well-kept yards. As in most parts of El Paso, the neighborhood identity covers a huge stretch of land called the Lower Valley, the second-largest of the nine independent school districts in the county. Some signs of disarray have begun to appear in the area: graffiti, several yards filled with old cars and other objects. Residents, with formal, contractor-built home subdivisions hooked into water and sewer systems, own relatively valuable land that generates property tax. In Texas, local governments depend on property and sales taxes for revenue.

The new periphery lies outside the city limits. Approximately 150 *colonias* have sprung up in El Paso County, where developers have subdivided farm and desert land into sizable lots to sell under contracts of sale. This legal distinction put occupants at greater risk than would land sales registered with the county until a change in Texas law went into effect in 1996. In the new periphery neighborhood, located on high desert and far from water lines, residents either dug their own wells (potentially contaminated with runoff from nearby septic tanks) or bought water and hauled it to their homes. Trailers and houses are built *poco a poco* ("little by little"), gradually improved or completed with accumulated savings. Residents tend to store equipment or used cars in their yards.

The displacement of residents in El Paso's core neighborhoods corresponded with an expansion of *colonias*. Those with resources crossed the city border and tried to realize the dream of home ownership in El Paso County. Since then other new crossers have arrived from a variety of places, as we will see in Chapter 5. Upon arrival, some are courted by social networks involved in collective organizational battles over annexation, water districts, and funds for water and sewer line construction.

Border Identities
Although the census classifies 70 percent of El Pasoans as "Hispanic," the household residents we talked to have many more labels for themselves. They add subtle nuances to the generic term *Hispanic: Mexican American* (the prevailing terminology in the media), *Mexicano, Mexican, Latino, American,* and *Chicano.* In Figure 1, we see these many subtleties, including the 42 percent who call themselves *Mexican* in English or *Mexicano* in Spanish.

El Paso is home to sizable numbers of legal migrants from Mexico whose identity does not disappear on U.S. soil. As we will see later, many residents speak Spanish in their homes, especially in the core and new periphery. Linguistic hegemony does not exist in El Paso, for even local and state government offices recruit bilingual speakers. Children learn in both monolingual and bilingual classes, but most bilingual education is designed to assimilate students into English-language classes.

In El Paso households, 40 percent of the residents with whom we spoke claimed birth in Mexico. A majority are citizens; 22 percent are legal migrants or "permanent residents," complete with "resident alien numbers," some of whom have lived in El Paso for decades. Households are frequently a complex mosaic of migrant parents and birthright citizen-children. For these reasons, immigration surveillance affects people's lives in significant ways, as we will analyze in Chapter 5.

People identify themselves in narrative form, to which we can give numerical shape, as in Figure 1. The three El Paso neighborhoods we studied correspond to census tracts. Only in the new periphery area, part of a large census tract outside the city limits in

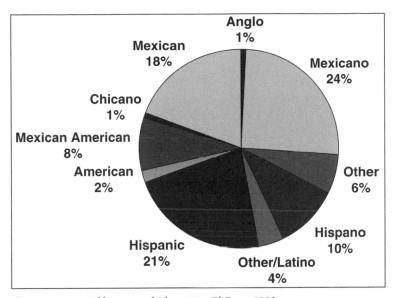

Figure 1   Self-Reported Identities, El Paso, 1992

Note: The English questionnaire asked: "What would you say is your race (ethnicity)?" The Spanish questionnaire asked: "¿A que raza pertenece?" Figures do not total 100% because of missing data.

Source: Household interviews in El Paso, respondents' answers to open-ended question.

El Paso County, did the community have coherence and a neighborhood name. In Table 4, which gives official figures, tract population numbers are rounded off to the nearest thousand, and the self-employed to the nearest ten, in order to protect the anonymity of the neighborhoods. Survey self-employment counts, reported later in this chapter, depart dramatically from these official figures.

Compared with El Paso as a whole, low-income neighborhoods populated largely by census-defined Hispanics are overrepresented in our survey. But, given El Paso's median income of $23,000, the entire research, with that overrepresentation, allows us to understand the experiences of El Paso's bottom economic half in relatively representative terms.

Our household interviews paint a richer and somewhat different picture of these neighborhoods, particularly when it comes to the various ways incomes are generated or enhanced by crossing the

Table 4   Official Census Neighborhood Statistics, El Paso, 1990

	Self-Employed/ Population	Hispanic	Own Home	Median Household Income
Core	40+/3,000	99%	15%	$7,100
Old periphery	20+/8,000	93%	68%	21,000
New periphery[a]	280/8,000	72%	87%	28,000

[a]The *colonia* is one pocket of this tract.
Source: U.S. Census, 1990.

border to take advantage of low prices for goods and services in Juárez (see Table 5). I analyze the U.S. side more fully than the Mexican in these terms. Informality extends our understanding of El Paso neighborhoods far beyond what the census categories allow, but informality is no secret in Mexico.

Residents' informality is not readily visible to the political and policy community. Besides, neither political agendas nor policies legitimize informality. Residents who earn income and build homes informally are relatively unorganized, in part because of their noncitizen status, but the channels of political participation are weak as well, as we will see in later chapters.

Juárez Neighborhoods

Ciudad Juárez is a political community with extensive civic participation, much of it based in partisan politics. As in all of Mexico, one party, the PRI, dominated municipal politics under the guise of multiparty democracy through the 1970s. With the national economic crisis of the early 1980s, PRI lost its grip at the northern frontier. Defectors shifted their support toward the Partido Acción Nacional (PAN) with its agenda of economic liberalism (in the classic and Latin American sense). Among these defectors was an influential group of industrialists and entrepreneurs, dubbed "neo-PANistas" by their critics inside and outside because of their seemingly shallow commitment to the PAN's socially conservative historical agenda, born during the 1930s.

The PAN won the municipal presidency from 1983 to 1986. In the latter year the municipal president lost his bid for state governor. It

Table 5   Household Survey Portraits, El Paso, 1992

	Core	Old Periphery	New Periphery
Call themselves *Mexican/Mexicano*	67%	21%	38%
Speak Spanish in homes	85%	41%	79%
Household income range/week	$40–638	$85–1,766	$20–2,000
Median household income/week	$200	$400	$240
Informal work/business	32%	38%	30%
Occasional informality	40%	36%	41%
Cross border for goods	50%	46%	55%
Cross border for services	52%	28%	49%

was widely believed that the PRI-controlled electoral machinery refused to recognize his victory. He tried again in 1992, and this time won both votes and official recognition. His economic liberalism matched the agenda of the Salinas presidency far more than the policies of the PRI's leftist archenemy, the Democratic Revolutionary Party/Partido Revolucionario Democrático (PRD). The PAN's control of the state overlapped with renewed victories at the municipal level, where it gained the local presidency from 1992 to 1995 and consolidated its hold in the election of 1995.

Part of the PAN's appeal was its passionate commitment to decentralization in the highly centralized Mexican "federal" system.[41] Mexico City extracts from the state the value-added or sales tax, income taxes, and international bridge tolls, returning a fraction (in the eyes of city leaders) based on an officially undercounted population and political alignments. Juárez must cope with national policies that spur industrial and population growth, along with border crossing, yet it lacks the resources to manage and respond to that growth and activity. The municipal budget of Juárez is equivalent to U.S. $43 million; the city of El Paso has a budget of $376 million for half that many people.[42] More recently, Juárez changed the name of a key thoroughfare, Ejército Nacional (National Army), to Municipio Libre (free municipality), a striking symbol of commitment of the city's industrial and commercial class. Even the PRI-identified members maintain an uneasy relationship with Mexico City, whose agents' behavior is characterized as *"terorismo fiscal,"* or fiscal terrorism, to use the strong and vivid language of the popular media.

In classic machine style, the PRI had long organized its grassroots supporters and patronage recipients along occupational and neighborhood lines. The city is divided into approximately 200 named *colonias,* or neighborhoods. *Colonia* leaders worked with *jefes de manzana,* or block leaders, to mobilize residents, not only during elections, but between elections as well. A certain sense of community is created, however top-down in orientation. Friendship and kinship underlie the political machinery, as families bond with one another to struggle for services. Yet shaping this superficial community is the reality of Juárez as a city of many migrants. Grassroots organizations that cut across neighborhood lines bemoan the *"por mientras"* ("for a while") mentality "that plagues border communities."[43] Borders are transitional places.

Several ideologically based popular organizations operate in northern Mexico. The most important in Juárez is the Popular Defense Committee/Comité de Defensa Popular (CDP). Under CDP leadership, settlers "invaded" publicly and privately owned land to create new *colonias.* The CDP founded thirty-one *colonias* in Juárez from 1976 through 1992, settling approximately 10,000 members.[44] CDP leaders maintain a dense, top-down organization reinforced with weekly meetings. Residents post the CDP acronym and symbols near their front doors to demonstrate their affiliation.

Both the PRI and the PAN have had uneasy relationships with the CDP, ranging from hostile confrontation to coexistence and support. CDP "protects" its unpaved streets from incursions by police, who are sometimes fearful of entering the winding *colonia* roads that lead to deadends and potential entrapment. In the past, the CDP protected residents from eviction and the penalties associated with utility piracy. During the 1990s, however, residents sought the security of land title deeds and stable utilities, despite the user fees and the property taxes that follow land registry documentation.[45]

The PAN reproduced neighborhood organizations under new processes and a new name, the *comités de vecinos* ("committees of neighbors"). Staff of the municipal government's Social Development Department issued a *Directorio y Manual de Procedimientos Públicos para los Comités de Vecinos* ("Directory and Procedural

Manual for the Committees of Neighbors") so that residents could elect their own representatives and become "living, autonomous entities that take their own initiative" in working for neighborhood interests, according to the officials we interviewed. The rhetoric has a populist cast. One official said, "The administration wants communities to be their own doctors"; no longer should "college boys (*chavos*) go into the *colonias* and tell them what they need."[46]

The PAN's Straight Citizen Program (Programa Ciudadano Derecho) offers a sixteen-point set of principles to which citizens and their leaders subscribe. The code emphasizes family values, integrity, hard work, environmental soundness, and a drug-free life with moderate alcohol consumption. Point 15 is civic: "A straight citizen is democratic; he or she votes in order to elect government officials." Once the civic mode is inculcated, the hope seems to be that participation will be contained in an individualized voting relationship.

The household interviews for Juárez uncovered little variation in median earnings and income informality. Earnings hovered around the equivalent of U.S. $90 a week, which, as we will see (Chapter 4), includes multiple earners and strategic users of cross-border opportunities, especially in the core and old periphery neighborhoods. Within the old periphery, two neighborhoods sit side by side. Dwellers in the owner-occupied, government-built INFONAVIT apartments earn three times the weekly income of their mostly CDP neighbors. The old periphery had more informal businesses than the core or the new periphery, but in all neighborhoods the proportion of informal employment hovered near a third. In the new periphery, informal housing is extensive (see Chapter 5).

In Juárez, the core neighborhood is located near the commercial district downtown, in a old neighborhood of one-family dwellings. As in many Latin American countries, Juárez's city center retains a mixture of middle-class residents and people working in service and tourism jobs. One sees PRI slogans painted on walls, even between elections. The large elementary school, with its walled schoolyard, received some federal funding under the National Solidarity Program/Programa Nacional Solidaridad (PRONASOL) to improve the school grounds. Signs bear the three colors of Solidarity—white, red, and green—which match the colors of the PRI. Solidarity committees organize the community's contribution to this municipally and federally funded community development program.

An interview with Norma, a *comité de vecinos* member, paints a picture of neighborhood initiatives.[47] Norma and her neighbors are working to create a park for children on donated land. Every third day, families get together to water the grass. Committee members avoid discussions about parties or religion, but once they invited the local Catholic priest to come to a meeting (he never came, according to Norma). The government promised to install drinking fountains, but never came through; officials did, however, provide paints, as promised. Local businesses donated benches, as long as their names could adorn the seats. Residents worry whether gang members (*cholos*) will wreck their park; graffiti are everywhere.

The government-constructed, owner-occupied, housing of the old periphery sits between paved side streets. The units, which look like townhouses, are approximately twenty years old and, on a street-by-street basis, more or less spacious, seemingly according to the residents' more or less privileged formal employment. The INFON-AVIT homes are solid, but generally modest in size, built according to precise specifications with public utilities included.

The CDP neighborhood next door is named after a political milestone. Bumpy and unpaved streets are connected in a mazelike pattern. Houses made of cement blocks and cartons sit side by side. Although CDP signs adorn many front facades, the organization no longer has the same hold over residents that it once had. Still, our research team and interviewers informed CDP leaders about interviews in advance in order to get their implied consent.

Both neighborhoods contain visible signs of self-employment. Small stores, *tienditas*, dot the residential area. Some houses have "selling windows" or signs posted about the sale of sodas and food. Traders approach people on the street with jewelry to sell.

Although the poorer neighborhood is changing politically, the CDP still draws residents to weekly meetings. Patricia, a CDP representative, worried about the commitee's inability to get services from the municipal government; at least when the PRI was in power, they would get things, she told an interviewer. The CDP tried to negotiate a deal whereby residents would contribute 25 percent of the cost of paving the streets, but most could not afford it. Some residents had approached the municipal Social Development Department about establishing a *comité de vecinos*, but CDP people viewed this as an attempt to break *colonia* unity. A lawyer came to fix land title deeds, collected money, and never returned, Patricia said.

In contrast, the INFONAVIT neighborhood is well organized. Its *comité de vecinos,* mostly women, had a spokesman for interviews. Their priorities include creating green areas and cleaning up a local canal that might contain infectious wastes. The canal is also a gathering place for *cholos,* say leaders. Municipal officials share this perception, worrying that gang members prey on their prosperous neighbors. Graffiti and deteriorated buildings can be found in some streets, but not all. Besides its *comité,* the more prosperous side of this area organizes a *ciudadano vigilante,* or vigilant citizen group, on the lookout for crime. (El Paso also has neighborhood crime watch programs.)

The new periphery neighborhood is part of the urban sprawl extending from the southeast of the city. It is a bedroom community for nearby *maquila* plants. The homes are new, small, and not yet painted. The area is dusty, for no internal roads have been paved (except for the one in front of the founder's home). Like many others, this *colonia* made the transition from PRI to PAN organization. We will take up neighborhood politics and the successful struggle for public services in Chapter 6.

Portraits in the Popular Media

Poised for NAFTA and Beyond

In the early 1990s, the border global city of El Paso/Juárez stood at the brink of the North American Free Trade Agreement (NAFTA). Mexico's 1986 entry into the General Agreement on Tariffs and Trade had eased formal cross-border trade in a region that was already commercially integrated through extensive formal and informal crossings of people, goods, and capital.

Selected newspaper headlines paint yet another picture of the borderzone (Box 1). The headlines (chosen from more than 200) carry us from 1991 beyond the anticlimax of the official agreement, which took effect on January 1, 1994 (famous also as the date when the Chiapas rebellion launched the Zapatistas into Mexico's popular imagination). They also reveal other important preoccupations at the border: professionalizing the Mexican customs, managing cross-border informal trade between those quintessential free traders and the street-level bureaucrats with whom they negotiate, the customs agents.

On the eve of NAFTA, the border was as leaky as ever,[48] much to the dismay of those concerned with trade deficits. Informals contribute to leaky borders and trade deficits in ways that have never been fully documented. Had financial observers been watching for historical patterns, they might have predicted the fateful 1994–95 peso devaluation. With their numerous petty regulations involving licenses and payments, governments bureaucratized formal commerce and privileged it as legally compliant. Formal businesses can pay lawyers and accountants to decipher and comply with the ever-changing rules. Governments are less able to control informals.

Cross-border informal commerce is sometimes called the *fayuca* ("contraband") trade. *Fayuca* networks are said to stretch all the way into the interior. From Chihuahua City's El Pasito ("little El Paso") market, five hours drive to the south, to the grand-scale *fayuca* markets of Mexico City, such as El Tepito, traders resell goods from all over the world at prices well below those of established businesses. Moreover, Mexican consumers, rightly or wrongly, view these foreign-made goods as superior to national products. Established business owners complain that they face a level of competition from cross-border commerce that officials in Mexico City do not fully understand.

Truck and van drivers involved in the *fayuca* trade make their way into the interior, striking deals with officials in agencies and at highway checkpoints. Meanwhile, the *fayuca* trade makes its way into the popular discourse and imagination through widespread coverage in the local Juárez newspapers. An extensive investigative series in *Norte de Ciudad Juárez* involved the CDP's effort to branch out into informal commerce. But not even the CDP can control all the informal commerce.

People seem to comply with official transcripts; in fact, as we will see in later chapters, they ignore, negotiate with, or resist petty rules. Rules protect formal businesses and government revenue extraction. Although NAFTA emphasized the reduction of bureaucratic obstacles and complicated tariff schedules, inefficient and labyrinthine machinery continued through 1997 to mystify the process for many, especially those without customs brokers or the CDP brokers labeled "corrupt" by the establishment.

Box I. Selected Headlines: The Juárez Media from NAFTA's Eve to Anticlimax

"Nueva Policía Fiscal: Idealismo, Contra Desprestigio y Carencias," *Norte de Ciudad Juárez,* December 6, 1991
New replacements fill posts vacated with the departure of 185 former customs agents who were "retired." The median age of the new agents is twenty-seven; they are described as devoted to the law.

"Es Más Restrictiva la Aduana Mexicana," *Norte de Ciudad Juárez,* November 30, 1993
Juárez residents may bring home up to $50 worth of goods from each trip to the United States (no more than $350 monthly for food and clothes), considerably less than the $400 worth of goods U.S. residents may bring home from each trip to Mexico. Taxes and fines also differ. If Juárez residents exceed the $50 limit, they must pay a 32.8 percent tax. If they do not declare the merchandise, they pay a fine of 400 percent of the amount, and may have their vehicle seized.

"Justifica PRI Contrabando," *Norte de Ciudad Juárez,* December 7, 1993
The practice of extortion and corruption on the part of the fiscal police must be punished, says the PRI Municipal Committee chairman. He says that these practices will continue if free imports are not authorized, without bureaucracy. Used goods merchants bring in their goods through bribes (*mordida*).

"Fayuca Inunda a Juárez," *Norte de Ciudad Juárez,* December 8, 1993
Contraband (*fayuca*) supports a powerful subterranean economy that increases corruption and leads to bankruptcy for legally established commerce. Car motor oil is an example. [Note: This article was part of a series that sustained headlines on reactions and investigations for a month.]

U.S. motor oil has saturated local markets without generating tax payments, only the *mordida* for customs. The CDP "king of contraband" controls this highly profitable trade. The most important storage centers are located in the CDP *colonia* Tierra y Libertad. These supply more than half the oil sellers registered with the Municipal Commerce Department.

"Opiniones," *Norte de Ciudad Juárez,* December 14, 1993
What is your opinion about the accusations that customs agents have failed to pay attention to contraband?

President of CANACINTRA (Chamber of Industry): Accusations must be investigated and results published; otherwise people won't respect the authorities.

Director of CANACO (Chamber of Commerce): These illegal actions create unfair competition [*competencia desleal,* literally "disloyal competition"] between smugglers and merchants.

Democratic Revolutionary Party (PRD) spokesman: All products from our neighbor city [El Paso] should be duty free. That way, all residents could gain from NAFTA, for right now the wealthy entrepreneurs have all the advantages.

On January 1, 1994, NAFTA went into effect.

"Lentitud en Importaciones," *Diario de Juárez,* **April 6, 1994**
New importation procedures are holding up imports. One importer of waterproof paper says the procedures are the same, but the process just takes longer.

"Mantienen Control de la Importación," *Norte de Ciudad Juárez,* **January 5, 1994**
Permits have been liberalized, but duties have increased up to 270 percent for those without previous permits from the Secretariat of Commerce and Finance. The CANACO vice president says that SECOFI keeps control of imports, even after NAFTA. She says it is impossible for Juárez commerce to compete with commerce in El Paso under these conditions.

"Duplica México Compras de EU," *Norte de Ciudad Juárez,* **January 14, 1994**
Juárez residents spend an average of $20 weekly in El Paso, according to the Bank of Mexico's Economic Research Department. It registers a trimester deficit of $343 million, down from a trimester deficit of $599 million in 1992.

"Solo Más Importaciones," *Norte de Ciudad Juárez,* **July 1, 1994**
After six months of NAFTA, the hoped-for benefits for the city and the county have been limited. While the opportunities for export have not been capitalized on, imports have increased.

Conclusion

The El Paso/Juárez area has long been integrated through the movement of people, goods, and capital. Both cities deal with migrant populations and distant capital cities that try, with limited success, to control the border.

A preview of the changing global economy is on display at the U.S.–Mexico border. Both cities underwent unique but related versions of structural adjustment: El Paso going from high-wage to low-wage (apparel) manufacturing; Juárez experiencing maquiladorization linked to foreign capital. The borderline creates wage advantages for industrial investors.

The portraits we have seen of the global city establish a context for subsequent chapters. Official portraits of El Paso and Juárez reveal a region divided into economic enclaves, seemingly rich at the north and poor at the south. Yet El Paso is a poor homeland compared with its mainstream, while Juárez is relatively well off, even with a majority of residents working below the poverty line. Only in Juárez does the predictably high level of informality associated with a global economy appear in official statistics. Neighborhood portraits, however, reveal considerable informality on both sides of the border. Political community, top-down in origin, makes neighborhoods cohere more readily in Juárez than El Paso, a coherence with potential payoff in multiparty competitive elections. The borderline itself creates opportunity for comparative price advantages that informal traders use but that will, ironically, probably decline as official Free Trade is consolidated.

CHAPTER 4

Finding and Making Work Within and Across Borders

The Informal Underbelly at the Border

El tráfico "hormiga" de mercancías se sigue dando.
  Juárez journalist

At the border, people invest considerable informal labor in sustaining themselves and their families. They use ingenuity in identifying opportunities and circumventing constraints. The Juárez journalist who used the metaphor of "ant traffic" to describe cross-border merchandising,[1] conveys their persistence in the face of the official rules.

Henry Selby and others refer to family solidarity as a form of self-defense, a "Mexican solution."[2] Informal work and housing, to which many family members contribute in many ways, are part of this solution. In this chapter, we use information from households and individuals to explore whether and how that solution works at the U.S.–Mexico border.

First I discuss informality in the context of a border global city, including its multiple meanings in Mexico and the United States. After examining two factors linked to extensive informality, poverty and immigration, I turn to information from households. At least a third of households, on *both* sides of the border, participate in informal work. I also look at the borderline as a space over which people cross to generate informal earnings. I compare crossers and noncrossers within households, and then analyze *fayuqueras* ("contrabandists") for extra depth. Finally, I examine three of the six neighborhoods for connections between informality and immigration, poverty, or both. I contrast those findings with the data we gathered about street vendors, who operate on independent and contractual bases in public rather than private space.

In this chapter, we find no clear and simple relationship between poverty, migration, and informal work. Informal work serves, however, as a cushion that protects people from absolute poverty. In a larger sense, informality operates where people control resources beyond subsistence levels in opportune space that is relatively free from regulatory surveillance. But regulations vary, as do enforcement strategies and levels of authority. When it comes to licensing, taxes, and customs, people counter the hegemonic arms of petty business regulation. The grander shifts in immigration and monetary policy are harder to escape, as we will discover in the concluding chapter.

Informalization in a Border Global City

El Paso-Juárez, the aspiring global city at the border, presents a new kind of informalization beyond that already conceptualized in global cities. But its newness is deceptive, old wine in a new bottle. The bottle is late twentieth-century capitalism's globalized economy of porous borders, and the informalization itself recalls some of the earliest observations of southern countries' income-generating and income-stretching practices that fall through the cracks of modern surveillance.

In the seeming epitome of modernity, global cities, informalization expands. Saskia Sassen distinguishes two spheres: "One sphere circulates internally and mostly meets the demands of its members, such as small immigrant-owned shops in the immigrant community that service the latter; the other circulates throughout the 'formal' sector of the economy . . . through subcontracting, the use of sweatshops and homework."[3] Chapter 3 addressed El Paso garment factories. Households here show considerable amounts of social security noncompliance, one of several informality indicators, and one that is typical in garment factories and subcontractor operations.

To Sassen's two spheres, however, we must add a third: informal self-employment, also called casual labor.[4] Neither of Sassen's spheres fully covers all the ways people make paid work for themselves at the border. These informals rarely employ other paid workers (as in Sassen's first sphere, "shops"), and they circulate outside their own enclaves, contracting their labor and engaging in domestic work, gardening, and buying/reselling services within regions and across borders.

The concept of informality, born in "developing" countries (the euphemism for the low-income countries of the south), is most frequently applied to people with limited resources and skills. Consistent with the market-led approaches of the 1980s and thereafter, poverty-reduction strategists problematized both the credit squeeze and the regulation burdens on budding microentrepreneurs. This is the standard analysis of international aid agencies and determines their prescriptions for reforms.[5]

Mexico has more poverty than the United States, in both absolute and proportional terms. Thus, one might expect more informality on the Mexican side of the border. Modern countries of the north, such as the United States, distance themselves from international development problems and solutions; informal labor is viewed as aberrant or criminal, and rarely recognized as self-employment or work. But when informality *is* identified in the United States, at a minimal or a substantial rate, is it a poverty issue?

Mexico keeps track of informality among its economically active population. Mexico's 1988 employment survey (Figure 2) shows half of informal workers earning less than the minimum wage, compared with a fifth of formal workers.[6] (Formal institutions are, of course more easily monitored for labor-law violations, including subminimum wages.) Still, the same survey shows the largest block of informals earning between one and two minimum wages.

How feminized is informality? The answer has some bearing on informality's connection to poverty. Gender disparities in earnings are ubiquitous and global, not confined to the United States and Mexico.[7] A gender hierarchy pervades informal work, rendering consistently less compensation for women than men.[8] The 1988 employment survey mentioned above showed a somewhat higher representation of women in informal work (38 percent) than formal (31 percent).[9] This is not evidence of female majority participation (i.e., feminization), but of relatively gender-balanced participation.

Informal earnings vary by task and location. At Mexico's northern border, informals' earnings are comparable to the earnings of many of the formally employed. Examining quarterly employment surveys from 1986 to 1987, Bryan Roberts found that "being self-employed earns significantly more than being employed in a large organization."[10] However, informals gain few or no employee ben-

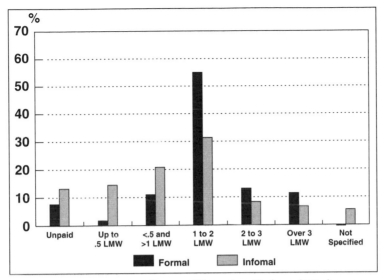

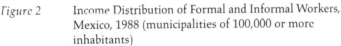

Figure 2   Income Distribution of Formal and Informal Workers,
Mexico, 1988 (municipalities of 100,000 or more
inhabitants)

Source: Secretaría del Trabajo y Previsión Social (STPS) and U.S. Department of
Labor (USDL), *The Informal Sector in Mexico* (Mexico City and Washington, D.C.:
STPS and USDL, 1992), 37b.

LMW = legal minimum wage.

efits from government health and social security programs (IMSS)
or from INFONAVIT.

Informal earnings may represent a more accurate indicator of
a market-based minimum wage than the politically set official
minimum-wage levels. Official commissions set minimum wages
in Mexico, where artificially low wages are supposed to minimize
inflation and to make Mexico attractive to foreign investment.

At the northern Mexican border, many formal earners work in
maquiladoras at minimum wages or slightly more. In 1992, when
we interviewed household members, the full-time minimum wage
was approximately U.S. $30 per week. One of the neighborhoods
surveyed contained what might be termed a bedroom community
for nearby maquilas in the Juárez new periphery. In Figure 3, we see
that those *maquila* earners make between one and two minimum
wages per week, with men making slightly more than women.

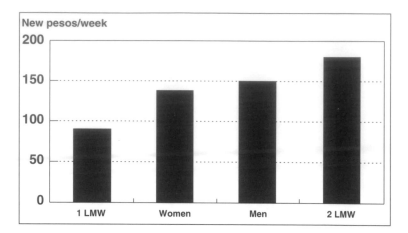

New pesos/week

Figure 3   Maquila Wages in the New Periphery for Women and
Men, Juárez, 1992

LMW = legal minimum wage. Three new pesos = $1.
Ns = 37 women, 59 men.

These differences can be attributed to the *plants* in which men work (transport and automotive, rather than garment and electronics) and the *tasks* to which men are assigned, recruitment and assignment constructions that overlap with gender.

Using Figure 3, we could make the case that *formal* work in export-processing industrialization is associated with poverty. The border economic context lacks sufficient numbers of formal jobs that pay above the (unofficial) poverty level (i.e., three times the minimum wage: see Chapter 3). To compensate, individuals work at multiple jobs in households with multiple earners.

We can therefore question any clear-cut relationship between informal work and poverty. Elsewhere in the Americas, it appears that informality cuts across economic class lines.[11] Furthermore, once it is clear that informality involves subcontracting—that is, formal businesses reducing costs through regulatory noncompliance—the break with poverty is even clearer, at least for those employers. Fine hierarchical distinctions among informal entrepreneurs emerge, from sweatshop owners and employees to used-car sellers and to food concession companies and the street vendors with whom they contract.[12]

Even the informally self-employed need *some* economic resources to get started (as is discussed below in this chapter). Those
who *produce* require start-up capital (usually savings) for equipment and raw materials; those who *provide services* require money
for mobility. In analyzing the households, we also learn that self-
employed informality is no more common in the poorest of the six
neighborhoods, El Paso's downtown. In this area the poverty is a
matter not only of limited cash but also of atomization and official
surveillance.

Informality and Immigration

Historically, migrants used self-employment and unpaid family labor for both subsistence and upward-mobility strategies. They may
carry cultural entrepreneurial baggage with them or acquire that
baggage in their new homeland for lack of other options. Immigrants draw customers and employees from those who share their
national origin. Often excluded from official and commercial credit,
they tap capital through kinship and social networks.[13] We might
expect informality to flourish among immigrants.

At the border, we can examine the relationship of informality to
migration among citizens, residents, and migrants. It would be a
mistake to assume that a group called *Hispanics, Mexican Americans,* or *Chicanos* can be lumped together with the category labeled
immigrants. Self-defined ethnics/non-U.S. nationals make up virtually all those we talked to on the U.S. side (see Figure 1 in Chapter 3) Many are assimilated into the mainstream through forces in
civil society, such as schools, public services, civic participation, and
workplaces. But the assimilation may be uneven, given the proximity of the border to their historic homelands in the south.

Immigrants are not immigrants forever. Many immigrants are
permanent residents, authorized to live and work in the United States
in a kind of citizenship limbo; others become naturalized citizens.
Even immigrants who remain undocumented may give birth to citizen children, potentially rooting households in the United States. Informalization might be expected to diminish under stricter border
control, to the extent that informality is associated with immigration.

Talking about "immigrants" focuses more attention on the people—perhaps on their economic vulnerability or on their cultural
baggage—than on the spatial characteristics of the economy in

which they are situated. But all these characteristics need to be explored if we are to comprehend the future spread of global economic effects in the heartlands.

Border space offers a myriad of crossing opportunities. Informal workers and traders not only work on their own side of the border; they also cross borders. One study distinguishes no fewer than eight types of crossers, ranging from day crossers to permanent crossers.[14]

Borderlands permit those with cash and risk-taking propensities to trade or to sell their labor on the other side. Nowhere is this clearer than among south-to-north crossers who buy goods for resale or who sell their services. Although crossing consumes time and generates risks for those without documents, the national price and wage differentials make crossing well worth while for people interested in generating central or supplementary household earnings, particularly in Juárez households. Were it not for crossers' uneven compliance with binational regulatory machinery (the official scripts), neoclassical economists might well applaud their use of "comparative advantages" at the border. We now turn to how crossers' earnings not only elevate their household income but also reduce persistent national and gender inequalities.

To the extent that informality is a work behavior best documented in countries like Mexico and those to the south, we might expect to uncover more informality among those households with one or more adult residents born outside the United States. We categorize those households as *migrant*, for their cultural baggage is assumed to be distinctive enough to produce different behavior. Households with *all* adults born inside the United States are classified as *nonmigrant*. While many nonmigrants continue to identify themselves as Mexican American/Hispanic, they are exposed to assimilationist hegemonic institutions on a longer-term, more regular basis. If it turns out that nonmigrants pursue informal labor to the same extent as migrants, then we must shift our focus from their cultural baggage to spatial factors and to the economy itself.

Measuring Work Informality at the Border

Regardless of their individual migrant status, policies and institutions affect people's labors and lives. Political institutions mediate or "channel larger political economic forces into settings that have impact on the lives of individuals."[15] Institutions mediate the visibility and viability of informal labor as well. Visibility is enhanced with reports, already discussed as extensive in Mexico, and indicators of measurement that make informality easier to identify.

I incorporate both U.S. and Mexican approaches here to document informality on both sides of the border. A bottom-line indicator is based on queries about self-employment, whether the occupation is primary or not. Another indicator of informality is nonpayment into social security. This approach is preferable to the earlier ones that defined informality largely as involvement in small business.

The considerable amount of informal work that goes on in Mexico has been incorporated into official and academic studies for the last two decades. Informal workers are so numerous that they constitute a politically significant group, particularly in local politics. Many participate in collective organizations whose leaders negotiate with officials to distribute benefits selectively to members, in clientelist fashion, or to protect members from enforcement of the numerous and complex regulatory laws. Protests and street vendors' "invasions" of public space are regularly covered in local media.[16]

The federal government extracts value-added (sales) taxes of 10–15 percent from formal and informal operations alike, though such taxes are enforced more easily in semifixed and fixed locations such as markets and commercial establishments. Employers are required to pay into the social security (IMSS) and worker housing (INFONAVIT) funds. At the municipal level, Mexican officials develop complex procedures to control commerce and extract revenue therefrom. Collective organizations extract political concessions in exchange for support. The municipal government sells commercial licenses at various rates, using procedures that vary in nontransparent ways from each three-year administration to the next. Northern Mexico's alternation between rule by the official, dominant PRI and rule by the opposition party makes commercial license procedures a window on local policy rhetoric and practice and a scale for measuring the viability of different political constituencies.

In Figure 4, we gaze (or glaze) at a flow chart illustrating the commercial licensing process in the PRI-controlled municipality before the PAN took control in 1992. The PRI made it possible for both individuals and organizational leaders to secure licenses, thereby politicizing the process and permitting leaders to augment their incomes with the extra fees they levied on members. Once in the po-

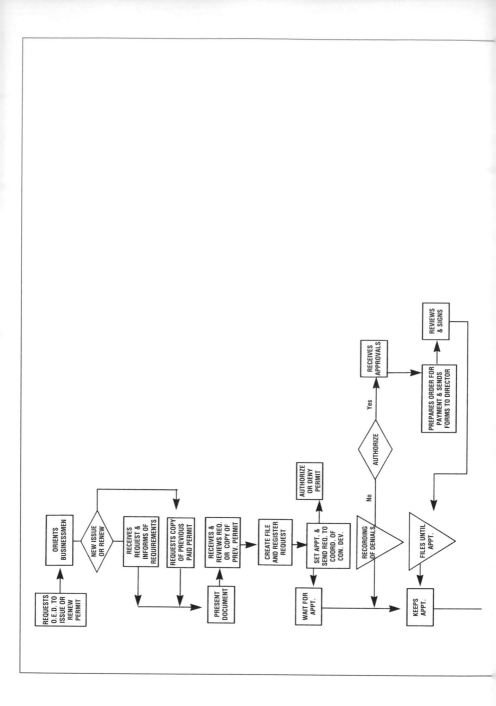

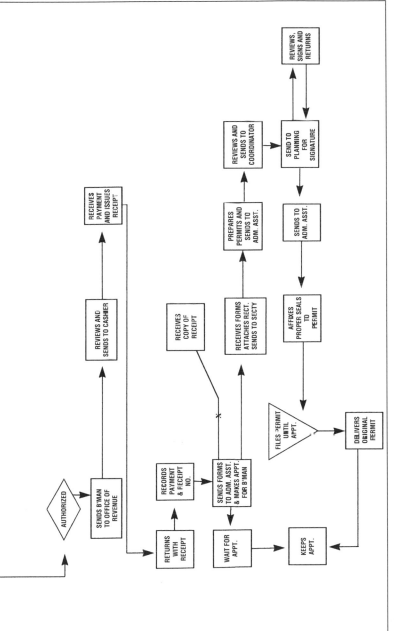

Figure 4   Process for Granting Licenses to Juárez Vendors Before 1992

Source: Data collected by Patricia Luna; layout by Larry White and Mike Cabral.

litical process, penalties for noncompliance can be swept away collectively, through negotiation and concession, and individually, through official fines and unofficial payments. As analyzed in other chapters, the PAN opposition government seeks to depoliticize the process, with varying degrees of success.

Informality's legitimacy in Mexico contrasts with its illegitimacy in the United States. Moving north, we find an equally complex set of procedures associated with commerce, self-employment, home-based work, and street vending. Several layers of government are involved: city (licenses issued by the comptroller, police checks for itinerant vendors), county (name registration, other licenses), state (sales tax, other licenses), and federal (income and Social Security tax). The procedures are relatively transparent, in the sense that consistent answers and figures are available in both oral and written form. But their uneven enforcement makes them as political in this bureaucratically driven system as they are in Mexico's constituency-driven system.

The U.S. Internal Revenue Service (IRS) treats informality as tax noncompliance, including noncompliance with the Social Security tax levied on the self-employed. Internal studies target the self-employed as "especially likely" to underreport income. One study differentiates three categories of U.S. businesses and industries, based on "the ratio of noncorporate employee compensation to total employee compensation": "suspect," "intermediate," and "well-measured." Service, home-based, and trade businesses fall into the suspect group, while large and publicly visible industries are in the well-measured group.[17] Despite surveillance, audits, and cross-checking, broad-based tax collection depends largely on voluntary compliance. Officials hope to deter noncompliance through criminalization or threats to criminalize unauthorized behavior.

This stigmatized informal labor has rarely been studied in a systematic or comprehensive way. More common is the use of vivid illustrations and small samples. The few systematic studies rely mainly on *indirect* estimates, or guesstimates, that hover around a tenth of the Gross Domestic Product.[18] Direct estimates of the number of informals or their percentage among workers are unavailable.

Vulnerable to prosecution as they are, U.S. informals rarely organize or affiliate with political parties as their counterparts in Mexico do. Perhaps their numbers are as large, perhaps not. U.S. informals' safest strategy is to melt into the woodwork and avoid surveillance and the criminalization associated with regulation non-compliance, whether those regulations are serious or petty. As a result, they lose the opportunity to influence policy or enforcement except in individually opportune ways. We shall try, nevertheless, to document the incidence of informality at the U.S.-Mexico border, based on migration and household income levels.

Informalization in the Border Economy

The international border divides two seemingly different worlds. Clearly, earnings and compensation levels differ, as do immigration and poverty levels. But do the different political and policy worlds matter for the incidence of informality?

At the time of our household interviews, per capita income was approximately ten times greater in the United States than in Mexico, though that gap narrowed in subsequent years (to rise again after Mexico's peso devaluation of late 1994). U.S. full-time minimum wages were approximately five times the minimum wages in the border states of northern Mexico (U.S. $160 a week versus $30 a week). Yet the economies are interrelated, as are the people who cross extensively to shop, to visit, and even to work with or without authorization.

Besides economic interdependence, residents on both sides of the border strive for similar material possessions and household conveniences. The incidence of these goods, uncovered in household interviews, tells us something about spending priorities, disposable income, and the goods that people deem to be common necessities.

In Figure 5, we see what consumer goods are found in households in El Paso and Juárez.[19] While houses are smaller in Juárez (see Chapters 5 and 6), comparable proportions of households had acquired televisions, radios, and kitchen appliances. Video-cassette recorders (VCRs) are somewhat less widespread in Juárez (two-fifths of households) than in El Paso (three-fifths). Material consumption does not vary as much as borderlines might suggest.

The Incidence of Informality

In our household interviews, people reported informal work and business at comparable rates on both sides of the border, with slightly more on its northern side. (As noted above, we measured

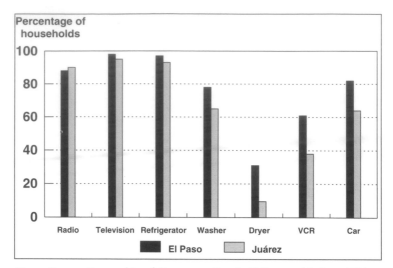

Figure 5   Ownership of Consumer Goods, El Paso and Juárez, 1992

the informal provision of legal goods and services, *not* illegal ones, such as drugs or gambling.)

In Figure 6, we can compare various kinds of informality. The first bar shows the percentage of self-reported informal businesses among the households surveyed. These businesses include self-employment and contracted services. The term *contractor* conveys the general idea but smacks too much of written agreements, enforceable through contracts. Informals generally do not leave paper trails, and they comply unevenly with regulations.

For each informal job or business, householders answered a four-page questionnaire supplement about start-up costs, capital, and clientele. This added considerable time to the household interview. If anything, Figure 6 underreports self-employment, for despite assurances of anonymity, people may have worried about jeopardizing the security of their income.

Figure 6 also reports the proportion of households with workers who are not covered by social security. These figures embrace those workers whose employers do not comply with social security payment laws. Here we see higher levels on the Juárez side.[20]

Yet another way to measure informality is the *occasional* provision of informal labor and services (bar 3). Here, the El Paso house-

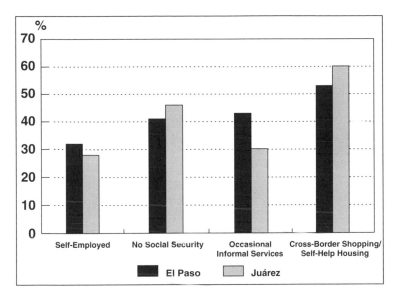

Figure 6   Informal Work, El Paso and Juárez, 1992

hold figures jump up, even as the Juárez figures remain similar to the first bar.

The final bar departs from most conceptions and measurements of informality. If we accept self-help housing as a labor-intensive and income-substituting category of informality, then it is consistent also to embrace labor-intensive cross-border shopping for products (like legal drugs, electronic equipment) and services (like surgery, dental care) that can be had across the border at a fraction of their hometown costs. Both self-help housing and shopping "on the other side" flourish, free of surveillance, over hospitable city/county and international borders. Both activities involve risks, time, and maneuvering skills. Figure 6 suggests the extensive *income-stretching* behavior of people at the border who cross to the other side for comparative price advantages. More than half of the households on both sides have members who cross the border to purchase goods and services at marked savings.

Juarenses cross to El Paso to purchase food, clothing, and electronic equipment. As we saw in Chapter 3, U.S. policy encourages cross-border shopping with Border Crossing Cards (BCCs). The Government of Mexico has pursued several contradictory policies on this matter. Its high tariffs, protecting what many consumers thought were low-quality goods at high prices in Mexico, discouraged U.S. imports. When Mexico entered the General Agreement on Tariffs and Trade in 1986, this official protectionism began to be dismantled (a process that continued with NAFTA).

Until 1992, however, the Mexican government simultaneously provided incentives for northern Mexican frontier residents to shop across the border. People could bring home goods valued up to $350 every month. At customs barriers 28 kilometers south of the border, officials would check to ensure that goods for border use did not leak into the interior. Popular organizations like the CDP, however, got "concessions" to trade foreign goods more deeply in the interior.[21] Markets like El Pasito in Chihuahua City and Tepito in Mexico City offer a full range of international goods at low prices due to nonpayment of tariffs and taxes. The $350 border limit was subsequently reduced to $50 to decrease this officially induced "trade imbalance." Many people perceive the customs machinery process as negotiable, even corrupt, despite a massive reorganization in the early 1990s.

The El Pasoans we surveyed crossed the border to purchase services, especially in the health field. Most household crossers report visiting Juárez to seek assistance from medical doctors, dentists, and hospitals. The cross-border pharmaceutical trade in Juárez is particularly brisk, as customers acquire drugs without prescription at a fraction of their cost in El Paso. Although El Paso County funds public health clinics for low-income residents, hours are irregular and waiting time considerable. People take health care into their own hands through cross-border consumption. Yet this relatively free trade in drugs has medical consequences, such as the overuse of antibiotics.[22]

Informal activities generate costs and benefits for both sides of the border that policymakers and economists do not always anticipate or appreciate. First, northbound crossers stimulate retail trade in El Paso and the extraction of sales tax revenue. With little to no marketing cost, El Paso retailers gain from a huge consumer group in Mexico. Mexicans pay the hefty $8\frac{1}{4}$ percent Texas sales tax, which is difficult to retrieve for all save the bureaucratically gifted. When the peso is devalued, U.S. border retailers are hurt; only Mexican consumers and the State of Texas sustain more damage.[23]

Second, Mexico-bound crossers seek low-cost goods and services in income-stretching strategies. In particular, those who seek dental, medical, and hospital services are compensating for lack of insurance or public health care. To the extent that Mexico's public facilities are utilized, cross-border activity also burdens the Mexican public sector. This fact is rarely heard in U.S. anti-immigration (frequently, anti-Mexican) harangues. U.S.-bound medical service seekers cross for alternative or upgraded care. Private hospitals hire professional staff to tend to the needs of paying, often privileged crossers. In El Paso's popular imagination, pregnant women cross to give birth in the United States as a citizen-rooting family strategy. While such deliveries occur, the chief of the county hospital minimized their number, citing data from before and after the Border Blockade.[24] The Blockade did not eliminate Border Crossing Cards (BCCs), although monitoring became somewhat stricter. In the tradeoff between more trade and more citizen-children, both prevailed in recent regional history, for BCCs facilitate movement.

Third, cross-border shoppers exploit comparative price advantages, ignoring nationalist buying strategies. Odd as it may sound in a global economy, commercial interests in Mexico publicly criticize the penchant for buying U.S. and foreign goods. The Juárez media use the phrase *Malinchismo commercial* to refer to such treasonous commerce: Malinche was the woman who, according to myth and legend, betrayed the Aztecs to the Spaniards in precolonial Mexico. *Competencia desleal* ("disloyal" competition: see Box 1) became a rallying cry for Mexico's Chamber of Commerce (CANACO), and was echoed in former President Salinas' address at CANACO's 1993 convention.[25]

The Official Scripts: How Informals Ignore, Comply, and Resist

Whichever side of the border they work on, self-employed informals are the quintessential free traders. They distance themselves from regulatory embrace. They do not burden state-subsidized credit, for start-up capital comes from their own savings or that of relatives.[26] What are informals' special skills? They are able to maneuver on both sides of the border, without calling official attention to themselves, using uneven enforcement of policies and regulations to lower their business costs.

In our interviews with householders, we learned that self-employed informals ignored regulations on the whole. In response to questions about permits, less than a third claimed these were necessary: 22 percent in El Paso, and 29 percent in Juárez. Fewer still said they held permits. Those who did paid sales tax or license/permit fees. On the Juárez side, at least one permit was outdated: one woman said she paid fees to the administration of Francisco Barrio (the municipal president from 1983 to 1986)! Among Juárez street vendors, the municipal government faces a majority of *prestanombres*, or "front people," who are named on the licenses.[27]

When queried about the costs of permits, respondents provided a wide range of figures, from nothing to 650 new pesos (about U.S. $215) in Juárez and from nothing to $400 in El Paso. The inconsistency is not surprising, for official decisions on matters like these are neither transparent nor stable.

Yet few informals said they had problems with authorities: 10 percent in Juárez, 7 percent in El Paso. Many informals do not expose their business. Visibility is the key to encountering or avoiding authorities. Rummage sales, for example, are visible home-based (actually garage-based) occasional or regular businesses. In El Paso, local law limits the number of sales annually, the number of consecutive sale days, and the placement and type of signs. When informals encounter enforcement authorities, however, the interactions and outcomes can have chilling consequences, as we will see in Chapter 7.

Individual Earnings: Gender and National Inequalities

Among the self-employed, income-generating strategies fall into gender patterns, but at relatively balanced rates (60 percent men, 40 percent women). The division of labor matches the division of normative value, with consequences for earnings.

What is "men's work," viewed through an informal lens? Men do repair work on houses and cars. Other men buy and resell used cars. They work at construction and brick masonry. Some work of this kind connects people to formal contractors, but not to benefits. Still other men work in gardening and landscaping services.

And what does the informal lens reveal for women's work? Women work as maids or care for other people's children in their own or the employers' home. These jobs connect women to employers who are probably legally obliged to pay social security and minimum wages. People are aware of the usually minimal burdens that the privileged bear. ("[We had a] laugh over Zoë Baird.")[28]

Other women provide beauty services, cater food for parties, or sell snacks. Several trained practical nurses, originally from Juárez, give injections in El Paso, charging by the shot or accepting gifts. Several women signed on with national distributors of beauty and household products. In that and other neighborhood businesses, friendships are social capital, forming a customer base.

Other work is gender-neutral. In Juárez, both women and men buy new and used goods in El Paso and resell them in Juárez. Crossers watch for sales in large discount stores, which advertise in the Juárez newspapers as well as those in El Paso. They take out memberships at warehouse-sized retailers that offer low prices to members. Crossers rummage through garage sales and *por libra* stores (which sell used clothing by the pound rather than the piece). On both sides, men and women sell from their homes, from garages, in storefronts, and from stalls at flea markets. They occasionally run video-rental operations from their homes.

Much informal work and business occurs within the cities where people reside. Overall, informal earnings hover around $60 weekly for three categories of people: women in both the United States and Mexico and men in Mexico. U.S. resident men earn double that amount weekly. In Juárez, informals' average earnings represent approximately two times the minimum wage; in El Paso, self-employment earnings are invariably less than the minimum wage. As meager as these earnings are, informality in the United States privileges men compared with women, but equalizes Mexican men and border women from both sides.

In Figure 7, we peer into windows within windows of information extracted from the households. We see the subgroup of self-identified informal businesspeople and their self-reported weekly incomes by gender; within that subgroup, we see the smaller categories of crossers who earn above or below official minimum wages, as defined in their national economies. Crossers use border spaces as enclaves of economic opportunity, selling goods and labor on the side that maximizes their comparative advantage in wages and profit.

The earning power of informal labor is weak on the U.S. side. Only 29 percent brought in the equivalent of a weekly minimum wage. Informal work in El Paso supplements low wages and irregular jobs, rather than providing central earnings for household maintenance. Women's informal activity rarely pays off in figures even

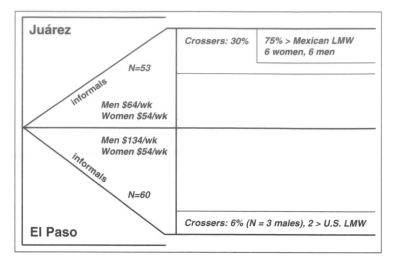

Figure 7   Border Households' Informal Earnings, 1992

LMW = legal minimum wage. Figures are in U.S. dollars. The highest male ($2,000) and the lowest female ($0) were removed to prevent skewed results. Income data are unavailable for nine households on each side.

close to the minimum wage, a poverty wage. Informal opportunities U.S.-style aggravate the unequal worth of men's and women's work contributions.

The contrast with Juárez is great. Approximately two-thirds of informals report earnings more than the official minimum wage. In fact, the average was two to three times the minimum wage. Crossers acquired U.S. supplies for their carpentry and mechanical businesses, bought consumer goods for resale, located used goods to resell at tremendous markup, and stocked their small grocery shops (*tienditas*) with some U.S. products. Women worked as maids, earning the Mexican weekly minimum in a day or two. Obviously, those earnings do not reach the U.S. minimum-wage level, even though the labor is performed on U.S. soil, attesting to uneven enforcement of minimum-wage and immigration policies.

Women are found in larger proportions in the lower-earner group. Of those who earned less than minimum wages, all except one were female. Eight crossed the border to earn and three did not, but those crossers went on *occasional* buying-for-reselling shopping trips, thus qualifying the work as part-time. In contrast, the noncrossers ironed, provided child care, and worked as maids, among other tasks, earning a poverty-level income. Only when they crossed did Juárez women help to diminish gender inequities in earnings.

Although El Paso men maximized their informal earnings, the ratio to Mexican men's earnings was about 2 to 1. This ratio, though unequal, is less exaggerated than the ratios for minimum wages (5 to 1) and per capita income (10 to 1).

Mexican women informals used border opportunities to their advantage. They crossed to work or to buy for resale, or both. Crossing involves risk and border negotiation; crossers comply with some rules but circumvent others to keep business costs down. They use local passports to cross, but masquerade as ordinary shoppers for their home-based business (much to the benefit of El Paso retailers).

Shoppers, Traders, or Contrabandists?

Women's risky behavior is more richly understood through another sample of crossers, known as *fayuqueras*. This ominous term ("contrabandists") represents the business of buying on the U.S. side and reselling in Mexico. In 1992, we talked to thirty-six women who responded to a two-page face-to-face interview after familiarity and rapport had been established in semiethnographic style.[29] Mostly, we conversed on the buses that in those days crossed the international bridge connecting downtown El Paso and Juárez. Mexico had entered the GATT in 1986, but the women's activities suggest that the open economy was still not open enough to supply consumers' demands at the right prices.

Women crossed to purchase items that customers had ordered or for which there was a likely market. They purchased clothing and shoes especially, followed by jewelry and cosmetics, electronic, household, and seasonal items, and toys. The majority of women sold from their homes, setting aside space to display goods or using their homes to deliver individual orders. The second-largest number of traders sold in regional markets. They traveled south to deliver orders to customers deeper in the interior. Such work involves risks, for at government checkpoints people must negotiate passage or pay for their imports in official and unofficial ways. A few women sold goods they had purchased to stores or directly to maquila workers at the plants themselves.

The special challenge *fayuqueras* face involves posing as shoppers rather than as traders. Success thus depends on minimizing the size of bags or making more frequent trips. Labor time can be considerable, given the congestion at the international bridges. *Fayuqueras* also face relatively heavy surveillance. Among the thirty-six women, twenty-one said they had been harassed by the authorities, all but one of them Mexican customs agents. Some women talked their way out of the situation, others paid fees, and still others were stalled at the bridge until relatives brought money so they could pass.

As a business, informal cross-border trade offers several benefits. Start-up costs are minimal, as low as $200, but high enough to suggest that these women lived at the upper end of the carless or single-car-owning working class. Women used savings to begin, but relatives and husbands were a secondary source of loans. Friends and relatives already involved in the trade offered advice. Given the widespread desirability of U.S.-made goods over those made in Mexico, markets are ever-present.

Earnings are reasonable, and women exercise relative autonomy over their time. They keep no accounts, so that numbers cannot be verified, but they report turning a 50–100 percent profit on each good trip, and 0–30 percent on each bad one. These figures do not compute the value of time on hourly or other bases. One trip's profit can easily surpass the weekly minimum wage of a maquila worker ($30 in 1992).

Fayuca is also useful to the men who operate stalls in public and private markets. Juárez is home to numerous public markets where traders have a stable place from which to sell goods. In return they pay rent and tax. These traders are thus partially or fully formalized in terms of compliance with regulations. The international development literature refers to businesses like these as "scaled up."[30]

Traders' cross-border activities have some bearing on the viability of their businesses, as we learned in 1993 from talking to thirty-three market vendors in two markets.[31] Few report problems with the authorities, for all businesses are registered with the federal treasury and pay sales tax, and all are licensed with the municipal government. One market is a privately run cooperative, affiliated with the once-dominant PRI; a dynamic women leads this market, having managed other businesses in Los Angeles and Juárez.[32] The other market is one of some thirty public markets with spots rented from the municipal government.

The private co-op market exudes success in terms of the volume of trade and profitability of its enterprises. All but one of the seventeen vendors we talked to there crossed the border to obtain provisions. In the less successful market, just half of respondents crossed. While success has much to do with the markets' locations and leadership, traders' cross-border sourcing also responds to market demand for U.S. goods, whether new or used. In both markets, and many others in Juárez, used clothing is openly sold, obtained from U.S. garage sales, flea markets, and *por libra* stores. Used clothing is a prohibited import, but it is everywhere in Juárez markets; this is a big business for informals and small business people.[33]

From Individual to Household Strategies

Thus far we have focused on individual earnings. But an examination of poverty or its absence would be incomplete without attention to the household and its neighborhood context. In households, we see the common practice of multiple income generating strategies, including self-employment. The "Mexican solution" transcends the border.

In multigeneration households, members piece together pension checks and the earnings of two, three, or four adults. In both cities, low-income people rely on cash gifts from adult children living away from home. Usually, most income comes from wage work (with or without benefits) away from the home. But informality augments household resources and thus contributes to solutions, no matter how meager the earnings on the U.S. side may be.

The household interviews allow us to examine expectations about poverty and immigration previously discussed in this chapter. Poverty and immigration might seem to be obvious factors in the extensive informal labor at the border. After all, incomes on both sides of the border are low, at least relative to the mainstream United States. Moreover, significant proportions of census-defined "foreign-born" residents have made the border their homes.

But it is important to look beneath that veneer to specific informal workers and to specific neighborhoods, along with the relative conditions therein. Looking at three neighborhoods, we learn that the relationship of poverty and immigration to informality is not so clear-cut. This sort of in-depth look necessarily reduces the large number of original households to smaller neighborhood subgroups and the still smaller sub-subgroups of informal businesses and those self-employed therein. The gain in specificity brings with it diminished numbers and reduced certainty about generalizations.

Poverty, Immigration, and Informality in Different Spaces

To understand the relationship of poverty and immigration, let us examine one neighborhood in Juárez (the core) and two in El Paso,[34] the core neighborhood and the middle-income old periphery neighborhood. We then turn to the downtown streets, analyzing several vendor samples.

Neighborhood Space

Both downtown neighborhoods are close to the international border. Public services are extensive and nearly universal, even for the most modest of homes. Some of the El Pasoans, however, live in tenement buildings or in federal housing projects. The vast majority of downtown El Pasoans rent, at rates ranging from $95 to $250 monthly but less in subsidized housing. In Juárez, downtown dwellers may be homeowners and renters.

The proximity of the border makes short-term pedestrian crossing possible and quite probable if people have the appropriate papers. Short-term crossers are especially common from Juárez to El Paso. This crossing is legal and legitimate, for two-thirds of Juárez downtown households sampled have one or more members who hold a *pasaporte local* or Border Crossing Card (BCC). Local passports facilitate commercial exchange, a godsend to the many El Paso retailers who depend heavily on Mexican customers.

In the United States, much attention is focused on northward crossers, but the movement has a southward dimension as well. U.S. citizens and permanent residents live in Juárez, as the household sample reveals. One-sixth of Mexico's downtown households shelter U.S. crossers; the individual totals add up to fifteen U.S. citizens and eight permanent residents who are authorized to live in the United States. Questions might be raised about the burden *they* place on local government, when numbers are multiplied to estimate the others who live elsewhere in the city. Mexico's federal system allocates few taxing and spending powers to municipalities, and its formula-funded programs are based on undercounted populations.

But the sort of migration relevant to Juárez is primarily from the interior of Mexico, especially from states to the south and southeast. To examine the poverty and migration expectations, we will divide the self-employed into the following groups: households with all adults born in Juárez versus those with adults born outside Juárez; those with incomes above the neighborhood median versus those with incomes below the median. Such finetuning requires caution in interpreting results, for, once again, the relatively large neighborhood samples are now minuscule.

Birth in Juárez and income level have little impact on the propensity to work informally in downtown Juárez. Households with informal income generation above the neighborhood median of $90 are just as active as those below the median. Juárez-born adults live in all but three of the households with informal income-generation. Migrants are more likely to be stuck with maquila jobs than with informal options.[35] Few can live on the 1–2 minimum wages of export-assembly line work, though one formally employed worker brings in social security and health and benefits for the whole household.

El Paso's downtown is home to long-term crossers. Of eighty-one households, just fourteen had *all* their adults born in the country. Given the high percentage of migrant households, it is predictable that most informal businesses came out of such households. Yet three nonmigrant households reported informal business/work. More clarification comes in the old periphery neighborhood, with a greater balance of migrants and nonmigrants, to which we soon turn. First, however, let us examine poverty in the downtown area.

By U.S. official standards, the whole neighborhood is poor. Yet the proportion of informality is comparable to that in other neighborhoods. In relative terms, the poverty connection looks different: only four of the fifteen El Paso households with informal earnings fall below the $200 median weekly neighborhood income. The rest generated more than $200 in household earnings per week. Even informals require some start-up cash, or cash that permits mobility. As Roberto said, "I have no papers, no money to elevate myself."[36]

Sheer will works wonders for some. Susana had to pay for her brother's bail bond. "I did everything I could—crossed the river five times, sold everything: plants, burritos. I became very commercial, even though I am shy." But hard work does not always pay off. María learned she was legally entitled to receive hourly wages, with

Social Security. When she told her employer, she said, she was fired. After that, María crossed to Juárez to work for less pay.

How do people manage in these circumstances? Approximately a third report, in addition to earnings, needs-based benefits that citizen-children and legal immigrants are entitled to claim (or were entitled to claim, before the 1996 welfare reform). The most common benefit is food stamps. Enrique bought food stamps at half price (he is counted neither as a beneficiary nor as an informal).[37] Older people reported Social Security payments, at barely livable amounts such as $62.50 weekly. Several receive disability payments, or housing subsidies, or both. Gloria and Jesús report with an aura of expectation: "We're waiting for November; our girls can apply for food stamps."

At local, state, and national levels, in the United States, the trade-offs associated with burgeoning immigrant populations are debated. El Paso is no exception. Do spending patterns, including the sales and property taxes, exceed spending for hospitals, clinics, schools, roads, and other public services? Do highly motivated immigrants add quality and value to the workforce? Is the existing workforce underutilized and undercut by competition, or is it becoming more competitive with the mammoth global pool? Such questions cannot be answered here. But these immigrants, spenders, service-users, and members of the labor pool are also community residents.

A third of the downtown households use food stamps. This number may appear high, but the financial burden is redistributed to the national level, and the financial payoff to local grocers is considerable. Perhaps a more important issue is why *only* a third claimed food stamps, when far more were eligible. Welfare *underutilization* receives far less attention in political debates than its utilization. (To its credit, the Commission on Immigration Reform acknowledges underutilization, and studies in California show less dependency on benefits among migrant than citizen households.)[38] Studies of U.S. schools also highlight higher performance among immigrant than third-, fourth-, and nth-generation households mired in poverty and racism.[39] If and when the structure of opportunity dwindles after migrant residency, naturalization, and subsequent citizen generations, perhaps more of the same can be expected.

Immigrants are probably less disposed to seek assistance than citizens for two reasons. First, the application process is intimidating, for information is sought that may put some household members at risk. In these checkerboard households, applicants run the danger of revealing too much information to government agencies that may share (or check) information with immigration authorities. Box 2 summarizes the contradictory messages of the all-purpose assistance application used in Texas. The form, coupled with bureaucratically driven enforcement changes,[40] may put applicants at the mercy of street-level bureaucrats.

Second, immigrants may be predisposed to underutilize services because of work-oriented values brought with them or presented to the public world. On the one hand, pride will not permit dependency. On the other hand, people worry that a record of public dependency could undermine applications for citizenship or amnesty, should the opportunity of 1986 be repeated (see Chapter 5).[41]

Utilization of services involves females, on the whole. This is a mixed blessing for women because it reinforces a division of labor that engenders dependency.[42] Women pursue the politically risky behavior of engaging with government agencies. In so doing, they expose or conceal information about the possible mixed status of household members. When regulations or congressional representatives change, honesty might backfire on basic living standards. Needs-based benefits are subject to reduction if incomes rise, augmenting the risks of visible informal work. Surveillance and complaints about the business by neighborhood snitches could curtail the household's basic food supply. The ultimate instability is a "voluntary departure," the name of an Immigration and Naturalization Service (INS) form that undocumented people sign when they are returned to Mexico.

An atmosphere of surveillance pervades downtown space. Between the authorities and the gangs, people are fearful about going out at night. In our household interviews, Don said, "The girls stay in all the time; our niece was raped in ——, and there wasn't enough evidence to charge anyone." Drugs are openly sold and used in the neighborhood; drunks occupy alleyways. In response to the question, "Who could you call for assistance?" householders commonly cite "the police." Yet, ironically, many also cite police for problems ranging from lack of timely response to neglect or even abuse.

"We always call, but they don't come," people told interviewers. "They come in two hours." And another variation: "They never show up when you need them." "We see them driving around, but

Box 2. Department of Human Services Application for Assistance (Excerpts)

Following are extracts from Form 1010–07/92 (Food Stamps, AFDC, Medicaid). The whole form contains four pages, in Spanish and English.

Amid detailed demographic, income, housing and savings questions are queries on

- U.S. Citizenship? Legal Alien? Social Security Number?
- Household members getting cash, gifts, loans from relatives?
- Household members on strike?

The cover sheet promises "confidentiality," "strictly for eligibility determination." Attached is Form 1847 (January 1993), "Declaration of U.S. Citizenship/Legal Alien Status."

> For each member who is not a U.S. citizen, you must show documentation from INS or other proof of immigration status. We submit information to INS to verify eligibility of non-U.S. citizens. Information received from INS may affect your houshold's eligibility and level of benefits.

Penalties for false statements on Form 1010–07/92 are specified. For food stamps, the penalty is ineligibility for six months for the first offense; twelve months for the second offense; permanent ineligibility for the third offense. Those making false statements may be fined up to $10,000 or jailed up to five years or both, and may be prosecuted under other state or federal laws.

As for AFDC (Aid to Families with Dependent Children):

> If you give wrong or misleading information, you could be prosecuted, and be sentenced for up to 10 years in prison. You could be asked to repay benefits, have your check reduced, or be disqualified from receiving AFDC. . . .

they don't come." One elder, Veronica, queried about specific problems, said the police entered her home with guns but without a warrant. "How was the problem resolved?" went the questionnaire prompt. "They said, 'sorry,'" Veronica answered. Yet the police remain a buffer in a world with threatening streets.

Another threat comes from the ubiquitous Border Patrol agents. Although our questionnaire did not ask residents to evaluate the Border Patrol, a significant number (in this and other neighborhoods) spontaneously gave the Border Patrol a low evaluation, implying intense feelings. From Leticia, Juan, and Fred we heard the following: "They're always around, but they don't do anything for the community." Sometimes it is just the "Mexico look." "Hey, *nopal!*" "He stopped me for no reason."[43] (Chapter 5 addresses some specific problems with "La Migra," slang for the Border Patrol).

In El Paso's old periphery, residents' lives are comparable, in terms of income, to the lives of average El Pasoans. Their houses, mostly built in the 1950s, are affordable and provide inside space and outside yard room.

More adults in this neighborhood than in others studied were born in the United States. This is where those identifying themselves as "Hispanics" reside (See Fig. 1 for all three El Paso areas). Many people have Anglicized first names. In multigenerational households, considerable numbers of elderly residents were born in Mexico. As in other neighborhoods, householders report minimal organizational activity: several parent-teacher affiliations, a few past union memberships.

Although connection to Mexican heritage is more distant than in the downtown and the new periphery, old periphhery residents use the "Mexican solution" to enhance household livelihoods: multiple income earning. One finds a sibling, a cousin, or a retiree with pension joining (perhaps recruited by) a dual-earning nuclear family.

While the median income for households was a modest $400 a week, depressed by retired pensioners, those households with double the median income (or more) exhibit patterns worth a deeper look. Their multiple earnings, some of them around minimum-wage levels, follow.

$1,250/week:	two teachers, regular participation in weekly swap meets
$1,110/week:	two earners, own land on which trailers are rented
$1,110/week:	five earners, all engaged in unskilled and service work
$850/week:	three earners
$845/week:	four earners
$800/week:	three earners
$800/week:	two earners
$800/week:	two earners

One household, striking because the woman of the house brought in three times the man's earnings, fell in between the median and the higher-earning group. Rose cared for three special-challenge foster children. The value placed on child care in this form is strikingly different from the amount authorized in welfare or assumed in drawing the poverty line.

The relationship between the pursuit of informality and immigration is far from clear. If informality is cultural baggage from elsewhere, then a culture of informality may be emerging in this "elsewhere," the U.S. border, or generally in the globalized U.S. economy. While total numbers are small, the pattern is there: eleven informal workers are U.S.-born and seven are Mexican-born. Old periphery informality is *not* limited to immigrant populations.

Old periphery residents have considerable capital in human and economic terms, compared with other neighborhoods on both sides of the border. Most U.S.-born resident adults have high school diplomas and some have even higher credentials. They also have sufficient financial capital to save small sums for sideline self-employment. This neighborhood exhibits a healthy proportion of informal activities, with eighteen businesses in sixty-two households. Several pursue weekend flea market vending, or hold multiple garage sales (more than the three allowed annually, according to municipal ordinance!). Catering services generate sporadic sales. Jay, who stays with his brother and sister-in-law, is "in-between jobs"; he cooks buffalo wings for *fiestas* and is looking for a restaurant to turn into a more permanent business.

And what about the relationship between pursuit of informality and income level, following up on expectations about poverty connections? Again, numbers are small, but a pattern is there: twelve informals earn above the neighborhood median; six earn below it. Informality in the old periphery is *not* limited to the poor.

Our household information reveals no clear relationship between poverty, immigration, and informal work. Informality has taken hold in free space among those with the wherewithal and aptitude for self-employment. Let us look at a different spatial setting, public streets, for its immigration connections.

Street Space

When moving from neighborhoods and households to individuals, different patterns emerge. The street vendors are largely poverty-level immigrants, only some of whom are connected to formal businesses.

In 1992–93, El Paso and Juárez experienced a surge in the number of street vendors who occupied downtown public space.[44] Conflicts emerged among the vendors, downtown merchants, and local officials. From face-to-face interviews with 117 vendors in both cities, and analysis of a universe of 89 criminal citations issued between September 1992 and April 1993 in El Paso, the following portraits emerged.

The disposition of street vending police citations is recorded in the El Paso Municipal Court. The vendors are an international, mostly Spanish-speaking group. Among those cited were seven Asians, a single African (nationality unspecified), two Peruvians, a Puerto Rican, and two Cubans—one of whom is a six-time "repeat offender" who variously claimed to be Mexican, Spanish, and Cuban. He called himself Batista, probably a joke that was lost on the police officers. All remaining citations labeled offenders *Mexican* or *U.S.;* all had Spanish surnames. No citee was identifiable as *Anglo,* the southwestern term for *white* or *Euro-American.*

El Paso-based vendors, with whom we conducted forty-six interviews, sold mainly prepackaged foods and drinks. A few sold untaxed cigarettes from Juárez, subjecting them to periodic scrutiny from the Bureau of Alcohol, Tobacco, and Firearms. This mostly male group, commonly in their twenties and thirties, worked primarily on their own.

A handful of vendors were in their sixties. Pedro, born in 1918 according to the citation for his repeated offenses, could barely sign his name. One of Pedro's tickets turned into a warrant for arrest, but he appeared in court to plead his case on the other charge and was pronounced "not guilty." A full 54 percent of the citations advance to warrant status, for vendors (or their bosses) do not pay the $62.50 fine or appear in court.

Thirty percent of El Paso vendors said they worked for a "boss," "*jefe,*" or "*el patron.*" Thirteen percent more do other work besides vending, including four who work in the chile fields. The younger and underage vendors called themselves the "Mendoza boys" (a pseudonym supplied by the author). Pay arrangements varied, with half to three-fourths of receipts going to bosses. Vendors' earnings averaged $20 to $30 on "good days," enthusiastically defined as Saturdays, but $10 on bad days. Among those cited for offenses, 49 percent listed an employer, and eight of them listed the same home and employer address.

The earnings of the Juárez vendors—a balanced group of seventy-one men and women—varied widely. A fifth earned the equivalent of $10 a day; a fifth earned $30. They sell prepared and packaged foods, cigarettes, balloons, flowers, religious artifacts, and other dry goods. Wives (*"mi mujer,"* as some said) prepare food for husbands to sell on the streets; women also sell their own concoctions. If the unpaid wives "counted," women would be a majority of informals.

Only one El Paso vendor belonged to an organization, though many more longed for an organization to protect their interests. Jaime said his organization (which sounded more like a racket) involved a biweekly fixed fee in exchange for the return of confiscated goods from "La Migra" (Border Patrol agents). Forty-one percent of the interviewed vendors cited problems with the authorities, mostly harassment from "La Migra," but also police citations.

In contrast, twenty-one of the Juárez vendors belonged to organizations, which ranged from PRI affiliates to vendor unions or syndicates and the CDP. Vendors said they joined organizations to "avoid problems," "so the authorities don't harass us," because it is "required"—or some combination of those reasons. Organizational leaders insisted on attendance at meetings; the fees they charged for permits ranged wildly in reported price, for some leaders added their own fees for a package deal.

Street-level informal workers in El Paso offer a contrast to home-based workers. Immigrant and poverty status *are* part of their experiences.

Conclusion

Informal work is an omnipresent part of reality on both sides of the U.S.–Mexico border. While the prevalence is predictable for Juárez, the comparable figures for El Paso are surprising and striking. People generate self-employment for themselves in permanent and occasional ways; they work at wage jobs without social security; they stretch their incomes through strategic cross-border consumption of goods and services.

The viability of informality varies according to the side of the border on which people work. On the U.S. side, informality in the form of self-employment is merely a sideline activity that generates extra income, but informality in the form of cross-border service seeking allows people to cope without health insurance and public medical services.

Among the U.S. households sampled, we found differences by neighborhood and gender. Informality occurs in middle- *and* low-income areas. Even in the middle-income old periphery neighborhood, residents use multiple earning strategies to realize the middle-class dream—a dream on which those in minimum-wage low-skill jobs have a tenuous hold. Male informals generate twice as much income as women, reflecting the comparable worth of gendered tasks on U.S. soil. Car repair has a higher market value than child care and domestic work.

On the Mexican side, income from informality is more central to household survival. Informality generates twice the minimum wage, thus making it more profitable than assembly work in maquilas. Informals are freer to chose their own schedules, but they get no fringe benefits or connections to Mexico's major pension and health programs. While gendered tasks produce unequal earnings on Mexican soil, too, female informals who seize cross-border opportunities are able to generate considerable resources and thereby reduce gender inequalities. They do so through their own risks and hard work, rather than through government or organizational protection.

Nevertheless, the earnings of Mexican informals are lucrative only in relative terms. If informals lived just five to ten miles north, contained in a different homeland, their earnings would be considered as paltry as those analyzed above for the U.S. side. The relatively free movement of people and goods permitted by the border prior to 1993, allowed Mexican informals to reduce the obscene income gaps of 5 to 1 (minimum wage) and 10 to 1 (GNP) to 2 to 1, compared with their U.S. counterparts. In other words, they share a more egalitarian relative poverty.

Hegemonic institutions stretch their rules, regulations, and street-level bureaucratic procedures to enfold informals, but without complete success. Informals work and cross according to their own imperatives and perceived opportunity. They have managed to ignore, resist or negotiate with the petty regulations that would extract revenue from them and add to their costs of doing business and making work. Neither does the U.S. "rule of law" protect them from exploitation or treat them with respect.

A critical mass of Mexican informals, particularly those who operate in public and visible ways on the street, organize to protect themselves from the long arm of government. They use the rhetoric of public discourse that legitimizes informality to avoid criminal labels. But local petty regulations are different from those that emanate from on high—from capital cities or the centers of global capital. As we will see in later chapters, grand regulations that block borders and devalue currency are more difficult for informals to counter.

As for the immigration and poverty hypotheses, connections to informality are mixed. Among visible informals like street vendors on the U.S. side, sizable numbers are migrants who earn minimum wages, at best. In the United States, minimum wages are poverty wages in multiple-member household contexts. Among the home-based self-employed, informality is rooted among the nonmigrant middle class as much as the predicted migrant poor. Informality is not just limited to immigrant or ethnic enclaves in the El Paso area.

Globalization has enveloped the border area, but the demography and political economy of the border may spread to the heartlands. With more studies like this, we will learn whether globalization, and its attendant consequences like downsizing, insufficient job opportunities, and informality, will in fact reproduce border life elsewhere. Is the "Mexican solution"—multiple earners, with one foot in wage work and the other in informal work—taking hold beyond the border? I believe that it is, and that this solution is a *global* one, as households respond to structural adjustment—a topic we take up in the concluding chapter.

Neighborhood businesses on a paved street just outside an unpaved *colonia* (Juárez). *Photo by Luis Aguirre.*

Political identifications on Juárez homes. The signs identify the residents as supporters of the Popular Defense Committee/Workers' Party (CDP/PT). *Photo by Luis Aguirre.*

A home-based business in Juárez selling *ropa usada* (used clothing). *Photo by Luis Aguirre.*

Home building, *poco a poco* (little by little) in El Paso County. *Photo by Magda Alarcón.*

A vegetable vendor in El Paso County. The semifixed stall advertises that Lone Star cards are accepted for food stamp purchases. *Photo by the author.*

Semifixed stalls in a public market in Juárez. *Photos by Luis Aguirre.*

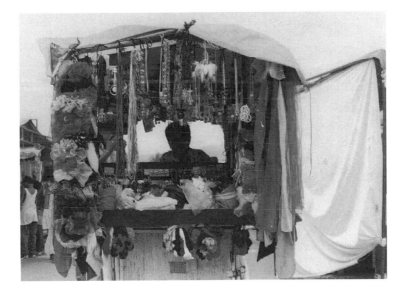

The NSF-supported researchers in the Franklin Mountains, on the El Paso side of "the pass." *Photo by the author.*

An *FBI* ("Fun But Illegal") tag on a campaign sign for congressional candidate Silvestre Reyes (El Paso). The sign had been tagged for crossing the line into FBI space. Reyes is well known as a designer of the Border Patrol's Operation Hold the Line. *Photo by the author.*

Sex-typing in some maquiladora job recruitment advertisements in Juárez newspapers. Note the pictures and the feminine or masculine language forms. *Photo by the author.*

Prominent officials, mostly Mexican, at Seeds Across the Border conference held in Juárez in October 1995. In the center, FEMAP President Guadalupe de la Vega shakes hands with Juárez municipal president Ramón Galindo. *Photo by FEMAP.*

CHAPTER 5

Moving Within and Across Borders for Land and Shelter

We came for the land.
We're building little by little.
  Household residents,
  New periphery household interviews, 1992

Space is central to thinking about communities, poverty, and identity. Borders are drawn around land for purposes of identity, official census counts, nationality, and political representation. Crossers fit awkwardly inside such units. Crossers can foil the best of official plans through politics, sheer will, and hard work.

Space also has economic dimensions. Poverty and wealth are associated with spatial metaphors. Witness the use of *north* and *south* in global analysis, or the use of *central city ghetto* and *suburb* in discourse about U.S. urban areas. Economic space and language often come together in symbolic ways. Official spatial separation, or *apartheid*—a chilling Afrikaans term ("apartness") once reserved for South Africa—has been used to describe conditions in the United States. In *American Apartheid,*[1] Douglas Massey and Nancy Denton focus on housing in urban ghettos and white flight beyond city boundaries to suburbs. At the U.S. southwestern border, however, to go beyond city boundaries is to go beyond surveillance.

On the U.S. side, the movement from the city is a flight to colonize cheaper, less regulated land. It is a flight to *colonias,* a word that means "neighborhoods" in northern Mexico, but has hotly contested meanings in the United States.[2] Both English and Spanish speakers use this Spanish label, for in El Paso, says Pablo Vila, Spanish is the language of poverty.[3]

By 1990, the U.S. General Accounting Office (GAO) counted 70,000 residents in 250 El Paso County *colonias,* as we see in Map 3. Greater numbers of *colonia* residents are counted in South Texas. All along the Texas border with Mexico, *colonias* make up a land mass larger than the state of Louisiana.[4] The rise of *colonias* has

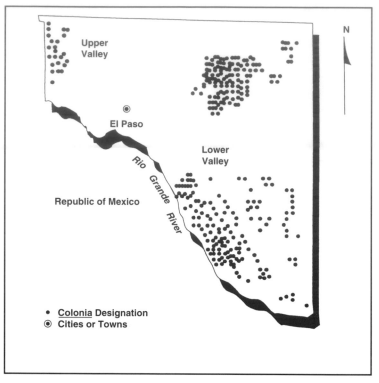

Map 3   *Colonia* Locations in El Paso County
Source: "Rural Development Problems and Progress of Colonia Subdivisions Near Mexico Border" (Washington, D.C.: U.S. General Accounting Office [GAO/RCED-91-37], November 1990).

been linked to the restructuring of El Paso industry from high- to low-wage manufacturing, especially in garment industries.[5]

In 1988 the Texas Department of Human Services surveyed a 10 percent sample of *colonia* households, which then numbered 139,873 residents. Home ownership was high (85 percent), but a quarter of households had no potable water, and 44 percent had outhouses or septic tanks. While 38 percent worked for minimum wages ($3.35 at the time) or less, 41 percent reported that they were unemployed. Given that only 20 percent of El Paso *colonia* residents were receiving food stamps at the time, and 4 percent were getting welfare, residents must have generated income in other ways not detailed in the report.[6] Then and now, self-employment probably figured into residents' antipoverty strategies.

Despite the common Spanish tag for poverty, people label places differently on both sides. Inside El Paso's ever-expanding city limits, places have geographic referents (east, northeast, south, west, northwest), except for the large tracts that hug the river valley (lower and upper valleys).

On the Mexican side, labels are multitudinous. The whole urban area is divided into *colonias* and social conditions range from poverty to affluence (the upscale ones are also called *fraccionamientos* in Juárez). In central cities, which are also commercial centers, neighborhoods are mixed, ranging from elegant mansions to older middle-class and working-class areas, the latter increasingly occupied by those who service downtowns through their labor.

One can count around two hundred named *colonias* on Juárez maps. People refer to places not by geographic cross-streets, but by evocative and memorable names, themes, and dates: victims of political assassination; patrons, parties, and people; historical figures and moments. Thus, labels include *Emiliano Zapata, Lucio Cabañas, Quince de Enero* (Fifteenth of January), *Tierra y Libertad* (Land and Liberty). Not coincidentally, this 1910 revolutionary cry has been usurped by the CDP in northern Mexico.

This chapter focuses on migration and settlement. In the first section, I analyze the movement of people within and across borders along with the risk taking that border crossing implies. The atmosphere of surveillance that surrounds northward crossing has consequences for people's lives and movements on the U.S. side of the border. Household residents give voice to these risks. In the second section, I examine the political players involved with land and housing. In the third section, I draw on household interviews to discuss land and housing, focusing particularly on figures for ownership and improvement.

People on the Move

On both sides of the border, many residents are migrants in their own land as well as migrants across national boundaries. The migration decision is a momentous one, a considerable risk taken with the goal of achieving a better life.

Are these migrants upwardly mobile, highly work-oriented, budding capitalists, compared with their counterparts back home? Although we do not have any data comparing Juarenses with their counterparts in the south, northern Mexico's regional culture is considered dynamic, fast-moving, and individualistic. About half of Juarenses migrated from the center-north or north-eastern states of Zacatecas, Durango, and Coahuila. Earlier in Mexico's history, patriots from the heartland complained that the north was losing its cultural soul to the United States.[7] If borders are transition zones, they have potential to mix and meld elements from their own margins.

When migrants cross national boundaries, the risk is magnified, for they are also crossing citizenship, regulatory, currency, and language boundaries.

Do migrants bring the wherewithal to survive, even thrive, in the new setting? Many factors figure into the answers to this question, including destination spaces, resources brought, and era of arrival. In the household sample, northward national crossers exhibit a range of responses to the legal boundaries they transversed: they might comply with the paperwork, or ignore it, or negotiate a change of status upon arrival, or use a mixture of these strategies.

Crossing to the United States

U.S. immigration rules are complex, changing, and difficult to fathom in multiple languages. Those with resources consult specialist lawyers to cover all the angles. Those without talk with friends, neighbors, and relatives about their experiences. If all else fails, one can call the Immigration and Naturalization Service (INS) and make use of its machine-answering service, which exhibits its own categorical logic. In Box 3, we see the many options available. Option 8 envelops callers in the surveillance process itself.

Talking to householders evokes the vast checkerboard of their birthplaces. The majority of adults were born in Mexico, while the majority of children were born in the United States. It is not unusual for husbands and wives to have been born in different states, or in different countries (the United States and Mexico). In U.S. downtown and new periphery neighborhoods, it is rare for all

members of the parental and grandparental generations to have
been born in the United States. In the new periphery *colonia*
neighborhood, five of eighty-eight households exhibited such uniformity.

In the checkerboard household, a mixture of legal statuses has
implications for citizen participation and entitlements. Citizen-
children live with permanent-resident- or citizen-parents or grand-
parents. Most adult *migrants* have maintained the in-between
status of "resident alien." They are legally able to work and reside
permanently in the United States, but they cannot vote. After five
years of such status, they are eligible to apply for citizenship, but no
special incentives propel them to do so, other than the periodic dread
inspired by hostile, anti-immigrant political climates, such as that of
the mid-1990s, and the welfare reform that promises to cut off assistance to legal immigrants in 1997. In 1996 resident aliens had to

renew cards issued before 1979, a process that included picture-taking and fingerprinting.

Encounters with the Border Patrol
During the period of our household interviews, Border Patrol agents pursued a policy of surveillance and apprehension, not only on the border, but in El Paso and other border communities as well. The ubiquitous Border Patrol agents, roaming in their green cars and vans, would apprehend people who looked as if they might be undocumented. Box 4 details the special apprehension authority in the hands of Border Patrol agents. Wide latitude is allowed, with the potential for abuse. The Mexican "look" is not always so different from the resident alien (from Mexico) "look" or even the Mexican American "look." Writing about a decade ago, Debbie Nathan describes the El Paso Border Patrol's "256,000 arrests. That's more than a quarter of the 1.3 million made in the entire country. . . . If you want to arrest 256,000 people, you have to stop a lot of folks, and there are only about 600,000 living in the entire region covered by the El Paso district patrol."[8]

Border Patrol surveillance has spawned a literature that speaks to a common experience of borderland El Pasoans, the overwhelming majority of whom are crossers (or descendants of crossers) from Mexico.[9] A high school principal who struggled to keep Border Patrol agents off his near-border campus may soon become a hero in a Hollywood movie.[10]

Although our questionnaire asked for no evaluations of the Border Patrol, residents spontaneously offered comments during interviews. Residents of the downtown neighborhood were particularly apt to cite specific problems with "La Migra":[11]

"They're always around, but they don't do anything for the community."
"He stopped me for no reason."
"I was strip-searched."

If people act in ways deemed suspicious, such as running or walking fast, they run the risk of encounter or apprehension by Border Patrol agents. Said Blanca: "He wanted to take my passport because I was in a rush to the clinic."

Even in the old periphery, a purely residential middle-income area, people cited problems. According to John: "My mother was

Box 4. Immigration Officers' Constitutional, Congressional, and INS Policy Authority (Summary)

You May, Without a Warrant or Consent:

1. Question a person concerning his right to enter or be in the United States if you have a reasonable suspicion, based on specific articulable facts involving more than mere ethnic appearance, that he is an alien (except at the Border or its functional equivalent, where you may question anyone);

2. Detain, short of arrest, a person (e.g., a pedestrian or employee on the job) if you have a reasonable suspicion that the person is an alien illegally in the United States;

3. Arrest an alien if you have probable cause to believe that he is present in or entering the United States illegally and is likely to escape before you can obtain a warrant;

4. Arrest a person if you have probable cause to believe that he is guilty of committing a felony relating to the immigration laws which has actually been committed and you believe he is likely to escape before you can obtain a warrant; . . .

[Items 5–10 concern frisking, seizure, search, and vehicle stops.]

11. Search a house *ONLY* under *RARE EXCEPTIONAL* conditions. . . .

running for the bus and the Border Patrol thought she was running from them." [How was the problem resolved?] "She showed them her papers."

Jenny said: "I was stopped by immigration."

Her husband joked: "Were you wearing a Mexican embroidered dress?"

In the old periphery, George, hostile to immigrants, took a gun with him on his personal patrols and strolls along irrigation ditch banks. He would see Border Patrol agents stopping people. The day agents stopped George brought a rude awakening.

The Border Patrol increasingly uses sophisticated technology to maintain surveillance. The millions of undocumented people who remain (the precise number is unknown) are testimony to the human ability to take advantage of space and enforcement cracks. But just as the minute percentage of tax audits have a chilling effect, deportations and their memories have an impact on people's willingness to engage government for accountability and change.

Encounters with the Schools

Immigration control (or the lack of control) is supplemented by other institutions that educate and assimilate crossers and their children. Respondents cited equivocal experiences with public schools, which all residents have the right to use since a Texas challenge was resolved in a 1982 Supreme Court decision.[12]

Adult residents of the old periphery recalled being "swatted for speaking Spanish in school." Downtown residents gave mixed evaluations of the public schools. Some parents had helped out at school and formed mothers' associations affiliated with the schools. Others thought schools were "like jails"; one person said that they had "lower expectations than schools in Mexico." One simply said, "They don't like Mexicans."

Yet U.S. educational opportunities had prompted some to move in the first place. Several residents in the new periphery neighborhood answered our narrow survey question under housing history ("Why did you move?") with broad, border-crossing responses linked to perceived school quality: "We wanted a better education for our children."

Crossing Toward the Urban Periphery: El Paso and Juárez

Although the move to the new periphery involves the search for land and home ownership, it also offers some relief from the surveillance of the city. In Map 4, we see residents' movement into the new periphery. In the United States, new periphery residents migrate from the city, from across the border, and (to a lesser extent) from other states in the western United States, part of a step-by-step migration that originated in Mexico.

Residents of the new periphery in Juárez also searched for land and home ownership opportunities. Map 4 shows movement mainly from the old periphery, where people rent or wait until they hear that land is available. Mobilized through settlers' organizations, *colonos* (as they call themselves) move en masse, with or without the implied consent of authorities. They construct their homes through self-help and savings. On average, household survey residents paid 800 new pesos (approximately $275) for a tiny 10 by 17 meter plot of land. Gradually, they hope to negotiate regularization for a land title deed.[13]

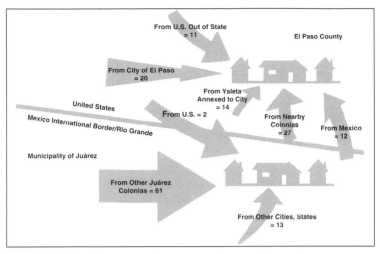

Map 4   Movement to the New Periphery *Colonias* (data unavailable for five households)

Land and home ownership involve different sets of players in government and the marketplace. To these players we now turn.

Political Players: Land and Housing

The hunger for home ownership transcends the border. People look for a piece of land on which to construct their homes. On the U.S. side, this hunger spills over into city-to-*colonia* movement. In Juárez these housing moves are politically charged and visible, while in El Paso they seem to be privatized and embedded in the market. These divergent approaches have implications for media visibility and public accountability.

As earlier chapters suggest, I view self-help housing construction and improvement as income-stretching activities that constitute one dimension of informality.[14] At little or no cost to government, people invest considerable labor in constructing and improving their homes. This practice, however, offers little potential for government to extract permit revenue, or for banks and contractors to extract profit and interest. Once visible to property-taxing authorities, residents will gradually be tapped for property taxes.

The Market: A Shroud for Politics?

Lots of official players influence land settlement and housing in both cities. In the United States, public administration projects the appearance of technical oversight for a market-driven process in which housing and land customers exercise choice. In Texas, a myriad of state, county, and city agencies have a stake in land sales, registration, taxation, and service provision. Federal agencies provide public housing and vouchers, loan guarantees, and community development funds for housing improvement. Land developers and real estate agents, along with aspiring residents, have material stakes in extracting value from property. In 1995, scandals erupted over developers' contributions to El Paso's congressional representative, who was active in securing benefits for *colonia* residents (and thereby also augmenting the value of developers' nearby land). Occasionally, political scandals undermine technical illusions.

The Political Marketplace

In Juárez and Chihuahua, land settlement and housing are just as obviously political, but ordinary people organize collectively around that politics and have gained visibility in the local media. The process seems more open and transparent, and also time-consuming, ripe for opportunism, and difficult for people to manipulate. Under conditions of ruthless media capitalism, several newspapers compete over reportage about the majority of citizens in the "popular classes." People rarely operate under the delusion that the process is merely technical.

Migrant job seekers, drawn by the maquila industry, add enormous numbers to the city population. (Half of them, as we saw in Chapter 3, were not born in Juárez.) New periphery settlements have become rather like maquila bedroom communities. However, as Map 4 shows, those *colonos* frequently migrate from one house to another *in* the city, hoping to find land on which to settle and build.

People settle on land, public and private, often without formal contracts of sale or land title deeds. These *colonias* are generically termed "irregular settlements." Settler leaders use land hunger to organize followers; municipal officials use land to consolidate political support and to undermine their opponents; opponents use slowness and corruption to discredit officials. Ultimately, officials hope to extract property taxes, one of the few sources of revenue under municipal control.

In Box 5, selected media headlines, with content summarized in English, suggest the diverse interests that have a stake in settlement, and trace the transition from PRI to PAN governance and the PAN's consolidation through populist gestures that echoed the PRI. The selection of these articles (from a file of 150) does not erase contradictions, for these simultaneous realities are important for the political space that people exploit, whether they are officials, leaders, or residents. Leaders, sometimes legitimate, sometimes fraudulent developers, organize settlers in a common pattern: occupation, followed by modest construction, then political work aimed at title acquisition, and, finally, home construction. The latter two steps may overlap, given the length of time necessary to acquire title deeds. Added to these strategic players, we find officials at various levels of government, including federal and state housing authorities; political parties; municipal agencies (with partisan appointees); and private contractors.

Housing and land are probably the most pressing everyday political issues around which people organize and engage government. For many people, the most essential question is: Who can deliver a piece of land on which to build? Because both the PRI and the PAN comprehend this, they have tolerated or negotiated with settlers, leaders, and owners to "regularize" land occupation. Both parties advertise their accomplishments in this realm when they campaign for elections.

The PAN came into office wary of popular organizations and PRI-affiliated leaders who settle residents. Within a year of taking office, the PAN began to negotiate with former PRI mayors to acquire land in the path of urban growth, to the south and southeast. The ex-mayors, along with family members, had purchased a huge tract near the large new airport and *colonia* construction. Newspapers discussed the possible "donation" of this land. Meanwhile, an aggressive newcomer, *Norte de Ciudad Juárez*, published a series of investigative reports in April and May 1993 on ways in which former PRI mayors manipulated growth and enriched themselves in the process: "Juárez: 15 años de voracidad" ("15 years of greed"). The resulting groundswell of criticism prompted unusual action on the part of the conservative PAN: expropriation (with promised compensation) of land belonging to the industrial and business class,

Box 5. Selected Headlines: The Juárez Media Cover Land and Housing

"Ni los Muertos se Salvan," *Norte de Ciudad Juárez,* June 14, 1993
The Revolutionary Front of Popular Organizations, a PRI-affiliated group, invaded land in an area that includes a cemetery. The owner says she is under heavy pressure to settle.

"Un Esfuerzo que Transforma," *Diario de Juárez,* July 7, 1992
Paid advertisement for Ayuntamiento [Government] de Juárez: From 1989 to 1992, of 9,600 title cases and 6,000 cases involving regularization of settlements, the administration resolved 8,100 titles and 5,800 regularization cases. New files have been opened for 3,200 cases affecting 108 *colonias.*

"Califican de Injusto el que Quieran Desalojarlos," *Norte de Ciudad Juárez,* June 14, 1993
Residents of the *colonia* San Antonio are fed up with court-issued warnings that they will be removed. The *colonia* has been in existence since the 1950s, and most residents have two titles to the property. Residents say threats occur every time a new administration takes power, and they believe the authorities are harassing them unfairly.

"Lideresa de Anapra Exige Varios Cobros," *Diario de Juárez,* February 3, 1993
A leader, affiliated with the PRI, is accused of charging residents of the *colonia* excessive fees, as follows: 100 new pesos for mediating a new lot, 120 for membership in the *colonia* organization, 60 for a down payment, 75 a month for financing, and 10 for a contribution to a proposed clinic and her travel expenses to visit President Salinas. [Note: in this period (from 1992 to December 1994), 3 new pesos = 1 U.S. dollar.]

"Satura Municipio Previas con Denuncias Contra Lideres," *Diario de Juárez,* February 2, 1993
To prevent saturation of the courts, cases against *colonia* leaders will be classified as "special" and will fall under the jurisdiction of the Social Development Department. The PRI accused PANistas of instigating a campaign against its members. Currently two leaders are in jail, and arrest warrants have been issued for five others.

"Lideres Colonos se Aprovechan de las Posibles Soluciones a la Tenencia de la Tierra, Dice Funcionario," *Diario de Juárez,* April 24, 1992
The state director for social work and urban development discusses the process of applying for a land grant from the municipal territorial reserves. One must have lived in the city for at least six months and show a marriage license or children's birth certificate, and a letter proving one has no assets.

"Brindan Plazos Morosos de INFONAVIT para que se Pongan al Corriente en Sus Creditos Ante Esta," *Diario de Juárez,* **December 6, 1991**

Five hundred owners of INFONAVIT homes have until December 31 to catch up with their payments. There are also 130 civil charges pending against those who have violated INFONAVIT law by vacating, leasing, loaning, or selling their homes.

"Evaden 52% de Empresas las Cuotas del INFONAVIT," *Norte de Ciudad Juárez,* **April 21, 1993**

INFONAVIT estimates that 52 percent of the companies are evading required contributions into the national pool for worker housing. In Juárez, with 2,500 companies on the register, close to 1,300 have evaded contributions, at an estimated cost of 200,000 new pesos. Companies have 45 days to make arrangements with the agency or face the consequences.

"Piden Constructores Bajar Intereses para Vivienda," *Diario de Juárez,* **March 3, 1993**

Contractors blame the slump in medium- and high-cost housing production on excessive interest rates. The current rate ranges from 34–36 percent. [In fact, credit card rates sometimes exceeded 100 percent in the mid-1990s.]

"Promueven Desarrolladores Abaratamiento de la Vivienda," *Diario de Juárez,* **May 1, 1993**

PROVIVAV members, whose members perform 80 percent of the (formal) construction work in Juárez, meet with federal, state, and local authorities to discuss problems and offer solutions. The PROVIVAV president suggests reducing paperwork and permit costs, permitting decisions to authorize construction within thirty days rather than six months.

"Colonos Juarenses Invaden EU," *Diario de Juárez,* **April 4, 1993**

According to local officials, every day there is a housing shortage of fifty families. As a result of this crisis, at least two homes in *colonia* Anapra have been constructed on the U.S. side. Juárez police have orders not to prevent invasions, and the Human Settlements Department has halted charges against leaders because internal problems have reached senior administrators.

"Los Planes de Desarrollo, a la Media de Ex-Alcaldes," *Norte de Ciudad Juárez,* **April 27, 1993**

In 1978, some former [named] mayors bought land in south and southeast Juárez. A year later, the mayor commissioned an urban growth plan that called for growth in that direction. Meanwhile, family members of a subsequent mayor purchased a tract of land almost half the size of Juárez. During his term, southward growth was fostered, with new settlers becoming PRI supporters. Other irregularities were related to new airport construction and unlawful purchases of farm land.

from which the PAN itself drew its supporters. (In fact, despite the populist rhetoric, both the PRI and the PAN draw their local leaders from this class.) Although the PAN's populist strategy had the capacity to polarize elites, it would have been more difficult for the PRI to pursue such a course against its own industrial and business-class supporters.

The PAN also exploited divisions within the two-decade-old CDP, which had broken into factions under feuding leaders. The PAN's social development director, soon to become the PAN municipal president for the 1995–98 term, aggressively pursued criminal charges against allegedly fraudulent leaders. Newspaper coverage of popular organizations moved from the front pages of the local-news sections to the police pages. Most significantly, the PAN went into several big CDP neighborhoods, long overdue for land regularization, to offer titles and public services.

The PAN used visuals to promote its short-term publicity and long-term modernization agendas. The municipal president's initial ventures into this seemingly hostile territory involved photo opportunities, intended to showcase the party's accomplishments in newspaper advertisements and in a polished book whose text and cartoons were designed to appeal to all types of audiences. *Colonia* leaders, drawn as scruffy, hairy, and overweight men seemingly straight from rural ranches, were contrasted with drawings of professional looking, suited men with slicked back hair.[15]

Technicians in the Land Market

In Mexico, planners trained as architects work under political direction. Urban planning began in Mexico City, but it spread to other municipalities under legislation passed in the Echeverría administration (1970–76).[16] Some call those the "palmy days" of planning; critics joked about three kinds of planning, or *planificación: socialista* (in socialist countries), *indicativa* (indicative, a guide) (in France and Scandinavian countries), and *decorativa* (decorative, in Mexico).[17]

Juárez got an early start in planning through the creation of a Planning Department in 1970.[18] In the absence of a civil service, however, turnover among planners corresponded with the three-year electoral terms for municipal government. Only in 1994 did the state legislature in Chihuahua authorize a Municipal Planning Institute, with planners' tenure extending beyond electoral terms. Opened with fanfare in 1995, its staff numbers twenty-six.[19]

El Paso issued its first city plan in 1925. Its professionals are planners and public administrators (or aspire to such status, for few are so credentialed). As elsewhere in the United States, city planning divides land into commercial, industrial, and residential uses. The City Planning Research and Development Department has thirty-nine staff members, for a population half the size of Juárez's. Moreover, the City Public Inspection Department, which monitors building contractors and home-based occupations, is a separate, more generously staffed unit. The county has an attorney's office, but no planning department (or planning authority).

Housing construction in the City of El Paso is highly formalized through building contractors. Most housing is constructed at subdivision scale. Regulation is more enforceable with formal contractors than with numerous informal income-stretchers, for company workers and their equipment are more visible than part-time resident constructors. Within city limits, strict building codes make it difficult for self-help to prevail. Moreover, commercial and public credit are biased toward formal business, developers, and building contractors for whom contractual obligations can be enforced in courts. Thus, banks help police the process and privilege formal contractors in home construction and remodeling. The city gains through delegating the extension of public services (water and sewer lines) in large subdivisions, but at the cost of more expensive housing to buyers and diminished numbers of constructors.

A large public inspection staff monitors building and remodeling activities, for which permits and/or bonded contractors are usually required. While inspection offers a service linked to public safety, its fees are high enough not only to recover costs, but to net the agency considerable revenue.[20] The costs of enforcement, however, are borne in municipal court through the criminal justice system. Those cited for an offense must pay or appear in court (and probably pay fines), or warrants are issued for their arrest.

In Juárez, the building permit and land regularization processes are highly charged politically. Partisan gains and losses riddle the decision-making process. The current administration is working to create a central data bank on land, building, and taxes,[21] a resource that would reduce the importance of personal factors and discretion in street-level bureaucrats' negotiations. However, with self-help construction for the majority of housing units and property tax collection rates of 30 percent,[22] negotiation and compromise continue. PAN officials idealize a "zero toleration of negotiation" policy, but collective organization and the sheer size and visibility of informality make negotiation necessary, as we will see in Chapter 7.

The World Bank estimates that 55 percent of all housing units in Juárez are built informally, while a study by PRONASOL (National Solidarity Program) reports 65 percent. Formal construction through private contractors accounts for a mere 10 percent; and publicly subsidized home ownership for formal wage workers, another 35 percent.[23] The acquisition of land title deeds, a source of anxiety for residents, offers many political opportunities to leaders and officials who promise to deliver them, as we have seen.

The Housing Program for Juárez in 1989 reported a mixed picture for housing and *colonia* conditions. Housing stock is relatively good: two-thirds of houses consist of stone or cement blocks; the rest are less adequate adobe or wood. Housing stock is obviously related to residents' security; residents are reluctant to invest labor and savings without title deeds. Over time, residents of Juárez tend to occupy larger houses. In 1960, 47 percent of houses consisted of one room, but by 1989, only 6 percent of houses had one room.[24]

Housing and land sales are organized differently in Juárez and El Paso. Politics undergirds both systems, though it seems more muted in El Paso, with its public oversight of markets in which customer choice depends considerably on income level. The household interviews will help to deepen our understanding of people's housing and land circumstances in both Juárez and El Paso.

Housing and Home Improvement: Household Economy

Housing is a high priority in everyday lives. Our household information provides comparative data on home ownership/buyership, title deed acquisition, and rental housing (Figure 8).

As we see in Figure 8, Juárez reflects strikingly high rates of ownership/buyership (over 80 percent), compared with El Paso (less than 60 percent). Downtown El Pasoans swell the rental category, and thus overall numbers. However, title deed acquisition is problematic in Juárez. The discrepancy between title and attempted purchase is nearly 25 percent. The land onto which settlers move ("invade" in a literal translation from Spanish) is generally a mix of private and public property.

In Juárez, private owners are not always willing to sell at prices that either settlers (or their leaders) or the government can offer. Permission to settle public land is a political decision, and partisan calculations enter the decision-making process. Officials worry that some seemingly poor settlers are disguising their true wealth and multiple home ownership (see Chapter 7). Among settler households in the new periphery, we will discover that two "leaders" fall into this category.

Workers in formal occupations benefit from publicly subsidized housing. Under direction from a federal agency (INFONAVIT), housing is built according to precise specifications. Formal workers and employers pay into a fund, and a lottery selects residents for these largely middle-income houses[25] that look like condominiums or apartments.

Space matters in people's ability to construct and improve their own homes. Table 6, conveys the similarity of the El Paso and Juárez new periphery neighborhoods in this regard.

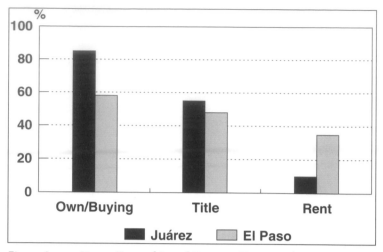

Figure 8   Home Ownership and Renting, El Paso and Juárez, 1992

Self-help housing, a variety of informal income-stretching behavior, is sparse in the older, established downtowns and widespread
in the peripheries, particularly the new peripheries. The highest
rates are found in the Juárez new periphery neighborhood, settled
in the late 1980s, where almost all housing is self-help. Its lower rate
of improvement is linked to the recent building and settlement, but
also to insecure title (as we develop in subsequent chapters).

New periphery residents in El Paso have accumulated savings to
put a down payment on land, make monthly payments, and construct homes or buy modestly priced houses or trailers, again with
monthly payments. Given existing income levels, most would not
qualify for a bank mortgage in other areas. Downtown residents are
generally stuck in rental units, with incomes and savings too low to
dream of a move outside the surveillance of the central city. El Paso's
new periphery improvement figure would be higher had trailers and
core room construction been excluded from the total; residents expand and improve these *"poco a poco"* ("little by little"), as many
described in interviews, but such improvements are viewed as part
of the overall construction.

The impressive title figures in El Paso's new periphery would
probably not square with those in the newer *colonias*, where title is
problematic. The new periphery *colonia* we studied is a settlement

Table 6   Housing and Self-Help Construction/Improvement,
El Paso and Juárez, 1992, in Percent

	Buying/ Own	Mortgage/ Title*	Resident- built	Improved
El Paso				
New Periphery	77	84	44	42
Old Periphery	70	97	3	39
Core	15	87	3	23
Juárez				
New Periphery	91	48	88	34
Old Periphery	82	68	55	55
Core	61	88	11	58

*Percentage of buyer/owners

approximately two decades old, and houses have been built and resold. Until 1996, when a new state law went into effect, *colonia* land was sold through sales contracts, with no equity built in. Under "contracts for sale," missed payments could result in foreclosure.[26] Even after amounts were fully paid, some unscrupulous developers required endless payments from those unskilled in English legalese.

The aspiration to own a home is high on both sides of the border. More people position themselves to do this—partly through political organizations—in Juárez than El Paso. Yet they are stymied by a land market through which politics is threaded in ways they cannot control. In both Juárez and El Paso, residents and settlers demonstrate impressive self-sufficiency, particularly in the new periphery. Space at the periphery provides room for housing informality to flourish. It is freer from surveillance, from both regulators and immigration officials.

Conclusion

The border is a crossroads for many. Here we consider that fact in immigration and housing terms. Many crossers move northward across the U.S.–Mexico line to face new lines that differentiate them on the basis of citizenship, housing, and language. Crossers on both sides seek opportunities for land and home ownership, despite modest incomes on the whole. In so doing, they face entanglements in the form of politics and bureaucratic rules that privilege formal building contractors. Such entanglements weigh more heavily on those with limited incomes, for they cannot exercise the kinds of consumer choices that surplus money offers to the relatively well off.

Yet despite these obstacles, many residents and crossers pursue an income-stretching form of informality that enables them to construct and improve homes. Impressive rates of ownership (or aspiring ownership) exist on both sides of the border. Does this residency turn into political community? To this topic we turn in the next chapter, focusing on new periphery *colonias*.

In public administration terminology, U.S. *colonias* represent *unplanned* settlement. *Planning*, of course, refers to the actions of officials rather than residents, for whom settlements are in fact frequently part of a planned strategy for upward mobility, security, and home ownership. Home construction and improvement occur largely through self-help and savings, and public services are extended gradually, if at all. Ultimately, though, residents need public services. Politics, and the associated potential entanglements, pay off in that realm, as Chapter 7 shows.

CHAPTER 6

Getting Public Services

Reflections on Political Community in the Urban Peripheries

> Unlike our northern neighbors, we have limited resources. But we are strong in organizations.
> Municipal Social Development staff member

The growth of El Paso and Juárez can best be observed in the residential sprawl that surrounds habitable parts of their peripheries. Residents pursue an upwardly mobile home ownership strategy, utilizing informal self-help to construct and improve houses. While conditions vary from city to city, such settlements generally begin with small homes in areas with unpaved roads. Public services like electricity, water, and sewage are extended only gradually. This reality transcends the border.

To many who study urban areas, public services are assumed. Services appear to fall within the domain of routine public administration, an aspect of government seemingly operated along technical and rational lines wherein public entitlements are available without political mobilization. One cannot take such matters for granted in urban peripheries.

Under conditions of new settlement, the political dimensions of public service outreach become clearer. And the comparative reflections of the U.S.–Mexico border further clarify this question: Which communities are better equipped politically to secure services, those in El Paso or those in Juárez? In the first section of this chapter, we examine public services in Mexico and the United States, both predominantly urban countries, focusing on both sides of the border with information from the household surveys. The heart of the chapter deals with the new periphery neighborhoods, where people build political community and meet neighborhood needs in the comparative political institutional contexts of Juárez and El Paso.

Modern life channels and contains most political energy in individualized electoral relationships between citizens and representatives. The political process privatized many public services, turning residents into customers. Vital issues are often absent from the campaign agenda, and technicians handle important matters within the bureaucracy. Witness the mainstream U.S. parties' silence on issues like job loss and free trade during the 1990s. This channeling is currently in process under conservative party rule in Juárez. At the border, a migratory crossroads on both sides, residents invent and sustain political community, however limited and flawed it may be. Through fledgling neighborhood organizations, many women and some men put vital issues on the public agenda.

Public Services at the Border

Whether a country is rich or poor, it takes considerable resources to construct water, sewer, and power lines. Virtually everyone uses or seeks these seemingly mundane services every day.

Public Service Outreach in Juárez

In Mexico, high population growth and extensive migration from rural to urban areas present fiscal challenges to municipal governments dependent on meager local revenue sources. The federal and state governments offer limited public financing for water and roads based on both political and technical calculations.[1] A federal agency operates locally to extend electricity, for which consumers pay installation fees and monthly service charges.

Many studies document the neglect of new urban settlements and the political energies that residents invest in getting services.[2] Popular organizations rise and fall according to their ability to "deliver" services or to act as intermediaries for residents and the public agencies that are supposed to serve them. Some of these organizations affiliate with political parties to strengthen their leverage, though affiliations permit capture or cooptation.

Despite the economic crisis of the 1980s, the government has made urban service provision a priority in the last decade. Both the 1990 census and special studies by the College of the Northern Frontier/El Colegio de la Frontera Norte (COLEF) tell us that access to public services is available to the vast majority of urban residents. Areas categorized as Economic Strata I to III (privileged to marginal) show impressive coverage, even in Strata III. Electricity and piped water are more commonly available than other services. Intriguingly, though, the COLEF study documented that border cities are less well served than those in the heartland.[3]

In Juárez, a full 95 percent of households had access to electricity, 81 percent to piped water, and 70 percent to sewer hookups.[4] The municipality of Juárez has expanded over the decades; it is a single-bounded unit, not one embedded in dualistic city–county structures, and cut across by other school and water district boundaries, as occurs in the United States.

It must be understood that the water piped into homes is untreated, though probably safe for drinking most of the time. During seasons or times of heavy use, water pressure drops. Sewage is emptied through collectors that deposit waste in what people call the *"aguas negras"* ("black waters") outside the city, contaminating groundwater and irrigation canals. Despite its huge size, Juárez has no wastewater treatment plant. An agreement reached in 1992 to build two plants was delayed and finally put on hold while negotiators debated about cost, cost recovery through user fees, and water-quality goals. Finally, the 1994 peso devaluation, in which pesos dropped to half their value the year before, killed this and other worthy projects.[5]

Paved roads are among the costliest of public services for neighborhoods in terms of building and maintenance. Residents can hardly pay user fees, for road use is indivisible. Paved roads in outlying areas and residential neighborhoods are uncommon, resulting in heavy dust and driving respiratory problems.

Public Service Outreach in El Paso

El Paso is divided between city and county and among different water and school districts. A privately owned monopoly provides electricity in El Paso, with people's interests ostensibly represented at the state commission level. Inside El Paso's city limits, private contractors build houses, usually in subdivisions, and city ordinance requires that water and sewer lines be laid. Outside the city limits, however, people settle in *colonias*, a veritable regulatory vacuum. Developers sell land with the promise but not the delivery of services. As we noted in the previous chapter, here the Spanish word for neighborhood—*colonia*—takes on an ominous tone.

The first El Paso County *colonias*, Sparks and Moon City, were settled in 1959. At the same time, changes occurred in El Paso's city core. Over a thirty-year period, low-cost housing in central El Paso declined by 55 percent, the result of several factors: the Chamizal Agreement returned disputed territory to Mexico and displaced residents; highway construction displaced others; and periodic enforcement of building codes for slum tenements razed buildings or drove up rents because of rehabilitation costs. Public housing units could not accommodate the many on waiting lists (with just 7,000 units, they still cannot). Even after Sparks and Moon City received electricity in the early 1980s, water was still being trucked in at considerable cost to residents.[6]

Outside the city limits, *colonias* in El Paso County grew to more than 150, with over 70,000 residents live there. The city has little material interest in annexing space with meager property tax returns and high costs for service.[7] Adverse publicity about *colonias* calls national, state, and local attention to their problems, particularly the public health problems (such as dysentery and hepatitis) associated with inadequate water and waste facilities.[8] Residents are responsible for their own water and sewer disposal, in the form of septic tanks, outhouses, and cesspools. Residents who do not borrow or buy water instead build their own wells, many of them too shallow to avoid groundwater contamination.

In the fragmented federalism of the United States, numerous state and federal agencies control much-sought-after funds, now threatened by the austerity programs of the last decade. It takes organization, resources, and commitment to acquire such funds.

In 1986 the newly created El Paso County Lower Valley Water District Authority began long-term negotiations with local, state, and federal agencies to secure grants and loans, with El Paso's Public Service Board (the water utility), to exchange water and waste treatment facilities. The lower-density settlement of *colonias*, compared with the City of El Paso (or even Juárez), makes the cost of providing service high, yet 5,000 connections were made in the early 1990s.[9] Water users pay for extension from main lines to their homes, bond issues, and high user fees. In the 1990s El Paso County water user fees were nearly double the city fees of $26 a month; they are expected to triple by the year 2000.[10]

In our household interviews, we queried residents about their access to and evaluation of various public services. Specifically, we asked about their access to piped water and sewage, electricity, trash collection, paved roads, and street lights. Residents also indicated whether they had indoor toilets. We can view the results in Figures 9–11.

Both cities resemble one another more than they differ. The downtown neighborhoods are almost fully serviced. Sewage and electricity coverage are universal. Paved roads, indoor toilets, and street lights are slightly more common on the El Paso side, while indoor piped water is slightly more common in Juárez. Several tenement buildings in downtown El Paso resemble the notorious *vecindades* of Mexico: one faucet for many residential units.

For the old periphery residential areas, services are similar as well, with one major exception (roads) and one minor exception (street lights). The lower percentage of paved roads in Juárez has a political aspect: one neighborhood in the old periphery was formerly controlled by the CDP. Its leaders have had uneasy relationships with both the PRI and the PAN governments. Residents' material interests in neighborhood improvements now lead some to "betray" the old popular organization, and others to affiliate with government parties. This area is in political flux.

The new peripheries are the main focus of this chapter. In Figure 11 we see some surprising achievements in Juárez compared with El Paso, not only in coverage, but in the time necessary to extend coverage. The U.S. *colonia* has been settled more than two decades, whereas the one in Juárez had been around for three years at the time of the interviews (1992). Water, trash collection, and street lighting are more widely available at the Juárez new periphery. Seeking installation charges and user fees for electricity, both state-owned (Mexican) and private monopoly (U.S.) providers extend access quickly to residents. Electricity coverage is somewhat wider in El Paso. More El Pasoans have indoor toilets, and their sewer facilities are their own: septic tanks and cesspools. Paved roads are almost nonexistent in both areas. One might have expected quicker provision of water lines in the "rich" United States. Politics (discussed below) helps explain why this did not occur.

Residents' evaluations of public services (Figure 12) offer a some-

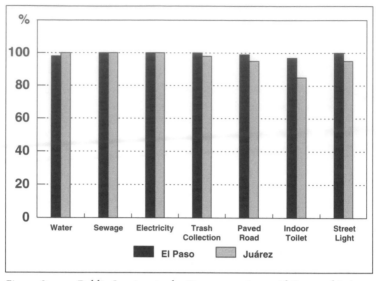

Figure 9   Public Services in the Downtown Areas, El Paso and Juárez, 1992

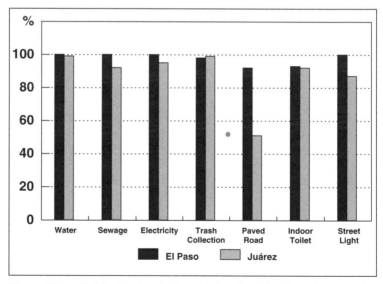

Figure 10   Public Services in the Old Periphery Residential Areas, El Paso and Juárez, 1992

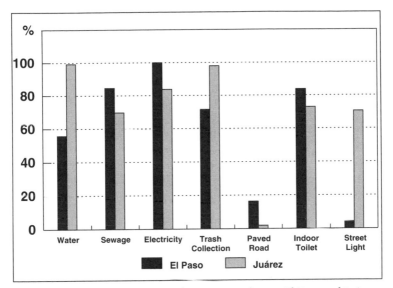

Figure 11   Public Services in the New Peripheries, El Paso and Juárez, 1992

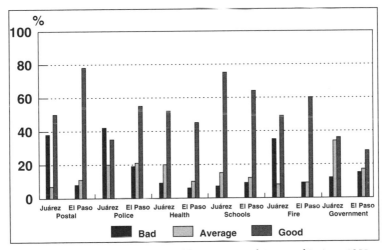

Figure 12   Satisfaction with Public Services, El Paso and Juárez, 1992

what different picture of both communities. Questions involved a broad array of public services: postal, police, health, schools, fire, and local government. Household respondents in both cities gave their overall governments similar ratings, with a majority finding them average to good. They also rated health and school services in similar ways, with a higher percentage of Juárez respondents evaluating their schools as good. The fire and police departments and the postal services drew a larger proportion of negative evaluations from Juárez residents.

Residents who choose to act on their evaluations do so through voting, individual contacts, and collective organization. To these topics we now turn.

Building Political Communities

Residents build political community within, outside, or in connection with official institutions specific to each side of the border. Through top-down organizational strategies, the multiparty system at Mexico's northern border offers channels for participation amid populist rhetoric and patronage. To the north, political representatives in El Paso monitor public agencies that operate according to uniform technical rules. The politics is muted compared with the situation in Juárez, but it is certainly there in the skewed patterns of political engagement.

The Institutional Contexts

Strong citizen–representative relationships require mutual knowledge, contact, and accessibility. Our tallies from the household interviews show that few residents made contacts with officials, or even knew their correct names at legislative levels. From the interviews, we know that voter registration rates are high in Juárez (85 percent), but low in El Paso (38 percent), due to citizenship requirements. Among U.S. Latinos, the adult noncitizen population exceeds the number of voters. Texas Latinos are a quarter of the population, but 15 percent of those on registration rolls have Spanish surnames.[11]

Collective organization adds value to voting. It offers a bridge to representatives and officials. Collective organization is particularly useful to politically marginal communities because it offsets the usual class bias of participation, at least in the United States.[12] The Saul Alinsky organizational model has been adopted in various Latino communities. In Alinsky's model, leaders mobilize members through institutions of social trust, such as churches, to seek local political accountability through occasionally confrontational means. Los Angeles Latinos work in UNO (United Neighborhood Organizations); San Antonio Latinos in COPS (Communities Organized for Public Services); South Texas residents of *colonias* and towns in Inter-Valley Faith; and El Pasoans in the El Paso Interreligious Sponsoring Organization (EPISO).[13]

EPISO operates in a virtual party vacuum, for the political parties are weak and personalistic organizations at the county level. City elections have been "professionalized" since 1957, when they became nonpartisan. Representatives appoint business and organizational leaders engaged in the political process to boards and commissions on which policies are discussed. The Mexican-American Legal and Educational Defense Fund (MALDEF) runs leadership training to recruit new pools for those appointments. The Southwest Voter Registration Project promotes registration and voting with its "Su voto es su voz" ("Your vote is your voice") campaign. Potential voters send another message with their low voter turnout.

Mexico's machinelike dominant party, the PRI, has gathered various affiliated organizations under its wings at national, state, and local levels. Under two PRI municipal terms from 1986 to 1992, *colonia* leaders worked with block leaders, who are known as *jefes de manzana*. The radical CDP occasionally affiliates with the PRI and with leftist parties whose names and programs shift according to the ideological fine points (or personality conflicts) over which leaders haggle. The CDP represents approximately thirty *colonias*, whose residents it helped settle through land invasions.

Why do people join organizations and sustain their commitments? According to James Q. Wilson, various incentives operate, material, solidary (social- and status-related), and purposive (goal- and ideologically oriented).[14] Some case studies in Mexico portray seemingly ideological groups as working with neighborhoods to secure public services,[15] but members' incentives are just as likely to evaporate once services are delivered. To avoid that outcome and maintain their organizational base, leaders promote free riding or pirating electrical and water lines.[16] Others pay, of course—municipal water agencies that lose fees or neighbors in nearby *colonias*.

Political parties also adopt top-down, neighborhood-based organizational models based primarily on material incentives, though delivery does not guarantee support from voters. Despite dense organizational nets, the PRI lost the 1992 municipal election in Juárez. The National Solidarity Program (PRONASOL) spent considerable sums for social programs before the election, and publicized them in three-color signs that match PRI's "tricolor" and in local solidarity committees. Teachers could be observed just outside the polling stations on election day reminding voters about the money spent to dignify school buildings. The conservative PAN won a three-year term instead, revisiting its 1983–86 triumph, which had initiated streamlined administration.[17] The PAN's strategy to individualize the relationship between citizen and government undermines the largely PRI-based neighborhood organizations, along with the PRI's occasional coalition partners, the CDP.

From 1992 to 1995, the PAN appointee Ramón Galindo served as the municipality's social development director. He pursued a vigorous campaign to criminalize allegedly fraudulent leaders. With great media fanfare, PAN also moved into CDP's increasingly factionalized neighborhoods with integrated land-regularization and public service outreach efforts. The municipal president's initial visits, accompanied by photographers and antiriot police, gradually turned into routine populist patronage and ultimately featured strongly in the PAN's presentations of its program accomplishments.[18] Ironically, though, they bestowed at least as many rewards on these former opponents as on more supportive neighborhoods. Such is the fate of collective organization amid scarce resources, clientelist politics, and patronage; neighborhood residents, ultimately, do not pull the strings.

The PAN replaced the PRI's neighborhood organization with its own machinery, known as *comités de vecinos* (neighbor committees: see Chapter 3). The *comités* were operating in 192 *colonias* by the middle of the PAN's 1992–95 term. The PAN put considerable energy into advertising its program in the local media and in publishing its own materials, including directories explaining how to contact officials and offices. Many of the issues that the PAN vigorously publicized are bureaucratized in El Paso. Box 6 contains an outline for the PAN's "State of the Municipality" address.

Voters elected Ramón Galindo municipal president in 1995, and the PAN took a majority of *cabildo* (council) seats, a number

Box 6. First State of the Municipality Report: "Your Vote Initiated This Work" (Municipal Government of Juárez, October 9, 1993)*

This is the programmatic outline of a five-page insert from a local newspaper, itself condensed from a forty-seven-page document. Five thousand copies of that document were published in its first edition. One copy is on file with the author.

Public Security (one-third of municipal budget)
Construct new buildings, with help from state government
Decentralize services throughout city
Train and professionalize police
Create "Group 16" to improve communication with schools, neighborhoods, and factories
Map crimes spatially, to target police resources
Operate special programs on car theft, drugs, etc.
Monitor private security companies
Purchase additional equipment
Combat corruption
Initiate programs to reduce auto accidents
Modernize public transport (concessions to taxis, buses, vans)
Improve firefighters in collaboration with El Paso Fire Department
Improve public ambulance service
Reform prison

Sanitation
Improve garbage collection
Organize transfer points for garbage removal
Operate special programs
Decentralize operations

Human Settlements
Develop agreement to standardize land occupation and ownership
Increase title deed issuance
Pursue citizen outreach to deal with thirty-year backlog

Planning
Establish the nation's first technical planning institute that transcends party-based municipal government
Create general rules for urban development
Modernize land registry, beginning with aerial photographs
Establish a Geographical Information System
Plan four new traffic routes, with assistance from the World Bank

Public Services**
Maintain and improve urban services, such as street lighting
Increase public parking

Improve slaughterhouse
Establish more road markings and signs
Increase space for parks and gardens

Public Works**

Increase pavement and drainage for rain run-off, with help from federal and
state governments
Work on neighborhood-specific projects

Administrative Efficiency

Pursue audits and anticorruption campaigns
Coordinate formula-funded, cost-shared programs with state and federal
governments
Reduce the inherited debt from previous [PRI] government [note: an en-
larged sidebar accompanied this text]
Maintain vehicles
Encourage employee performance through 15 percent pay incentives
Increase revenue-generating efficiency (timely payments, evasion detection)

**Community Development (Under Social Development Depart-
ment)**

Promote comités de vecinos [a PAN state program]
Promote PRONASOL Committees, to obtain federal resources for the improvement of school facilities, homes, green areas, and neighborhood
watch groups)

**Social Assistance (Integrated Family Development/Desarrollo
Integral de la Familia, DIF)**

Provide school lunch and breakfast programs with community kitchens
Program for the elderly and against child abuse
Assist the needy with health care
Dispense food

Environmental Protection

Inspect vehicles at nineteen verification centers
Work with FEMAP [a private community development organization] to
promote alternative fuels for brickmaking
Program for other needs, investigating complaints, and monitoring waste

Routine Government

Completed ordinary (13) and extraordinary (12) council sessions
Issued documents (13,092 government and 4,243 judicial)
Orchestrate resettlement and dialog over formal and informal commerce
Parking

*The title uses the familiar tu, "you," rather than the formal usted. The municipal
president's address also contained familiarly-phrased remarks aimed at children and
women.

**Public Works and Public Services consume approximately a fifth each of the
budget, the next largest portion after Public Security.

roughly proportional to their vote. The *regidores* do not represent geographic districts, as they do on El Paso's city council and county board, reinforcing the need for neighborhood organization.

Political Community in the New Peripheries?

Collective organization is a neat and abstract phrase unmuddied by complicated everyday realities. The analysis of collective organization in the new peripheries illustrates the many incentives that motivate and sustain involvement, among them income generation, material benefits, and religion. In both household surveys and interviews with leaders, we found a picture of weak and sometimes flawed political community in both new peripheries.

Top-Down, Dense Organization: Political Payoffs

Early settlers arrived in the Juárez *colonia* in 1989, when the PRI controlled municipal government. Four "leaders," eight *jefes de manzana*, (or *jefas*, for the feminine form accurately reflects women's majority presence at this level), and four members of the emergent *comité de vecinos* help tell the story.[19]

Interviews with three of the four leaders took place in their homes, which doubled as offices. The office of one was striking for its artifacts and atmosphere. He had a desk adorned with a candy goblet, chairs, a couch, and walls covered with photographs of himself shaking hands with prominent people at different stages of the *colonia*'s development.

People use the generic term *leader* to describe several activities. At one level, leaders represent communities or serve as brokers to convey demands and negotiate benefits. At another level, they control a space and its residents for a party. Such control may be a delusion; this *colonia* switched sides from the PRI to the PAN with great media fanfare. At yet another level, some leaders are entrepreneurs and land developers. They work hard collecting fees for ends that are both legitimate (services, for example) and illegitimate (title deeds they do not control).

The founding leader mobilized settlers, who were selected on the basis of economic need and PRI affiliation. He organized settlement on publicly and privately owned land, and both the PRI and later the PAN governments negotiated with a private owner reluctant to sell at the offered price. Both state and municipal lands were authorized for sale, paving the way for land registration and title acquisition. President Salinas made a highly publicized visit to the area, an event at which some titles were conferred at prices that averaged $275 (800 new pesos) for a small plot.

As the *colonia* grew, new settlers and leaders arrived to compete with the founder. Leaders' backgrounds varied. One of the new leaders, loosely affiliated with the PRI, had moved up from the party's youth branch, while another claimed a revolutionary heritage. The third new leader supported the PAN from 1983 to 1986, after which he accepted a PRI appointment. The original settler criteria no longer prevailed; others arrived without the blessings of either leaders or the PRI.

Leaders circulated petitions seeking water, sewer, and electrical lines. Services came quickly, as we verified in household interviews, but installation charges varied widely. Lacking uniform installation rates, this process is subject to negotiation and corruption. Yet the user fees residents cited are similar, with most paying modest amounts compared with those in El Paso. Some residents complained about installation fee collection and rates, saying that some collectors gave no receipts and others fled with their money. Residents were not clear about whether the collectors worked for the agencies or for the leaders.

The quick extension of services is impressive. Are leaders responsible, with their mobilizations and threats of protest? Or have officials routinized the extension of services in high-density settlements, recovering costs through installation and user fees? Peter Ward's comparison of two PRI administrations in Mexico City periodizes a change: the politically charged distribution system, with services accorded to the leaders who could create the most disturbances, was replaced by a more efficient and streamlined distribution system, dependent upon residents' labor contributions and user fees.[20] PAN governance in Juárez from 1983 to 1986 reinforced the streamlined approach, which was continued in the subsequent PRI administration[21] and emphasized again from 1992 onward.

Yet officials have a political interest in appeasing constituencies. Why? First, threats of or actual political disturbances get wide coverage, creating a thorn in their side. Second, low-income residents, the majority of voters, can grant or deny electoral victory, assuming that vote counts are honest and accurate. This assumption is sometimes questionable; nonvictorious parties habitually shout "fraud" after elections. The PAN negotiates, as I demonstrate in Chapter 7; this is testimony both to its organizational viability and to the party's emergence from a political culture that prizes such behavior.

Colonia leaders respond to material incentives, just as members respond to the material benefits of participation. Some of the interviewed leaders received stipends from the PRI, while others spoke vaguely about acquiring "support." One was inspired to lead land invasions because, as a settler, he had been duped into making payments to a leader who never produced title deeds. Now he credits himself with leadership in eight *colonias*.

Over time, PRI-affiliated leaders lost some of their membership base. In our household interviews, residents complained that leaders charged weekly fees and required attendance at meetings; leaders said fees were voluntary donations for services rendered. After residents got services, however unpredictable the installation fees, little was left for that cast of leading characters to deliver. From our interviews, we learned that fewer than half of the residents held land titles, leaving a critical mass lacking this basic security despite payments they claimed to have made. Leaders denied receiving money for land, but they blamed each other for fraud, validating residents' concerns.

Once the PAN took control of municipal government, lingering incentives no longer could be offered. Under the PRI administration, *jefes/jefas de manzana* got discounts for water bills and could also nominate needy residents for discounts. Of course, such incentives paled in significance next to services and land titles. A majority of residents still await land titles, for which they are willing and able to pay.

The PAN did not leave neighborhoods in a political vacuum. It blanketed the municipality with its own version of top-down organization. In this new periphery neighborhood, the PAN appointed nine members of the *comité de vecinos*. Neighbors subsequently voted for members, amid competition and choice. The PAN forbade members to collect fees or require meetings. Residents' cynicism might have made such collection impossible anyway.

Comité members, most of them women, seek funding for neighborhood improvement. They encourage residents to plant trees and clear fields for a future park. To raise funds, they sponsor parties, bazaars, and raffles. More ambitiously, they once sought resources for road paving, but were ultimately unsuccessful in packaging Solidarity Program funds with municipal contributions and residents' labor. According to interviews with municipal Social Development Department staff, negotiations broke down over the amount of the municipal contribution; the National Solidarity Program reneged on its promised contribution.

Solidarity is a mixed blessing for opposition governments, for the program creates the appearance of PRI beneficence. While the PRI does not appear to reduce the amount given to opposition governments for formula-funded projects, some evidence suggests that the PAN cannot pursue public-debt financing for high-cost, long-term public works projects such as roads.[22] (PRI discretionary money is, of course, unavailable to a PAN-controlled municipality.) Yet PAN propaganda claims credit for Solidarity Program projects in which it had a partial hand.

Juárez is an organizationally dense municipality, a grid on which many parties compete in regular elections. These organizations are not autonomous, but tangled in top-down strategies that occasionally pay off for neighborhoods. Yet neighborhood organizations can sometimes be pawns in larger games that officials and entrepreneurial leaders pursue for their own interests. Unless technical criteria kick in (such as neutral formulas and schedules for service delivery), along with the government's material interest in putting land on the registry so that it can collect taxes, residents must await for opportune moments tied to elections to achieve their goals.

Bottom-Up Organizations: Uncertain Payoffs
The El Paso *colonia* was settled over twenty years ago in a high-desert region east of the city. In the typical pattern, farmers and ranchers sell land to developers (or they transform themselves into developers); the former farm land around the city is less and less profitable for agricultural purposes. Many developers exercise political clout through their contacts with officials and their contributions to electoral campaigns. The long-term congressional incumbent decided not to run in 1995 after a series of scandals over developers' loans and campaign donations. His work for *colonias* helped residents, but it also increased land values, thereby tainting the effort.

Settlers purchased lots that averaged a quarter to a half acre. They made individual, commercial transactions, rather than political ones in collective organizations. Land values have inflated in value over the years, but prices outside the city limits are considerably less than those inside, for basic services are under- or undeveloped.

For most residents, political engagement rests on the lowest common denominator: voting. Because only a minority of individuals in the new periphery neighborhood are citizens eligible to vote, voter participation is minimal. Of the 41 percent of adult citizens who are eligible to register, fewer than half actually do so. Of the registered, 35 percent voted in the big local elections of 1990 and 20 percent in the presidential elections of 1988.

In our household interviews, residents revealed little knowledge of political parties or their leaders and agendas. Of course, local political channels do little to facilitate this knowledge, with their nonpartisan, frequently personalistic campaigns. Yet half of the household residents say they sympathize with a party, most of them (two-thirds) with the Democrats. Others gave a politician's name, rather than a party name, or said, "The ones for the poor." Party differences are not always transparent. Besides, important regional decisions are often made through bureaucratic fiat, such as the Border Patrol's installation of the Border Blockade (Operation Hold the Line). El Paso has a virtual one-party system (the Democratic Party), but if two-party competition were viable, the opposition would not likely court new periphery residents.

Citizens have numerous elected representatives in the U.S. system of fragmented federalism. The county contains fourteen water districts, nine school districts, court and criminal justice offices, and city representatives; all city and school representatives are elected in nonpartisan contests. In partisan elections, citizens elect the county judge and four county commissioners, each representing roughly a quarter of the territory. Few household residents could correctly name area representatives, except for the county judge at the time, Alicia Chacón, who invested many years in *colonia* water issues.

Residents are more likely to know executive-branch officials in both El Paso and Juárez, but parties have some programmatic meaning in local Mexican politics. They have little meaning in El Paso. Moreover, parties in Mexico recruit candidates who, if elected, earn generous salaries, compared with the amateur salaries of most legislators at state and local levels in Texas, who depend on other jobs or pensions.[23]

The technical complexities of many rules, procedures, and standard-setting decisions are in bureaucratic hands, insulated from political representatives (and the people they represent). Moreover, Texas counties lack land use and planning authority, thus pursuing only minimal control over *colonias*. In recent years, though, the Texas legislature has expanded county attorneys' authority in order to halt further *colonia* development.

The two English-language El Paso newspapers provide minimal coverage of *colonia* settlement and residents' struggles for services, compared with Juárez newspapers. El Paso has no Spanish-language newspaper, although a local Spanish television station has captured about 10 percent of the news viewership, according to periodic ratings published in the newspapers. The major exceptions to news blackouts on ordinary settlers involves reports on health crises and scandalous "third world" conditions, loan/grant awards and their enforcement, and EPISO, the Alinsky-type advocacy organization that gives voice to residents' water and sewer needs.

Now in its second decade, EPISO mobilizes members through Catholic churches. When it was founded, the local political establishment viewed EPISO leaders as radical outside agitators. Leaders are trained in tactics that are sometimes confrontational; for example, EPISO has organized sit-ins and "accountability sessions" that make it difficult for public officials to avoid giving straight answers. Ironically, many adherents are socially conservative Catholics, who organize within the moral space of religious institutions. Friendly priests and nuns legitimize EPISO's agenda. After the early years, EPISO became a recognized and respected power broker for large numbers of low-income people who have been unevenly engaged with official politics. It has dedicated itself to bringing water and sewer lines to the lower valley, where many *colonias* are located. EPISO makes the most of its numbers by organizing members across *colonia* and neighborhood lines.

EPISO also works at the state level to promote higher-level changes in law and policy. It helped create a Lower Valley Water District Authority, an official body with which EPISO collaborates to apply for loans and grants that allow residents to extend water lines to their property. Yet water bills outside the city are double and triple what city dwellers pay, as we have seen. As far back as 1983, Texas Governor Mark White spoke publicly about helping residents dig ditches for water lines. Populist rhetorical lines go a long way in Texas, but high regulatory standards made lines to low-density settlements expensive. Residents pay part of the upfront costs of public services.

In the new periphery neighborhood, loans and grants have finally trickled down to residents, nearly a quarter-century after the first settlers came. Without EPISO, most residents mattered little politically. But at the time of our 1992 interviews, most residents still resorted to self-help.

In our household interviews, we found that a quarter of *colonia* households claimed affiliation with EPISO. Interviews with EPISO leaders validated this figure. EPISO leader Sister Mary Beth Larkin coordinated her work with people in neighborhoods who provide voluntary, informal leadership to their areas. In our interview, Larkin expressed pride over high attendance at EPISO's 1993 convention in El Paso's Civic Center. Support for EPISO and its convention was built through 180 home meetings in the Lower Valley, southeast of the city following the Rio Grande.[24]

The household interviews uncovered four more informal community organizations, which connect people over water sharing and food distribution from government surplus commodities and local donations. These connections are tenuous, dependent on a few volunteers who get little material compensation for their work, in contrast to party activists in Mexico and entrepreneurs who double as party activists.

What motivates people to participate in these formal and informal organizations? As in Mexico, material interests come into play, for households benefit from public services along with loans and grants to pay for those services. Public services improve land values, should residents sell their homes and property. However, once public services come (or incomes rise to buy services like deep wells), will organizational motivations continue? More than materialism is at work in organizations like EPISO. Organizations based on ideas and principles, whether religious or ideological, offer prospects for sustainability.

In the United States, religious-based organization is a safe space in which to connect, at a distance from government. On this side of the border, ironically, residents of mostly Mexican heritage organize collectively around religion, a practice that is rare in contemporary Mexico. There, ideology and culture drive, or supplement, the material agenda of many collective organizations.

Surveillance is a reality that U.S. residents live with every day. Public agencies collect considerable information from those seeking needs-based assistance. Immigration surveillance and enforcement wax and wane, for reasons beyond the control of ordinary people. *Colonia* residents live everyday lives that do not comply, or fully comply, with the myriad of regulations and rules. The more they expose to authorities, the more vulnerable they become. Thus, a fundamental paradox exists in those outreach strategies that seek to connect people with public assistance. The enforcement details of such programs can change at the whims of bureaucrats or the U.S. Congress, both of which are disconnected from *colonia* residents. Those who manage state-funded community centers in South Texas *colonias* count, according to their own charts, "client contacts" with "service providers" who have recently begun the "delivery of services."[25] People's needs for health and food are great, as the poverty and income data of earlier chapters document. But for many, the safest strategy involves lying low, avoiding agencies that solicit extensive household data, particularly for members who fall between the cracks of official regulations. Lying low also means avoiding the sort of attention political organization might bring. Yet without political organization, public service delays and neglect are probably inevitable, given the scarce resources of the property-tax-poor county.

Political channels that emphasize voting offer a perfect recipe for political quiescence. Informal work, low income, and citizenship limbo all conspire to reduce civic culture and democratic practice. When (if) people get their work and papers in official order, they can more openly pursue a formal, civic strategy. The Union de Colonias Olvidadas/Forgotten Colonias Union emerged in South Texas and built a successful ten-*colonia* coalition to demand water. It achieved its goal within a year.[26] The discourse, style, and speed of the effort are reminiscent of a Juárez organization. However, the cross-neighborhood coalition, plus its autonomy, set it apart from the party-dependent patronage of Juárez.

Once services come, will incentives exist to organize collectively? In contrast to their Mexican counterparts, *colonia* residents in El Paso County occupy land for which the acquisition of a title deed is usually transparent. Abuses exist, but once routine services are in place, delivered to customers in return for payments, residents may remain or retreat into political quiescence.[27]

Conclusion

In Juárez, *colonia* residents quickly acquired most public services. Their political organization, obviously flawed as a result of leaders' opportunism, helped explain their visibility to government. Both the PRI and the PAN court neighborhood constituencies in increasingly competitive elections wherein parties promise different approaches to local problems. The PAN capitalizes on an image of streamlined administration and uncorruptability, although it negotiates in ways consistent with the larger political culture.

In El Paso, the image of individualized, streamlined administration prevails amid the Texan political culture of minimalist government. Nowhere is this more obvious than in county government. Although party competition allegedly exists in county elections, organization is weak, personalistic, and rarely issued-oriented. Amateur politicians have the potential to oversee technical agencies, but they respond primarily to those with political clout and, to some extent, to voters, who constitute a minority among many alienated or excluded from voting. Noisy organizations like EPISO bring issues to the public agenda, but activists work long and hard with fragmented government agencies to secure funds for costly services that must comply with high technical standards. In the meantime, *colonia* residents wait and wait; residents of the new periphery *colonia* under study have been waiting for twenty years. And public health problems ferment, even though high technical standards were meant to protect the public from them.

At the base of fledgling organizations, women do most of the work and create most of the connections with neighbors. First-tier female leaders in El Paso's EPISO match a growing tradition in Mexico. Perhaps those female traditions were there all along, but invisible to mainstream political observers. The communitarians seeking lost political community in an increasingly individualistic United States perhaps need not look far for the key to its possible restoration. But will they be satisfied with political community that is female-built, shared between men and women, and strengthened by residents with or without the authorization of formal citizenship?

Colonia problems and solutions are similar on both sides of the border. They share the same air and water basins. Communitarians might also do well to rethink notions of old-style civic culture, where tolerance and solidarity stop at national identities and official borders, despite the shared heritage, economies, and realities on both sides. They might begin with a regional citizenship that extends the logic of commercial citizenship found in free trade agreements and in multinational corporate joint ventures. It is to these larger, macro-political-economic concerns that we now move.

CHAPTER 7

Engaging Political Community

Surveillance, Public Accountability, and Seeds Across the Border

> The municipality is the point of greatest interaction between the state and civic society, the point where the logic of the state and the logic of daily life interact.
>
> Jordi Borja, "Past, Present, and Future of Local Government in Latin America"

Whatever the civic and regulatory institutions do, people on either side of the border generate work for themselves, stretch their incomes, and build or improve homes with their own hands. Border crossing and the maneuverability it teaches facilitate these opportunities, but in the grim context of a global city of poverty, cheapened labor, and the special surveillance associated with the borderline itself. If people are to engage government in the construction of a political community accountable to themselves, the local level is where they can logically begin.

In this chapter, I take the research findings and apply them to action in nongovernmental organizations (NGOs) and in government, especially as it enforces public policies. Ultimately, the full meaning of policies develops in enforcement, rather than in stated intentions. The chapter is grounded in a normative assumption: however global the character of the border region is, people ought to be able to use political institutions to protect their livelihoods and free themselves from surveillance when they cause no harm to others. If people are intimidated, or if their organizations are counterproductive, then we must raise questions about what kind of democracy we have. Democracy, defined broadly as responsiveness and accountability to the governed, has its U.S. and Mexican twists. The institutional context matters, as I uncover in this chapter.

In this chapter, we examine the spectrum from nongovernmental organizations (NGOs) to government agencies and observe how their street-level bureaucrats (SLBs) behave at the borderlines of interaction with residents. Ideally, all residents would be viewed as *constituents:* the ones whom "public servants" or "civil servants" serve. Constituents exercise their voice when, as individuals or members of collective organizations, they engage those in government. Public administrators using the language of Total Quality Management might even term residents *customers,* implying that individual residents have choices and voices. The reality is that many residents are treated like *clients:* people often stigmatized by a government that aims to control them.[1] Consequently, residents do not uniformly seek political engagement, but rather distance from and even avoidance of government, stances that do not bode well for creating and sustaining political community.

In the first section of this chapter, I examine public administration at the border as an incomplete modernist project. After that, I analyze a potential constituent group of cross-border community bankers. For three years I have participated in a steering committee trying to transfer the model from south (Mexico) to north (the United States), attending meetings, planning and speaking at conferences, and guiding the collection of information across bankers' loan cycles. In the third section, I compare public policy practices on both sides of the border, elaborating on the enforcement aspects of those agencies with stakes in informal work and housing economies. I conclude with the case of a street vendors' organization whose members' collective action served to expose rather than empower informals.

Policy, Planning, and Public Administration at the Border: A Modernist Project?

Public administrators and planners face special challenges in an aspiring global city at the border, with its web of multiple rules that seek to embrace ordinary residents, opportunists, and crossers. Government workers ostensibly respond to problems associated with industrial and urban growth in a professional and technical manner. As such, they participate in what I refer to in Chapter 2 as a modernist project to implement policies in reasonably uniform and effective ways, based on informed, rational analysis. To do so, governments require public resources and political guidance.

How does a government get resources and guidance? At the border, the administrators are a complicated and diverse group, divided not only into different agencies, but different layers of government, in two governance systems, the United States and Mexico. Mexico has no formal civil service; instead, professional staff turn over every three years at the local level, reducing organizational memory after elections. But for many policies, the ultimate meanings and real practices are expressed in front-line administrators who interact with the public: street-level bureaucrats, operating with limited oversight and maximum discretion.

Who are these publics that contribute revenue and guidance? In U.S. cities, planners have been viewed as handmaidens to what John Logan and Harvey Molotch call "economic growth machines."[2] Thus bankers and developers are among the big players with material interests in administrative choices. In more neutral language, grounded in the banality of everyday administration, Peter Eisinger says local and state officials "usually treat employment and tax-based growth as compatible objectives."[3] Presumably, this orientation would add employers (especially those from visible, large-scale firms) as another group of players. The drive to generate revenue adds yet another set of players drawn from the administration itself. While taxpayers are part of the public, the revenue seekers from within the administration are more organized, with authority and technology to collect data and to maintain surveillance to the extent that resources and political direction allow. This is a recipe for an all-powerful state, but the institutional embrace is not nearly so complete as this modern image projects. Other groups counter this power, using material and ideological arguments plus ballot-box accountability. Still others, including the unorganized, ignore or resist control, using spaces of inconsistency, resource limitations, and occasional political leverage to protect themselves.

At borders—these territorial lines that divide one political jurisdiction from another—there is no monolithic state that acts in coherent fashion. Rather, fragmented agencies pursue various interests using different means, riddled with inconsistencies. Threaded throughout this in-between place, administrative agencies pursue their objectives more or less relentlessly, creating other in-between spaces that ordinary people use and abuse. Agencies are staffed with people, not machines, who make discretionary decisions with variable resources and supervision. The realities of demographically diverse, poverty-stricken public administration at the border raise questions about the effectiveness of this modernist project. But some administrators try and try hard. Law and lawlessness coexist, and enforcement is bound to be selective rather than uniform.

With what institutions do people engage? Most of the many public agencies planted upon societies are contained *within* nations; few are cross-border bureaucracies. But community development, human rights, and environmental NGOs do cross borders. Both the United States and Mexico claim to be federal governments, although U.S. federalism delegates far more taxing and spending authority to state and local governments than Mexican Federalism. Yet municipal governments in Mexico have considerable authority and autonomy to regulate space and local commerce and to extract revenue therefrom. In both governments, numerous public agencies have a stake in regulating citizen-clients who generate income and construct their own housing, and from whom they extract service, rent, or tax revenue. To avoid this entanglement, some people have opted for autonomy, self-sufficiency, and private fundraising even as they remain potential constituents. To one of the cross-border NGOs we now turn.

Nongovernmental Organizations: The FEMAP Case

The Mexican Federation of Private Associations/Federación Mexicana de Asociaciones Privadas (FEMAP) is a Mexico-wide private association focused on health and community development. Mrs. Guadalupe de la Vega, national president through 1995, presides over the Juárez FEMAP. FEMAP's foundation rests on grassroots volunteer *promotoras*, who began working in 1973 to expand family planning in their own *colonias*. Through private fundraising and user fees, FEMAP also built and maintained a hospital to promote maternal-child health, clinics, and a nursing school, all intended to address reproductive health in comprehensive ways. FEMAP illustrates the possibilities of engaging informals in political community, so that they can in turn engage government as constituents. Of relevance here is the *side* of the border on which political community is engaged. Context matters.

FEMAP on the Mexican Side

In 1988 FEMAP initiated an economic development unit, along with other new programs aimed at encouraging ecologically sound brick-making processes, a home- and neighborhood-based business in

Mexico. Respecting Mexico's own home-grown credit societies (*tandas,*) FEMAP began a group-based lending program known as *bancos comunitarios* ("community banks") to stimulate microenterprise. Community banks use trust and peer pressure, rather than salary or land title guarantees, to achieve remarkably high (more than 90 percent) repayment rates. Most bankers are low-income women who face a marked credit squeeze but enjoy relations of trust in their communities. In our 1992 household interviews, self-employed respondents used their own savings at high rates (63 percent in Juárez; 70 percent El Paso); most of the rest secured loans from relatives, rather than government or commercial banks.

FEMAP *promotoras* convene groups of neighbors who initiate individual businesses with strong *ganas,* or motivation, to succeed. FEMAP technical staff work with women who select their own leaders and governance procedures. Along with advice about bookkeeping, management, and markets, FEMAP staff make up to nine cycles of loans, starting with $80 in U.S. currency and increasing in slight increments. The loans must be repaid with interest (less than 10 percent, or rates lower than banks and credit-card firms charge in Mexico), thus replenishing a fund that can be used to stimulate new banks. Bankers must also save money; they put aside 20 percent of each loan amount after each cycle, transforming their savings account into a substantial sum at the completion of nine loan cycles.

This process represents FEMAP's definition of "sustainable development." Women employ themselves; approximately two-thirds sustain the work after completing the lending cycle; and they create an average of 3.8 jobs per loan.[4] Almost a third of the bankers go on to the next level of larger loans, starting small businesses and moving toward formal compliance with regulations.

Women from a variety of backgrounds start a variety of enterprises. The testimonies they provided at a public meeting focused, above all, on economics. One woman does iron work (windows and doors); others want to start a flour tortilla factory, to expand the tortilla making done by hand and sold at a smaller scale. María started a *tiendita* (small grocery stand) in her neighborhood, selling to place-bound customers.

> I started off my business by selling two cases of sodas and soon there were not just two but five, and then not just five but more. So then I asked my husband to build me a wooden stand and I started stocking

more items, and so I started seeing there was more money. Thanks to my old man and the bank, right now my business is no longer a little stand; it's a store.[5]

Socorro took in washing before the bank. "I was a slave to the washtub . . . to my children, to my husband." Now she calls herself a merchant and feels "a lot younger. . . . Even though I was only forty-five when the community bank was started, I felt like an old lady."[6] Guadalupe and Juana—a mother–daughter team—started a used clothing business whose proceeds allowed them to buy a pick-up truck to help make the business grow. For years, Juana said, "I tried to survive on my husband's minimum wage until one day I decided to start my own business."[7]

Personal politics prompt some women to launch into new directions. Leti sold prepared food, but used community bank money to start a butcher shop following the abrupt closure of a relationship with a man who had been supporting her financially. Another woman makes and sells cheese. She also makes and sells home-made *chorizo* (sausage), along with spices.

Most women's occupational choices are limited. Domestic service is at the bottom of the pay scale in Juárez. Maquila work is rigidly controlled, paying one or two minimum wages plus benefits. Sex work is fraught with risks and dependencies on bar owners and health licensing regulators.[8] *Clandestinas,* who escape regulatory control, are considered freer, though checked less regularly. Another woman named Juana, from the former sex workers' group, said

I learned to be a friend to other people because our relationship as sexual workers was just for work. . . . We also learned there how to handle a bank, when to speak up and shut up when it was necessary to listen to others. We learned how to set up rules because we realized that without any, the bank couldn't work. . . . We had rules and if we didn't follow them, we would fine each other and the fines were for savings.

For Juana, the most important outcome of steady income from the business was owning a home, rather than paying rent. "We're not like the crabs walking backward," she said.[9] She is also a *promotora,* giving talks on sex diseases and passing out condoms as part of her HIV-prevention work with downtown sex workers.

Bankers work in groups based on mutual trust. With the FEMAP connection, the groups formalize and develop new strands. Said Irma, from Chihuahua City, "We get together every Friday at 4 p.m.

The meeting is also a get-together for us as mothers. We share the problems we have with our children and even with our husbands. Thus, these meetings are a kind of relaxation for us where we provide support to one another."[10]

The *banqueras* who spoke represented the success stories, not the stories of those who dropped out. But in groups of ten to twenty, only one or two drop out for lack of interest, time, or family support. The *ganas* is there, and the organizational grid is known, trusted, and respected. Moreover, bankers have actionable ideas about market niches, and they use that space to develop businesses. Government regulatory surveillance diminishes the further one works from downtown.

Women's organizational relationship with FEMAP is itself multistranded. FEMAP connects people to health clinics, to technology training for local production like brickmaking, and, of course, to credit. More recently, FEMAP expanded into home improvement loans with support from a foundation that depended on cultivating NGO connections for its grassroots base. But FEMAP assiduously avoids capture in a political system saturated—for better or worse—with partisanship. Like other organizations, though, it creates photo opportunity events at which presidents or governors applaud members' efforts. Partisan connections are risky for NGOs when their collaborators are out of power.

FEMAP's economic development efforts rarely have a civic development dimension. If public intervention occurs, its staff and leaders provide the voices. They also pursue ambitious fund-raising efforts with foundations and corporate donors, co-hosting two binational conferences in the 1995–96 academic year. More recently, though, the downtown group with which Juana does anti-HIV work supported protests against official extortion, mostly from street-level bureaucrats.[11]

The public testimonies quoted above came from an event designed to engage the wider political community, including government officials. Through the connections of FEMAP's president, various dignitaries attended a day-long conference and gave testimonies themselves. For some, the conference made low-income women visible and public as a constituency. These included political players from both the public and the private sectors, mostly men: the municipal president of Juárez, the regional director of Banco Internacional, the general secretary of the Chihuahua Business Social Fund.

Other political men in attendance recognized *banqueras* not only as a political constituency, but also, perhaps, as a model of development for replication elsewhere. The general secretary of the National Population Council had just returned from the Fourth World Congress on Women in Beijing, where he was chief of the Mexico delegation. He expressed his commitment to developing a National Women's Program around two priorities: violence against women ("truly deplorable and disgusting. . . . Women are literally living out their lives in constant fear")[12] and lack of access to money. The local manager for Nacional Financiera, which funnels loans from the Inter-American Development Bank through FEMAP's economic development program, spoke about his agency's support for these efforts.

Political women also spoke. The wife of the governor, who heads the state's Integrated Family Development agency/Desarrollo Integral de la Familia (DIF), offered words of support. A former FEMAP chapter president had been appointed secretary of health and development in the State of Coahuila. She spoke of taking the FEMAP comprehensive community development approach to health *into* government, at the governor's encouragement. Not least among political women was FEMAP's president, long active in community development and part of a prominent family. She has used social networks to raise funds and to provide credibility for FEMAP's broad-based efforts. These cross-class dimensions of FEMAP are as startling as its cross-border dimensions.

FEMAP on the U.S. Side

In the early 1990s, FEMAP began working with a support group on the El Paso side. These civic-minded, mostly professional people supported FEMAP's work with fundraising and useful contacts, especially in health matters.

In 1994 a new initiative started, known as Seeds Across the Border/Semillas a Través de la Frontera. Seeds began, with technical assistance from FEMAP, to test the transfer of the community bank idea northward. This south-to-north transfer reversed the usual direction of donor-driven development. By late 1995 three groups were operating in new periphery areas of El Paso. Many women had recently arrived from diverse places in Mexico; few had encountered FEMAP in their hometowns far south of Juárez.

Although the El Paso–Juárez metropolitan area shares a common economy at one level, at another level it exhibits differences that posed challenges to the transfer. First, market spaces are not so plentiful as in Juárez, for formal businesses already occupy market niches with high-volume purchases that bring down selling prices. Can homemade *tortillas*, however fresh, compete with factory-made versions distributed through grocery chains?

Second, women generate low, even sporadic, earnings. In interviews we conducted relatively early in the cycle, earnings averaged just $40 weekly, the amount earned in part-time domestic service, a less-than-minimum-wage job. Informal earnings cannot sustain households, particularly when other earners bring in only minimum wages.

Third, informals perceive the level of government surveillance as high. This is especially true for people loosely connected to needs-based benefits, such as food stamps. Members of checkerboard households are even more fearful, worried that they are putting loved ones at risk for "voluntary departure" at the hands of the immigration authorities when they expose information about their identities. Seemingly minor steps in the FEMAP sequence, such as setting up a bank account, require a Social Security number. Formal license applications generally require one, though not verification of legal authorization to work, as immigration law requires for formal employment. People worry that numbers like these will attract busy bureaucrats' tracking systems.

Fourth, immigration itself carries baggage that discourages engagement with agencies. For example, Spanish-speakers worry that a phone call to a government agency will reap little information or turn into a translation nightmare, even though in fact many public employees speak Spanish. In Mexico, *primaria* (six years) and *secundaria* (three more years) education provides informals with basic skills; in the United States, however, nine years fall below high school diploma equivalency and the qualifications for some technical training at community colleges.

Finally, FEMAP's people, work, and logos are not part of everyday life in El Paso. In Juárez, community banks started well *after* a grassroots family planning outreach effort had fanned out and built a volunteer network. Besides, Juárez has maintained a tradition of volunteerism; ironically, this is not true in the land of Tocqueville and group efforts and of individual self-interest, enshrined by the Founding Fathers.

In contrast to the minuscule dropout rate in the thirty-one Juárez groups, a much higher proportion of women stop out and drop out of groups on the U.S. side. The neighborhood bonds, by no means ideal in Juárez, are undeveloped in the United States. One group, sustained with a meeting place and support from Catholic sisters, vacillated between too much and too little intervention by supporters in its organizational survival.[13]

Public outreach to low-income communities has generally involved delivering information and services to potentially entitled clients, not constituents. With support from the state legislature, a major Texas university builds state-of-the-art community centers in *colonias*. Two have been built in El Paso County. The university program director counted one center's accomplishments at a major *colonias* conference in 1995: "Of the 2,000 to 3,000 contacts the center has each month with *colonia* residents, 95 per cent or more are with women. . . . Service providers need to be sensitive to family roles when designing services."[14]

In FEMAP's eyes, U.S.-based community bank women are different from those in Juárez. FEMAP staff worry that these women do not have or have lost some of the *ganas* women exhibit in Juárez. These cultural attributions coincide with conservative PANista perceptions in Juárez and the individualism that prevails in northern Mexico compared with the south and central regions.[15] The *regidor* for the economy in the Juárez council told an interviewer, "The people of the U.S. are poorer than the people of Mexico, because the Mexican is more ingenious; the poor are poor because they want to be."[16]

Despite the complex, even chilling, conditions surrounding community bank development in the United States, and the relatively high stopout and dropout rates, the banks survive. Several U.S. residents gave public testimony at the FEMAP conference in Juárez. Organizational success stories were more common than economic ones. Said Olivia, "We learned to work in a group, and this has been very important because in a group each one gets help and support from the others. Ideas come out which one person individually can't get."[17]

At yet another level, political engagement is even more formidable on the U.S. than on the Mexican side. In policy and political constituency terms, low-income women count for little. Voter turnout is low; for permanent residents or undocumented people, voter turnout is nonexistent. Rare is the politician, or political appointee, who embellishes his or her career by serving a group perceived as marginal to the political economy.

Microenterprise is far too small for even the U.S. Small Business Administration (SBA), which defines *small enterprise* as one with 500 employees or fewer. As SBA forms warn, credit applications take up to 18 hours to complete, and the advice of lawyers and accountants is recommended.[18] Banks view low-income women as risky bets seeking too small loans at too high an administrative cost, should sizable numbers apply. And credit cards, easy enough for those with jobs and flawless credit ratings to get, charge nearly 20 percent interest.

We in Seeds Across the Border invited U.S. officials to the FEMAP conference. Just one city agency, the Economic Development Department, sent representatives. The Community Development Department, after repeated contacts, could see no connection to its work. Not even a "political wife" appeared as the gracious replacement for a busy husband. Of course, U.S. officials generally seem less willing to cross to the south than Mexican officials are to travel northward, even though either group, if traveling by automobile, would wait approximately thirty minutes to cross at the international bridges.

Cross-border community development offers insightful reflections on U.S.- and Mexican-style political engagement for informals. The bankers themselves illustrate the potential for people to strengthen their businesses, especially in Mexico, with its narrow or poorly paid employment options. Informals there have the makings of a political constituency, although interaction with funders and government has been mediated through staff and FEMAP leadership. Informals' work is legitimate and relatively free of surveillance, a marked contrast to the somewhat hostile climate in which U.S. informals operate, the intimidating net of surveillance they perceive, and the officials who view them as clients rather than constituents. The real and lost potentials of this microcosm case provide the necessary background for our look at governments.

Governmental Organizations

Numerous agencies in the federal governments on both sides of the border have a stake in informal regulation, control, and fund-generation. Although job creation is ostensibly at the heart of the

142 | *Chapter 7*

local government mission, public administrators rarely encourage self-employment. In the United States, job creation is encouraged once enough information has been solicited to create paper trails for potential legal actions and revenue collection. Even in Mexico, where self-employment is tolerated, informality is not part of the modern vision for economic development. Chihuahua Siglo XXI envisions job creation for the next century in terms of pictures of muscular arms and smokestacks.[19]

Map 5 shows the international border and a list of agencies that have a stake in informal work. Federal agencies appear in all-capital letters, state agencies in capital and lower-case letters, and local agencies in lower-case letters, with Mexico on the left and the United States on the right.

Comparative analyses reveal several important features of government oversight of informal activity. First, the number of agencies is itself of interest; fragmentation and inconsistency are chronic and probably inevitable.

Second, policies change somewhat from one administration to the next. The City of El Paso's elected representatives serve two-year terms, while in Juárez the terms are three years, with succession outlawed. Parties can succeed themselves, however, and for most of Juárez's twentieth-century history, the PRI reigned supreme. But in 1983–86 and 1992, Juárez made a transition from dominant to opposition party government. The PAN consolidated that transition with its 1995 electoral triumph, as earlier chapters analyzed.

Third, the street-level administration of policies and programs varies from one agency to another, but especially from Juárez to El Paso. Pockets of discretion exist in bureaucracy, among the seemingly powerless people at the bottom of the hierarchy or in the field and on the street: the street-level bureaucrats (SLBs). The commonalities between Mexican and U.S. SLBs are as great as their differences. Both sides are headed toward eventual convergence in regulatory schemes that individualize the relationship between government and informals, transforming them primarily into either serviced customers or controlled clients.

Both cities pursue costly enforcement strategies that are relatively ineffective. Enforcement makes work for low-level government staff who selectively enforce nearly unenforceable policies. Surveillance augments their efforts, from which informals seek protection through collective organization and invisibility. Juárez can

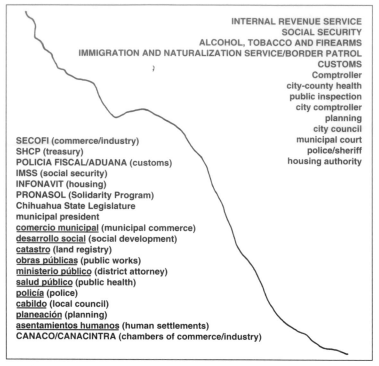

INTERNAL REVENUE SERVICE
SOCIAL SECURITY
ALCOHOL, TOBACCO AND FIREARMS
IMMIGRATION AND NATURALIZATION SERVICE/BORDER PATROL
CUSTOMS
Comptroller
city-county health
public inspection
city comptroller
planning
city council
municipal court
police/sheriff
housing authority

SECOFI (commerce/industry)
SHCP (treasury)
POLICIA FISCAL/ADUANA (customs)
IMSS (social security)
INFONAVIT (housing)
PRONASOL (Solidarity Program)
Chihuahua State Legislature
municipal president
comercio municipal (municipal commerce)
desarrollo social (social development)
catastro (land registry)
obras públicas (public works)
ministerio público (district attorney)
salud público (public health)
policía (police)
cabildo (local council)
planeación (planning)
asentamientos humanos (human settlements)
CANACO/CANACINTRA (chambers of commerce/industry)

Map 5   Informality at the Border: A Policy Map

be characterized as staff-heavy, facilitating street-level bureaucratic negotiation with those they ostensibly regulate. In contrast, El Paso is staff-light, facilitating sporadic enforcement coupled with an intimidating style that criminalizes noncompliance and reinforces the surveillance shroud. We have already considered the U.S. and Mexican federal-level agencies (Chapters 3 through 6). Below, we focus primarily on local policy enforcement—the place where logics of state and daily life interact, as the epigraph for this chapter calls to our attention.[20]

Policies Mexican Style: Juárez

Whether the PRI or the PAN controls municipal government, policy discourse recognizes informal work as generating income and housing for residents, but also as generating revenue in the form of fees and fines under local budgetary control. *Local* control is *prized* control for municipalities in a federal system where the central government sucks taxes, tariffs, and international bridge fees from the wealthy northern frontier, providing little in return, from the perspective of Juarenses. Francisco Villarreal, municipal president from 1992 to 1995, became a hero to people on both sides of the border for his defiance of the central government. Despite a life-threatening illness, he endured jail in his efforts to capture more local control of international bridge fees through symbolic collection boxes placed before those of the Mexican feds.

Local revenue generation is a chronic political issue for the PRI, the PAN, and commerce big and small. Municipal leaders criticize what they view as central government extortion to benefit heartland interests, from sales tax to tariffs and the tolerance of contraband trade. Where the budget is concerned, local control is a life or death issue. As one official poignantly stated in an interview, "We need income; we've got to be tough on regulations."[21] Several factors motivate the complex, staff-heavy enforcement process: revenue generation, land regularization (to increase property tax), "make-work" strategies for SLBs, and political realignments. We see evidence of all of these in three areas of informal work and housing analyzed below: street commerce, health, and housing.

Juárez manages the licensing and control of self-employment through the Department of Municipal Commerce, whose director is appointed by the municipal president. People make business and trade out of their homes, either autonomously or through subcontracting with formal businesses, but officials say that the latter is practically undetectable and thus not subject to regulation, making policy unenforceable.[22]

Federal officials have a stake in subcontracting because employers probably pay nothing into the national housing fund (INFONAVIT) or into the social security/health-care system (IMSS). Federal social security inspectors therefore roam about, seeking compliance.[23] Of course, informals have access to neither health care nor subsidized housing, unless other, formally employed household members are covered. In all of Latin America, informals' lack of coverage is problematic.

Municipal officials regulate street commerce, but they do not fully control it. License fees differ according to whether a business is located on the street, in a semifixed location, or in a fixed location. Licenses can be granted on annual, seasonal, or daily bases. Figure 4 in Chapter 4 shows the tangle of procedures associated with licensing under the former PRI administration, a tangle that, however, facilitated collective organization. The PAN removed the financial incentive for group applications.

Under the PRI, procedures allowed organizational leaders to obtain licenses for members. Leaders generally charged a fee for these services, after which they "protected" members from the long arm of government, including inspectors who confiscated goods. This strategy resulted in *organized* constituencies, often affiliated with the PRI or other popular organizations that coalesced with the PRI. The PRI gained political capital, and members gained protection. As is evident, informality represents a burgeoning set of income-generating opportunities, not only for traders, but also for leaders and inspectors. Still, not all vendors submit to organizational affiliation, with its fees and time commitments.

The PAN supports an individualized relationship between vendors and government. Partly, this results from PAN principles, which aim to clean up government, eliminate middlemen, and thereby reduce opportunities for corruption. But the PAN also has a political and ideological agenda. In contrast to the PRI's political discourse, which gives lip service and negotiation space to the "popular class," to the poor, and to informals, the PAN envisions a classless political culture. It worries about those who get away with things and get around the rules, using political space. As a result, it seeks to undermine PRI-affiliated organizations, build new organizations, and professionalize the relationship between citizen and government. Will low-income citizens receive the same consideration and efficiency as the privileged? The historical experience of low-income people makes this doubtful. The PAN worries less about well-organized commerce at middle and privileged class levels, a class from which many of its political appointees come.

Even while the PAN seeks to individualize citizen–government relationships, it recognizes that it is embedded in a political culture that prizes negotiation. Organization persists, a source of exasperation to officials. "They turn a subsistence problem into a political one," Mr. M., the director of municipal commerce, complained. "Each citizen should come for his permit personally, but there are leaders who manage about eight thousand people. They come with banners and protest groups."[24] Accordingly, the PAN has simplified and streamlined procedures. Officials claim the licensing process takes just three to seven days. They also claim to permit a grace period of six months during business start-up, so that informals can determine whether the work is profitable and worthy of formalization. In practice, no records are kept on the stage of business development.[25]

On the other hand, official procedures outline increasingly stiff burdens for noncompliance. Unlicensed traders are supposed to be *warned*, after which they are *fined* or have their goods *confiscated*. Approximately fifty street-level inspectors monitor public places to enforce the rules.[26] In practice, street vendors told us in interviews, goods may be immediately confiscated ("donated to charity," they are told), or inspectors may demand fees on the spot. [27]

At the top of the street commerce hierarchy is the fixed market stand, wherein vendors rent stalls. The municipality manages over thirty public markets filled with vendors in compliance, that is, who are formalized and more easily monitored. They also comply more fully with the sales tax to the federal treasury agency. In a showdown between the municipality and street vendors, several hundred agreed to be relocated to public markets, but these turned out to be poorly attended and ill served with buses.[28]

To create a favorable climate for formalization, and to quell the fears of established businesses, the municipality sponsored a two-day conference held on November 17–18, 1993, in the Municipal Palace. Conference presenters from Tijuana and Mexico City discussed architectural and program models wherein traders sell goods from rented stalls near acquiescent retailers. Many vendor organizations in Juárez boycotted the meeting, though, and the event ended a half-day earlier than it was supposed to because a bomb threat cleared the Municipal Palace.[29]

The public health department does not license food sellers or collect fees from them. But it does rely on "the good will of the people that they are, in their own interest and that of the public, going to observe the health regulations."[30] Its thirty-nine sanitary agents also offer training, distribute free water purification drops, take complaints, and close eating establishments with documented health hazards.

Municipal officials also regulate building construction. They require building permits for all houses larger than fifty square meters on registered land.[31] These permits advance official drives to spot unregistered land and thereby increase property tax payments. Because such taxes are collected *and* controlled at the municipal level, they are highly prized as a revenue source. But tax collection is inefficient: the World Bank estimates a 30 percent collection rate and self-help housing at 55 percent of construction. The city is divided into sixteen zones, to which street-level inspectors are assigned to roam about looking for construction. If houses are already built, officials say that residents are given judicial notices, with a grace period, to regularize the land.[32]

With 40 percent of the land irregularly settled, and officials working hard to negotiate with actual owners, full building-permit compliance is virtually impossible. Land settlement occurs on a complex mixture of private and public property. Officials worry that some settlers feign poverty and actually own several houses in Juárez. A fleet of ten street-level social workers patrols settlements looking for this sort of abuse. More than one official used the evocative term *urban latifundismo*, recycling a noun once reserved for large rural landholdings.[33] PAN officials perceive that most land developers who exploit public sympathy are PRI-affiliated. Under these circumstances, it is difficult for officials to determine who is "worthy" in land-purchase applications. Worthiness is determined partly on political grounds and partly in response to desperate housing needs (recall Box 5 in Chapter 5).

Regulation of informal activity is highly charged politically among both officials and the plentiful SLBs assigned to enforce the rules. Officials seek to professionalize land, building, and tax oversight with a central data bank[34] that would let them reduce discretion in negotiation or street-level bureaucratic behavior. Such a reduction would increase surveillance over informality and likely make it shrink.

Yet compromise continues. PAN officials idealize a policy of "zero toleration of negotiation," but collective organization and the sheer size and visibility of informality make negotiation necessary. Even officials occasionally negotiate, on the condition that leaders not reveal the process to members, as Mr. S confided. Leaders' credibility, of course, rests on members' perceptions that they can make deals. It is part of the political culture. As Mr. P. concedes, "The spirit of concession is the public way."[35]

Comparing El Paso and Juárez, we see stark official contrasts in policies and enforcement when it comes to informal work and self-help housing. Policymakers are oblivious to informality as a way of generating work or employment.

Housing construction is highly formalized through building contractors, and strict building codes make it difficult for self-help to prevail, at least within city limits. As noted in Chapter 5, commercial and public credit are biased toward formal business, developers, and building contractors. Not coincidentally, people from these well-organized formal businesses sit on boards and commissions, exercising their political voice. They "capture" the business of public service through local ordinances that privatize water- and sewer-line construction. People with money move into city homes that are equipped with services, but they borrow large sums and pay interest that doubles or triples the cost of homes over a span of twenty or thirty years.

The City Council and the County Commissioners' Court pay amateur wages to representatives elected to short terms in nonpartisan city and partisan county campaigns. In fact, the wages of *regidores* ("representatives") in Juárez exceed those of El Paso representatives, when one adds the lucrative *nomina confidencial* to the pitiful base pay.[36] Nevertheless, El Paso employs a professionally paid civil service that administers laws and policies. Their numbers are small, especially at the street level. Resource scarcity prevails, perhaps the result of misplaced priorities in allocating staff resources for some of the following regulatory dreams.

Property-poor El Paso, by its own accounting, has a $12 billion shortfall when compared with similarly sized cities around Texas. Using national comparisons, El Paso ranks fifth among cities over 300,000 in the ratio of service- to tax-generated revenue. In an understaffed system, policy enforcement is inevitably uneven. "We all depend on complaints," a councilman told me, putting the meaning of those skimpy resources in banal everyday terms.[37]

A complaint-driven process veers toward selective personalism, a practice decried in rational, modern government. Once a policy is enforced, momentum develops, moving noncompliance to criminality. Among a population stigmatized for lack of stable jobs, some of whom belong to households characterized by gradations of citizenship and uneven documentation, invisibility and subterfuge offer their best "protection." Collective organization makes little sense, as the experience of street vendors (see below) demonstrates.

Street commerce is heavily regulated across different agencies in different parts of this sprawling city. Although street vendors are far less numerous than in Juárez, they are burdened with many conditions for full compliance: one license from the city comptroller, another license from the City–County Health Office, a sales-tax number from the Texas Comptroller's Office (located twenty miles from downtown), and (for itinerant traders) fingerprinting at the local police department. Street vendors pay sales tax when they buy from retailers, whereas retailers who buy from wholesalers enjoy "tax-exempt status."

Until 1993, city ordinance required that street vendors move constantly. Feuds between vendors and retail shopowners led to complaints, sporadic enforcement, and ultimately a compromise providing thirty-two fixed sites. This solution increased vendors' start-up costs tenfold.

Bureaucratic enforcement staff are minimal, with ten health inspectors and only seven sales tax inspectors covering formal and informal commerce.[38] Voluntary compliance is expected, but only sporadically checked. The state comptroller's office, for example, stages surprise raids at two flea markets a year. Once complaints transform noncompliance into crimes, police officers become involved as enforcers.

El Paso is not the only city to equate street vending with crime. In Los Angeles, this misdemeanor earns up to 180 days jail time and a thousand dollars in fines, equivalent to drunk driving, the possession of more than one ounce of marijuana, and brandishing a knife.[39] In New York, fifty-nine police officers on peddler-control duty issue 25,000 summons monthly, even though most peddlers ignore them.[40] Once they are in the system, the machinery of justice goes after offenders with vigor: witness El Paso's Municipal Court, where garage-sale offenders who posted signs illegally cry over $200 fines but comply with court rules prohibiting chewing gum and tank tops.[41]

El Paso's Municipal Code contains detailed regulations for home-based occupations. Licenses are issued for those that offer no noise, nuisance, and traffic burdens to neighbors. The most common home-based businesses include child care, adult care, and craft production. The Department of Public Inspection issues approximately 1,100 permits annually, the fees for which ($44, $33 for renewals) cover inspection costs. The inspection follows the application, and a single inspector makes home visits annually, recovering roughly the cost of his job.[42]

Formal businesses are easier to monitor for compliance with license, tax, and Social Security regulations. Extension of findings from the 1992 neighborhood sample about the incidence of self-employment would have produced approximately twenty times the number of home-business permits actually issued for the city! In interviews with another category of home-based workers, a sample of seventeen child-care providers, who are required to undergo additional regulation and training, we learned that half of them operated under license.[43]

Income tax and Social Security payments depend heavily on voluntary compliance and complaints. Social Security has no inspector staff to monitor informal or home-based employment, though tax audits can catch those who underpay. (Some offenses are discovered when retirees seek benefits.) Noncompliance can result in stiff penalties, back payments, and interest. Central data banks or cross-referenced banks enhance oversight capability.[44]

The city's Public Inspection Office provides a formal contrast. A staff of ninety covers the more public activity of building and remodeling. *Inspection* is the generic word for construction oversight. Permits and bonded contractors are usually required, making formalization implicit. The office nets considerable revenue, not simply an even cost recovery for inspections rendered.[45] Outside the city limits, the minimal zoning requirements are enforced in the County Attorney's Office. The City–County Health Office extends inspection oversight to septic tank and cesspool installation, issuing citations and fines.

Long a given in U.S. housing policy, formal businesses are privileged in construction and remodeling. Commercial banks also police this process, if loans are involved. To be sure, such regulations provide contractual recourse should work be inadequate, but the additional costs also spread money toward important political and economic constituencies.

The city Economic Development Department is keen to stimulate jobs and improve the property tax base. Property tax is the largest source of revenue for the city, but El Paso's property-poor status compared with the rest of the state results in comparatively high tax rates. Since the state law changed in 1979, business and residential owners have been taxed at the same rate, but formal businesses have access to tax abatements in foreign and urban enterprise zones and other incentives not available to home-based businesses.

The presence of an international border at El Paso's boundary gives federal immigration policy a presence unknown in most U.S. cities. Border Patrol and Customs agents control the entry of people, commerce, consumer goods, and illegal substances. The Federal Bureau of Alcohol, Tobacco, and Firearms periodically shows an interest in the untaxed cigarettes that street vendors in downtown El Paso once sold openly.

The tangle of local and federal enforcement is apparent in El Paso's street vendor showdowns of 1992–93. Box 4 in In Chapter 5 suggested the authority of Border Patrol agents to stop and search under the relatively loose standard of "reasonable suspicion" (as opposed to the "probable cause" criterion the police must meet). Yet home entry is associated with a far stricter standard: "Search a house ONLY under RARE EXCEPTIONAL conditions." Home-based informal work is inconsistent with the surveillance agendas of modern government.

El Paso Street Vendors Engage the Government

Prior to the Border Blockade of September 19, 1993, U.S. Border Patrol agents roamed the streets of El Paso to identify undocumented people.[46] In the previous decade crossing was common, officially encouraged by the issuing of Border Crossing Cards that allowed residents of northern Mexico to visit the United States and shop for up to seventy-two hours. Before their stationary assignments for the Blockade, the SLBs of the Border Patrol tried to apprehend undocumented crossers, netting lots of citizens in the process.

In the summer of 1992, street vendors swelled in numbers, particularly on Saturdays, when Mexican pedestrian traffic was plentiful. Well-organized downtown merchants complained about congestion and competition. They encouraged the city to enforce an old ordinance requiring vendors to move constantly. Police officers issued numerous citations to Spanish-surnamed people and non-U.S. nationals, none of them Anglo, as reported in interviews and in citations stored in the Municipal Court (see Chapter 4).

Vendors watched over their shoulders, ready to flee and to warn others, should *La Migra* (Border Patrol agents) appear and, depending on their whim that day, decide to net some suspects. My interview with the director of the Immigration and Naturalization Service (INS) made it clear that agents usually had more important things to do than clear downtown streets of vendors. This task was therefore informally delegated to local police. Some Municipal Court judges sympathized with vendors' hard-luck stories and released them without a fine. Mostly, though, vendors did not appear in court, and warrants were issued for their arrest.

In the upcoming election year, a committee was invented to negotiate a compromise among vendors, downtown merchants, and professionals from various city agencies with a stake in regulation. (Merchants' sidewalk sales were not an issue.) A newly created vendors' organization, with support from an activist lawyer, pushed for an ordinance establishing fixed vending sites. Underneath this open struggle was a clash between two ice cream concessionaire companies with alienated kinship connections. None of the players realized how dramatically fixed sites would increase the costs of compliance.

Planners determined that a public, blind draw for sites, with thirty-two winners, plus alternates, would be the fairest process. Vendors crafted valiant schemes to use genuine and fictive kinship connections to maximize their chances for the sites; the leader of the vendors' organization, for example, became an alternate, but his wife (the organization treasurer) and his daughter made successful draws for authorized sites. In the end, vendors paid steep costs for the tax numbers, insurance proof, and picture licenses they were now required to display. Start-up costs, as noted above, were ten times as high.

Collective organization did little to advance the interests of street vendors. Their work was legitimate only insofar as they provided evidence of compliance with a complex application process and expensive fees. The newly invented arrangement offered striking surveillance capabilities, should the police use their time to monitor compliance.

Unlike civil servants and organized merchants, informals do not experience engagement with government in a way that works democratically for themselves. As long as they lack technical information, loans for start-up costs, and articulate voices, the shared vision of merchants and planners is bound to prevail, even in an election year, when accountability presumably reigns supreme.

Conclusion

In both Juárez and El Paso, informals make income-generating work for themselves at meager to relatively lucrative levels. Their actions demonstrate people's potential to become self-sufficient workers and political constituents, rather than dependents or clients. For the most part, the self-employed rely on local sources and markets, rather than on unaccountable political-economic elites in distant global cities.

In both cities, however, officials strive to eliminate or control informals. Enforcement strategies vary. Mexico's negotiation style and legitimizing discourse offer space for informals to obtain concessions, relief, or protection. The best protection for non- or partially compliant U.S. informals is to lie low, for once the criminal justice machinery kicks in, informals are ground under or subject to consequences wholly out of proportion to their efforts to make or supplement a livelihood. On balance, informals in a global economy ought to be able to spend more time and effort protecting their livelihood than protecting themselves from those who govern them.

Policy enforcement is uneven and selective, inevitably unfair and at odds with the uniformity expected of modern enforcement strategies. Public administration in the United States is an under-funded, undergreased modernist machine, whereas the PAN represents an aspiring modernist machine, greased with a willingness to negotiate with elements other than formalized businesses and well-off citizens. The control of informals is driven as much by revenue calculations and surveillance capabilities as by reason. Yet, when we consider the regulatory thorn in Juárez vendors' sides and the noose already around U.S.-based vendors' necks, it seems that ideological and material motives are also at work. A Juárez commercial leader, noting the paltry pay in the maquilas, asked, "Why should anyone want to work eight hours if they can make the same in two hours?"[47] If autonomous self-employment gets too profitable, capital may be less able to recruit low-cost factory labor. But the machinery of government has its logic as well.

Both cities operate under detailed rules and laws. Mexico, burdened with the baggage of Spanish colonialism, has been characterized as personalistic amid rigid rules that aim to proscribe personalism.[48] The enforcement of U.S. rules against informals, spurred by complaints and carried out by insufficient staff, appears personalistic. But instead of personal negotiation, rule enforcement instigates a series of legal maneuvers that entangle informals and provide them with perverse incentives to maintain even greater distance from those who govern. Any impulse toward voluntary compliance can backfire.

In this global economy, self-employment will not disappear. In all likelihood it will increase, as households on both sides of the border pursue a Mexican solution of multiple earners with multiple low-paying jobs. To draw on another healthy and adaptive Mexican tradition, however flawed the organizational practice, informals should move toward a "constituent" rather than "client" status as they engage with their governments. Delusions about everyone's assuming "customer" status will likely backfire amid existing social inequalities.

Having suggested that strategy, I can hardly pass on the opportunity to offer policy recommendations. I begin with broad issues. Through engagement with government, with its burdensome official transcripts, informals should discuss the following questions. Should formalization begin in earnest, to extend the modernist project (which not coincidentally extends regulatory control)? Or should space, free of surveillance, be provided in which self-employment and self-help housing can grow to a size and scale that warrant taxation and regulation? Or are "official transcripts" ultimately meaningless? After all, informals do a fairly good job of keeping their distance from authorities, even though they sacrifice the chance to scale up their work, make it public, and contribute to political community. In reality, however, the hands of the state and its SLB negotiators *are* meaningful and heavy for captured residents or those compelled to pay.

Once these matters are discussed, more specific policy recommendations can follow. These discussions should occur within a political space where residents can share their voices. They are probably best organized at neighborhood levels that connect to the larger political community. Such participation should not be limited to those with formal citizenship, but rather should be extended to others on the grounds of residence and public contributions like the payment of sales and property tax and the provision of inexpensive labor on permanent or occasional bases. Mexico has a long history of top-down party-affiliated participatory structures, which are problematic in many ways. The United States has begun to flirt with neighborhood associations,[49] although they are the exception rather than the norm. When Washington provides incentives to stimulate such organization, it often occurs in marketlike structures such as "neighborhood corporations" or "community development corporations" (CDCs). Civic, democratic components should be built into these structures.

If informals' participation is to be strengthened and perhaps formalized, policy enforcement must move beyond Orwellian "detection" toward reasonable rules, linked with the consent of the governed. Modernist visions inadequately enforced place a burden on those who can least afford it. Overly detailed policies invite nonenforcement, or sporadic enforcement based on complaints, so that the very idea of reasonable administration becomes a joke. Complex procedures, including nuisance taxes, generate more administrative costs than they reap, especially for those least equipped to organize of hire lawyers to protect themselves from their government. Effective law enforcement depends extensively on voluntary compliance and civic duty, and inspection officials cannot engender these. Politicized enforcement invites corruption and cynicism, not to mention the abuse of power associated with official (though informal) income-generating strategies.

Whatever the budgetary and political costs of compliance are, we must ask: Compliance with what? For what purposes? Regulation should serve the public interest in health and safety as well as in revenue collection from those able to pay. Rules should not cost more to enforce than the value they produce, whether that value is measured in revenue, health, or safety terms. Enforcement might even involve self-employed informals, who have a far better understanding of what is going on, at what public costs, than SLBs.

Fiscal regulation should be designed with "value added" in mind: training, property improvement, access to capital. Voluntary compliance will increase when informals are given incentives to improve their businesses and property. Compliance should involve civil, rather than criminal, enforcement.

Self-help housing should be encouraged, even subsidized. After all, home construction and improvement are subsidized and protected from competition through ordinance, loan guarantees, and loans, generally spent on formal contractors, landlords, and banks. Over the long term, this strategy predicts that scaled-up business and higher property tax values will generate more revenue than short-term compliance-detection strategies. Where people can "go public," visibility assures open accountability.

Value-added regulation should be dispersed into neighborhoods and communities, using the "one-stop" concept. Residents cannot engage with the regulation process if inaccessibility or multiple locations make compliance difficult. Signs and brochures should make the process, payments, and benefits transparent rather than negotiable for political concessions. Negotiation reproduces existing patronage and clientelist arrangements, excluding the unorganized or those unwilling to pay for organized protection.

Government should extend the idea of urban enterprise zones to include homes in residential zones, with technical assistance and tax incentives available to recover costs and generate revenue. Self-employment *can* generate jobs and serve market niches.[50] Government should nourish the viability of this work, rather than prey on informals. Once informals begin to be legitimized like formal businesses, they can scale up to formality, higher earnings, public presence, and tax payments.

Governments should make public spaces available, at reasonable rents, for production and services. Public markets that resonate with urban tourism offer space for informals to move outside their garages, seedy flea markets, and public streets onto more profitable turf.

Policies should support NGOs that engage with informals over technical assistance and credit. But NGO connections with officials should be expanded to include a civic component, giving a political voice to members who become active in a far wider political community. Nascent political communities exist on each side of the border, as well as across borders.

If informality is to be discouraged, decisionmakers should recognize that this cannot occur overnight. To ease the transition, policymakers should detach health and social security coverage from formal employment. Informals also work and shelter themselves, at little or no burden to the state. They deserve basic public services.

Wage earners should align formal minimum wages more closely on both sides of the border. This would require increasing the below-market-value Mexican minimum wage. Market-value minimum wages should make formal employment more attractive than informal work, as long as other attendant benefits are the same. Moreover, national wage inequalities need to be compressed in any case.

Until informals surpass the poverty line in both countries, policymakers would do well to lift the burdens placed on informality and instead offer incentives for job creation and scaled-up profitability. Until economic restructuring itself is transformed, the flexibility of informality will be with us. Above all, the voices of working people, including those working informally, must be part of a dialogue about further economic restructuring, one that improves and expands income-generating opportunities. The borderland is at the center of these debates; the heartlands may soon follow.

CHAPTER 8

Moving from the Border to the Mainstream

Conclusions and Implications

There are tensions at the border with the dominant society, at the frontier between liberation and oppression.

Regina Austin,
" 'The Black Community,' Its Lawbreakers, and a Politics of Identification"

Borders are increasingly used as metaphors to clarify relations between people and ideas, not just between governments and their institutions. A focus on the U.S.–Mexico border allows all of these aspects to come together: territorial lines, people in relation to competing hegemonies, the struggle over the construction of our future.

In this concluding chapter, I pull together all the pieces of a Gramscian framework: the state and transnational institutions that seek to embrace people, who respond in complex ways. By examining informal work, housing, and migration, we can gain new insight into how people ignore, resist, negotiate, and comply with public transcripts, both petty and grand. In the first part of the chapter, I summarize the results of that examination. I then consider how policy changes from 1992 to 1995 are likely to affect patterns outlined in the previous chapters. Many changes are momentous, from the stricter enforcement of immigration law at the border to peso devaluation and NAFTA. Finally, I address the meaning of these findings for the heartlands of both countries. From borders, says Pierre Vilar, "the history of the world is best observed."[1]

Informal self-employment and housing, as a sideline or principal household support strategy, are less than ideal. But they are an omnipresent reality at this globalized border in the Americas. What, then, is to be done?

From empirical analysis, we must move to some normative considerations, even anxieties, about that question. While informality offers flexibility to earners who can work without being observed by the authorities, it brings in meager earnings and lacks labor standards and security. To the extent that the late twentieth-century global political economy fuels informal growth, informals' meager success may sustain the contemporary global economy. Yet with insufficient work at wages above the minimum, how will people support themselves? Informal work and housing are here for a while, unless the global economy is magically transformed.

Border-crossers are also with us, temporary and permanent, including those officialized through formal naturalization ceremonies. A global economy that facilitates capital and job movement can hardly control people's movements. Perhaps awareness of these crossers reaches a peak at the borderlands, but crossers occupy many spaces and niches in major global cities in the heartlands. The border experience thus speaks to the mainstream in the ways outlined below.

Borders: Spaces of Informality

El Paso and Juárez represent an aspiring global city, internationalized both through a globalized political economy and by being a special location at which people and capital exploit comparative advantages in prices and wages.

The hegemonic institutions that prevail at this and other borders are not part of a single unit, but are multiple and contradictory. Those who man hegemonic institutions pursue policies and practices with chronically selective and uneven enforcement strategies. The people over whom hegemonic institutions seek cooptation, consent, control, or all three also respond selectively and unevenly; they accept, assimilate, modify, and reject those official policies and practices. They use the multiple and contradictory institutional approaches to create a space in which to pursue informal work and housing in self-sufficient ways. They cross borders in spite of rules and surveillance. But this self-sufficiency exists amid overall impoverishment.

National and gender constructs create lines that structure people's income prospects. Examined in per capita and minimum-wage terms, national inequalities are quite marked, as are gender inequalities. Examined in *informal* terms, national inequalities narrow, as do gender inequalities, although men situated in U.S. space still have an advantage. On the U.S.–Mexico border, with its market niches and cross-border opportunities, women informals on both sides earn comparable amounts—and also amounts comparable to the earnings of male nationals on one side. The amounts are still meager, however.

The high incidence of informality reminds us that *counter-hegemonic* practices are alive and well. Despite propaganda, rules, and surveillance, people continue to make their own history, in part, in low-visibility ways that add few public burdens or threats. Women counter hegemonies as much as or more than men do. The appearance of compliance and consent covers everyday resistance in earning money, crossing borders, and building shelter. Moreover, authorities consent to such resistance by overlooking noncompliance (tolerance), negotiating, claiming unenforceability, or shifting their enforcement resources to other priorities.

Some might applaud informality and counter-hegemony. Others might worry that they coincide with global structural adjustments that cheapen labor and reduce public responsibility for the social needs of workers. Linked to that coincidence is an expansion of women's responsibilities in the workplace and in households. Continuing job loss and corporate downsizing may well root informality in the United States, equally burdening women and men. The multiple-income-generating responsibility of household members has been called a Mexican solution, but it is a global solution in many economies undertaking structural adjustment.

Added together, informals represent a sizable force of resilient people. Their resilience is undermined by those who, sometimes swiftly and behind closed bureaucratic doors, alter the value of currency and impose military force along borderlines. The tenuous balance between consent and force shifts toward force.

Informals feign compliance (which looks like consent), but have little to no voice. This ostensible consent is backed up with occasional force when government touches informals in heavy handed, even patronizing ways. Force comes into play in the banal enforcement of regulations over licenses, construction, and garage and street sales, even when the rationale is to prevent public harm and health problems. The kind of self-employment analyzed herein rarely harms others, yet it is pursued quietly, at least in the United States, because of the criminalization of bureaucratic noncompli-

ance. If informality sheds its criminal image, which not coincidentally would reduce administrative enforcement costs, could real consent develop with organization and political community?

In Mexico, the discourse that legitimizes informal work is an organizing tool. With organization, informals secure some protection
from government, though not necessarily from leaders who use
them to generate income or political upward mobility in clientelist
relationships.

Mexican informals operate in a highly charged political atmosphere in which people are keenly aware of the political motives that
drive policy and enforcement. When we use Mexico to reflect on the
United States, we find a flawed democracy that produces some payoffs to low-income people amid partisan competition and populist
strategies.

Low-income informals are outcasts in the structurally flawed democracy that prevails in the United States. Professionalism and in-
dividualization seem to have replaced the political motives that
drive policy and enforcement. But informals and those without
clout are still suspicious. Such suspicions are borne out when informals try to engage government but lose. If people gain power
through the marketplace instead, they can buy land and public services. Those stuck near the bottom of the income scale have little recourse.

NAFTA: From Eve to its Anticlimax, 1992–95

Since 1992, the U.S.–Mexico border has seen momentous changes:
surprising policy shifts, predictable moves, and unanticipated oc-
currences. They fall into the following realms: border initiatives by
the INS, the enactment of NAFTA, and the Mexican peso devaluation that began in late 1994.

On September 19, 1993, on the seasonal eve of NAFTA's New
Year transition, the Border Patrol installed a Border Blockade, posi-
tioning its officers along the densely settled urban areas of the border to prevent the entry of undocumented people. This strategy de-
parted from the former strategy of identifying undocumented
people in workplaces, on streets, and at interstate highway checkpoints. Many citizens and legal immigrants had been harassed in the
process. The new strategy, in contrast, proved popular among a majority of El Paso residents, including people of Mexican heritage.[2]

Hegemonic institutions have begun to do their work, at least when it comes to refashioning identities along political-economic lines.

Seeking to evaluate the effectiveness of the Blockade, subsequently renamed Operation Hold the Line, the U.S. Commission on Immigration Reform (CIR) held public hearings in El Paso and other border cities. A panel of "experts," including the Catholic archbishop, spokespeople from the Hispanic and El Paso Chambers of Commerce, and an academic cited grave concerns about the Blockade's impact on poverty, family interaction, and commercial exchange in the highly integrated twin cities of El Paso and Juárez. Without prior consultation, and despite their divergent institutional backgrounds, the panelists' analysis and predictions were strikingly consistent.[3]

The CIR also commissioned research on the Blockade's effectiveness. Under the direction of University of Texas sociologist Frank Bean, researchers questioned the Blockade's effects on long-term immigration but found that it appeared to deter day crossers. The CIR's report to Congress praised the Blockade for discouraging street vendors.[4] Ironically, this relatively insignificant group, in numerical terms, had already experienced a setback—through a U.S.-style democratic consultation process—when the El Paso city government legitimized their presence in a fixed number of downtown streets with sharply increased fees and surveillance threats (see Chapters 4 and 7).

The Spanish acronym for the INS conveys in English some of the negative symbolism associated with immigration enforcement. The Servicio de Inmigración Naturalización (SIN) seeks to hold the line on the movement of *people* while other parts of the U.S. government facilitate the movement of *capital and jobs*. NAFTA came after a long sequence of policies that cheapened labor costs in a global economy and reinforced neoliberal strands in countries like Mexico. NAFTA promised that market-driven foreign investment and job creation would improve Mexico's standard of living, thereby paying off with stronger consumer demand for U.S. products. Mexico's official minimum wages were as low as ever, and they were not on the negotiating table, ready to increase with the transition to NAFTA. Only one losing candidate in El Paso's 1996 Democratic congressional primary election spoke to this wage issue, citing its potential to increase the standard of living and deter immigration. The victor instead was the former Border Patrol chief, Silvestre Reyes.

In already integrated border economies like El Paso–Juárez, people saw little change in the post-NAFTA world. Texan observers probably did not expect much change at the border, for the anticipated Mexican consumer demand was for high-technology products made in the Dallas/Fort Worth and Houston areas. Red tape in the import–export trade was even thicker and more elaborate.[5] However, one group felt the impact of NAFTA almost immediately: the garment labor force. A poignant graphic in *Unidad y Fuerza* ("Unity and Force"), La Mujer Obrera's monthly newspaper, lists fifty-five plants that had closed by the January 1996 issue. It named the plants on gravestones, under the title "NAFTA Cemetery: Plant Closings in El Paso Due to International Trade Agreements."

It is too early to assess the effects of a long-term trade agreement, grouping countries in what the World Bank calls a "regional trading bloc" rather than free trade.[6] NAFTA protects a geographic space from outside competition. It creates a transitional process wherein tariffs are reduced and phased out over ten to fifteen years. Some products remain protected from free trade, the outcome of political negotiations. The export–import process itself is still tangled in licenses and other fees that formal businesses employ accountants and lawyers to untangle. Informals cannot afford to hire experts, and their occasional leaders in popular organizations do not have the "technical look" of modern business. The bureaucratic tangle erects a kind of informal commercial blockade in the name of free trade. Do informals dare view the commercial blockade they face under NAFTA as a protectionist racket for formal commerce whose paperwork is cleaned up by accountants? However we view modernist, if bureaucratized, free trade regimes like NAFTA, they will probably destroy informals, the quintessential free traders, unless the latter find some new spaces to exploit.

Militarized blockades have been tried in other parts of the U.S.–Mexico border. Sophisticated technical support increases the surveillance capabilities of diligent SLBs: "electronic sensors, infrared radar, helicopters, closed-circuit television monitoring," and more. Timothy Dunn analyzes the implications of this militarized presence for human rights when a low-intensity-conflict foreign policy operation comes home.[7] U.S. election-year rhetoric aggravates the seeming costs of immigration, but the costs of surveillance and maintaining a border by force may have a deeper and more chilling effect on public resources and freedom, not to forget commerce, with its *rhetoric* of free trade.

In the meantime, the other face of INS/SIN is "Citizenship USA," reducing the backlog of citizenship applications amid the changing national political climate. On July 3, 1996, at a symbolic pre–Independence Day event, 4,078 El Pasoans swore their allegiance to the United States in a citizenship ceremony that was the largest event ever held in the city. An expected 16,000 naturalization cases are pending in this region. Most of the prospective citizens are crossers who moved north, some as many as fifty years ago.[8]

While this study and others emphasize the legal immigrants' *underutilization* of social benefits, the 1996 welfare reform act in Congress makes citizenship limbo a less and less viable alternative for border-crossers. Instead, loyalty oaths are in order should health fail or some other disaster occur. If social benefits are under threat today, will public schools be next? Some school districts have begun registering students with Social Security numbers, so increased bureaucratic surveillance may be on the horizon.

Less than a year after NAFTA went into effect, Mexico devalued two important values. The first event was a wrenching break in the hoped-for transition to democracy. The assassination of Luis Donaldo Colosio, the official candidate of an increasingly divided PRI, has yet to be resolved. It occurred just after the Chiapas rebellion, symbolically initiated the day NAFTA went into effect. The so-called dinosaurs of the dominant PRI flirted with the idea of having a progressive woman at the helm, but that lasted only a year.

Mexico's currency devaluation reduced the value of the Mexican peso to half its precious value in U.S. dollars in late 1994 and early 1995. Peso devaluations following Mexican elections are not unknown, but this one was bound to reduce consumer demand for U.S. products, thereby adjusting Mexico's trade deficit. Minimum wages dropped to half their former value, a considerable boon for maquiladoras. The number of maquila employees in Juárez increased by 20,000, to approximately 150,000. Given the continuing female majority in export-labor processing, that increase continued to inch up the proportion of women in the cheapened formal labor market.

Currency devaluation also affected *fayuqueras*, the cross-border shoppers whose money no longer goes as far in U.S. markets. As a result, U.S. retailers face a lower consumer demand for products at the border. All the petty regulations and interference from SLBs paled in significance next to the swift blow of devaluation imposed from on high. If history is a guide, these women will probably specialize more in used than in new goods until they rebound.[9] But *fayuqueras'* ability to rebound is tied to maintaining that space on the border, with its negotiable bureaucratic regulation. Meanwhile, more and more U.S. wholesale and retail outlets like Sam's Club and Wal-Mart are bringing cheap U.S. goods directly to the Mexican consumer.

Implications for the Heartlands

Informal activity is part of people's everyday lives on both sides of the U.S.–Mexico border. Lacking sufficient jobs above poverty levels, people pursue multiple income-generating strategies with multiple household earners. On the U.S. side, the work is not lucrative; on the Mexican side, it generates more earnings than artificially low minimum wages.

Shall we call this, as Selby and his colleagues do, the "Mexican solution"? Actually, it transcends the border, among native-born and immigrants alike. While the solution may have been born in poverty, at least conceptually, it encompasses those with aspirations, those claiming a middle-class lifestyle. The solution flourishes in opportune spaces, free of surveillance and enforceable petty regulations, on both sides of the border, or, for crossers, *on* the border itself. This solution is practiced in countries like the United States, which hardly sees itself among the poor countries. It emerges from a globalized political economy concerned far more with free trade than fair trade among people desperate for work.

What is to be done about seemingly free but unfair trade? Interim strategies are necessary until grand, global hegemonic practices shift. In keeping with my focus in this book, the strategies I propose involve informality, wages, immigration, and political community. The general strategy would allow self-employment to become more lucrative. At that point reasonable regulations should emerge in which people—whatever their citizenship or gender—can exercise their voice, moving toward public work around which people can organize. The strategy would also bring public authority to bear on reducing gaps between Mexican and U.S. wages, along with wage gaps within each country between rich and poor, men and women. The market appears only to aggravate those gaps and thereby stimulate immigration. With earning ratios of 10 to 1 and 5 to 1, immigration is a natural extension of people's decision to cross space for comparative advantage. Self-sufficient behavior is a skill people need to exercise as global economic players pull their strings, which will perhaps be tighter before they get looser. Self-help offers protected space, or refuge, from increasingly relentless hegemonic controls.

Self-sufficient risk-takers, these informals are not victims. They are not pacified through hegemonic institutions of social control and propaganda. While surveillance spreads into everyday life, people identify the cracks in the surveillance machinery and make the most of them until new mechanisms develop, at which point the cycle begins again. People's ingenuity and resilience offer testimony to the human capacity to counter hegemonic institutions. This is the spark and spirit necessary for transforming hegemony, a drive necessarily pursued through collective means. Building political community is the necessary counterpoint to economic self-sufficiency.

Yet people's counterhegemonic strategies are usually hidden, a practice antithetical to public debate and scrutiny. More ominously, counterhegemony generates avoidance, sabotage, and even deceit. That sort of behavior undermines the transformation of public life and the construction of healthy communities built upon trust. Counterhegemony engenders cynicism and mistrust, but trust and hope are the essential building blocks not only for political communities, but also for collective organization to transform, build, or rebuild community.

Counterhegemony makes the disjuncture between dominant institutions and socioeconomic reality more obvious. Its existence challenges people to transform or to rebuild political community in ways more compatible with humane and democratic values. But those who would romanticize counterhegemony would do well to consider its various consequences. If the challenge avoids public obligation in individualistic and hidden ways, it is unlikely to promote political or collective organization. Counterhegemony is a mixed blessing to those who dream of democratic political community wherein rights and obligations are embedded in open and public expression, responsiveness, and accountability.

Somewhere between the borderlines of lawful and lawless behavior lies a large middle ground of people working and constructing shelter in ways that do not hurt others. Law professor Regina Austin analyzes "the relativity of what is legal and what is illegal" to "folks who are situated somewhere between the middle class and the lawbreakers. In leading their everyday lives, these bridge people draw a sensible line between the laws that may be broken and the laws that must be obeyed."[10] Resistance to unfair and inconsistent law enforcement can be applauded and celebrated as testament to the human spirit. But where does one draw the line for resistance that harms others, that is counterproductive, or that targets "similarly situated minority folks"? Austin worries that some "rebellion is part of . . . conformism to the larger culture" of materialist consumption.[11] Her concerns have resonance for the ways in which informals respond to regulatory enforcement.

Regulations can be enforced in ways that foster voluntary compliance among people who respect as legitimize the content and enforcement of those rules. Looking at the many—too many—petty regulations and patronizing enforcement strategies from the point of view of informals especially those lacking resources, the rules about border crossing, or home and street sales, hardly seem legitimate, fair, and worthy of respect. Voluntary compliance is more likely if regulations are *reasonable,* if regulations touch the regulated with *dignity,* and if the regulated have some *voice* in both policy and enforcement decisions.

These three factors—reason, dignity, and voice—are inoperative among many policymakers dealing with informals. Rather, the rules are applied with a vengeance, whether people are being steamrollered into the criminal justice system, U.S. style, or are negotiating with willing SLBs, Mexico style. In both settings, the rules seem calculated to make work for government staff and to generate revenue for the local treasury, or even SLBs themselves. But some of those rules cost more to enforce than they generate in revenue. Thus, they fall into the category of what international finance experts call nuisance taxes.[12] Government-as-nuisance generates more than short-term expenses. It generates long-term cynicism and subterfuge. Selective enforcement of policies, seemingly according to the whim of those in authority, raises questions about the integrity, fairness, and justice of the whole process.

Whether bureaucrats are zealots or drones, their missions backfire when they enforce a machinery of petty regulations, with criminal penalties, for actions that cause no public harm but rather generate work for people or stretch their meager incomes. Busy holding the line against rummage sales or street vendors struggling to make a minimum wage, bureaucrats make expensive work for themselves. Will their work deter informal operations, or, instead, will the regulated devise new and more clever ways to avoid detection while breaking rules that seem unreasonable and illegitimate? Perhaps ordinary people's schemes are a match for officials' schemes, but the latter are backed up by the authority to fine, to confiscate, and to detain people trying to make a living.

The grander regulations are harder to escape or avoid. Immigration control is increasingly enforced through high-technology, high-speed coordinated data files. Monetary values are manipulated from on high, deep within the bowels of treasury or central bank bureaucracies. Decisions about petty regulations are made closer to home; the grand schemers are so far removed from people that even their elected representatives cannot get close to the decisionmaking process. Perhaps this is just part of the plan for suprastate, regional, or global trade organizations, as some have argued.[13]

Informals maintain a distance from government. In the United States, they melt into the woodwork as much as possible, while in Mexico they acquire leaders who offer protection rackets. Some organization is probably better than no organization, but a patron-client organizational style does little more than reproduce an unequal, hierarchical system. Mexican informals have coopted government discourse to afford themselves some protection, at some cost in time and money.

In both countries informals' participation is limited to enforcement rather than the policymaking process. By avoiding the latter they forfeit the opportunity to organize collectively to change regulations, regulatory enforcement, or the steamroller of bureaucratic machinery that criminalizes noncompliance, no matter how petty or unreasonable the rules are. A street vendor of prepackaged food cannot be equated with a drug dealer on school grounds. Meanwhile, seemingly intractable problems continue. Burdening the self-employed is a misplaced priority, taking time and resources away from overseeing the wage and safety violations that more privileged informals commit against their workers in sweatshops and other places.[14]

Colonias are special places in which residents are more or less embraced by government. People migrate for land, housing, and an escape from surveillance. Informal activity in the neighborhood reacts to space and opportunity as people try to construct secure shelter. But informals miss the opportunity to press for housing and land policies that would fairly redistribute public resources to themselves in a transparent and reasonably efficient process.

Meanwhile, residents and taxpayers tenuously forge social bonds and generate social capital to promote their common interest in obtaining public services. Those emergent voices are increasingly female, even as men continue to monopolize decisionmaking at the highest reaches of local government, not to mention state or global players. In the past, male representatives have presented a homogenized front to officials, even as women and men experience their work, earnings, and neighborhoods differently. With greater balance among those mediators, perhaps the gender differences will become public and thereby visible enough to affect policy and collective agendas.

On the U.S. side, many of these potential new voices belong to people who are not full citizens; others belong to legal permanent residents who pay sales and property taxes (on their own homes or through their rent). Their lives symbolize a more momentous act than the casting of a vote: they uprooted themselves in search of work and a better life for their children. Whether they apply for citizenship, as more and more are opting to do, or delay doing so, they represent the foundation for building or rebuilding civic engagement and political community.

The informals and political community builders standing front and center at our borders have crossed territorial, regulatory, gender, and employment lines in a region called North America. The southern line of that region was once northern Mexico; the NAFTA world shifted the line to southern Mexico. On either side of the U.S.–Mexico border, people share clear commonalities that range from informal housing and income practices to culture and kinship. Political communities also cross borderlines. Such transcendence occurs through occasional NGO partnerships, such as Seeds Across the Border, or through local government leaders' search for relief from the financial burdens of the infrastructure expenses of international free trade.[15]

Border people are changing the meaning of political communities. Let us all think about such changes, even if they contravene national and global hegemonic institutions. In so doing, we can reconstruct more meaningful communities that embrace our common concerns for responsive, accountable democracies that use public authority for fair trade and wages above poverty levels. A real civic culture cannot and should not stop at the border. Rather, it should extend through regions and on to an eventual global citizenship that can transform the grand hegemony that seeks to envelop us all.

Notes

Chapter 1

1. I acknowledge, among many others, Ellwyn Stoddard and Oscar Martínez. Martínez's latest book is *Border People* (Tucson: University of Arizona Press, 1994); his latest edited collection is *U.S.–Mexico Borderlands: Historical and Contemporary Perspectives* (Wilmington, Del.: Jaguar Books, 1995). Stoddard summarizes the evolution of the Association of Borderlands Scholars in the *Journal of Borderlands Studies* 7 (1992); 92–121. His own work has contributed enormously to these studies. Also see Lawrence Herzog, ed., *Changing Boundaries in the Americas* (San Diego: Center for U.S.–Mexico Studies, University of California at San Diego, 1992).

2. *Informality* generally refers to income-generating or income-substituting activity that tends to be unrecorded, untaxed, and partially regulated. Recent works that bring together this voluminous literature include Cathy A. Rakowski, ed., *Contrapunto: The Informal Sector Debate in Latin America* (Albany: SUNY/Albany Press, 1994); Bryan Roberts, "Informal Economy and Family Strategies," in a special 1994 issue of the *International Journal of Urban and Regional Research*, vol. 18; and J. J. Thomas, *Surviving in the City: The Urban Informal Sector in Latin America* (London: Pluto Press, 1995). See Chapters 2 and 4 for more analysis.

3. Renato Rosaldo, *Culture and Truth* (Boston: Beacon Press, 1989), 28, 198, 208. I am eternally grateful to Alejandro Lugo for introducing me to Rosaldo's work.

4. Ibid., 434. The definitive work on border cultural identities is Pablo Vila, *Everyday Life, Culture and Identity on the Mexican-American Border: The Ciudad Juárez–El Paso Case* Ph.D. diss., University of Texas at Austin, 1994; Austin: University of Texas Press, forthcoming).

5. Cheryl Howard directed extensive field work in order to develop the sampling frame. The team relied on random number tables for selection, tossing a die to determine which corner of the blocks to begin with. If a dwelling unit was uninhabited, a new household was selected using the random number table. If assistants could not conduct interviews after three attempts, the unit to the left was contacted. See Cheryl Howard (untitled manuscript, 1995), available from author.

Random samples were drawn from U.S. census tracts and Juárez neighborhoods, which are invariably larger than the small cross-cutting census tracts called las Areas Geoestadísticas Básicas (AGEBs). Census tracts rarely respect neighborhood integrity and identity. El Paso has 95 census tracts, while Juárez (with approximately twice the population) has 264. The named Juárez neighborhoods we selected cut across several AGEBs, making composite data difficult to estimate and rendering census tract boundaries less meaningful for comparative analysis. Can we generalize from neighborhood to city? Technically, no. But, roughly speaking, the neighborhood samples represent the bottom economic halves of the populations of both cities.

We decided to avoid rich neighborhoods for various reasons. First, we anticipated that interviewers would not be able to get beyond the fences, dogs, and maids on both sides of the border. Second, the material stakes of informality among the wealthy might make them more likely to conceal this practice. We suspected that the wealthy engage in informality at substantial rates, but we thought snowball sampling, rather than random neighborhood sampling, would be the appropriate methodology in their case.

Scientific sampling has its cumbersome, sometimes counterproductive, side. Student interviewers provided illustrative examples in their ethnographic journals. One politically charged neighborhood in Juárez is like a village: once interviewers became known and recognized, potential respondents would greet them warmly. From Patricia Molina's entries: "Several women approached, saying, 'When are you interviewing us?' I asked them where they lived, and they answered with a street we'd already completed. 'That's a shame,' they said." Irma Carrillo's entries express frustration with the complicated mazes, alleys, apartments, and tenements in El Paso's poor core: "People would ask, 'Who are you looking for?' They were suspicious when we had no name, just an address."

6. Interviewers' ethnographic journal entries, plus clues embedded in the interviews themselves, convince me that the incidence of informality reported here represents an underestimate. Despite interviewers' badges, university t-shirts, and self-presentation, some Juárez residents wondered if they were from one political party or the other or, even more troubling, from Hacienda, the federal treasury agency, which sends roaming inspectors into neighborhoods to ensure sales tax payments (from the journals of Luis Aguirre and Angélica Holguín). One particularly telling example is from Patricia Molina's journal: "I was interviewing a man when a child came to buy a soda. I asked him if he had a *tiendita*, and he told me no. But when the interview ended, I looked past a door and saw a table with chips and sweets. I think he did sell things, but he didn't want to say." Only when respondents acknowledged self-employment/business did interviewers continue that line of inquiry with a supplementary questionnaire. The quest to document the *incidence* of informality was frustrated in part by probable underestimation and the unreliability of self-disclosure. Conse-

quently, no tests of significance are conducted. A conservative estimate—for research in sensitive areas like these invariably involves estimates—is that one in three sample households participates in informality. If one adds self-help housing, the estimates rise.

I am wary of such numbers, no less and no more than I am about much census data. Many of the insights in this book have been obtained through "thick" readings of questionnaires and the search for patterns therein. A copy of the questionnaire is available from the author.

7. For example, Alejandro Portes, Manuel Castells, and Lauren A. Benton, eds., *The Informal Economy: Studies in Advanced and Less Developed Countries* (Baltimore: Johns Hopkins University Press, 1989).

8. James Scott, *Domination and the Arts of Resistance: Hidden Transcripts* (New Haven: Yale University Press, 1990). Chapter 2 draws on Gramscian approaches to the global political economy, a theoretical inspiration that heretofore has focused more on "hegemony" than on "counter-hegemony," as I do.

9. For one example among many of comparative urban studies in industrialized market economies, see David Judge, Gerry Stoker, and Harold Wolman, eds., *Theories of Urban Politics* (London: Sage, 1995). For a rare exception, see Lawrence Herzog, *Where North Meets South: Cities, Space, and Politics on the U.S.–Mexico Border* (Austin: University of Texas Press, 1990).

On mirrorlike reflections, see Edward Soja, *Postmodern Geographies: The Reassertion of Space in Critical Social Theory* (London: Verso, 1989), and his "Heterotopologies: A Reinvention of Other Spaces in the Citadel—Los Angeles," in *Postmodern Cities and Spaces,* ed. Sophie Watson and Katherine Gibson, (Cambridge: Blackwell, 1995), both of which draw on Michel Foucault's relatively short essay on space: "Of Other Spaces," *Diacritics* 16 (Spring 1986), 22–27.

10. Victoria Rodríguez and Peter M. Ward, *Policymaking, Politics, and Urban Governance in Chihuahua* (Austin: University of Texas, U.S. Mexican Policy Report no. 3, 1992), and *Political Change in Baja California: Democracy in the Making?* (San Diego: University of California Center for U.S.–Mexican Studies 1994); Vivienne Bennett, *The Politics of Water: Urban Protest, Gender, and Power in Monterrey, Mexico* (Pittsburgh: University of Pittsburgh Press, 1995); Diane E. Davis, *Urban Leviathan: Mexico City in the Twentieth Century* (Philadelphia: Temple University Press, 1994). Many earlier in-depth studies of Mexican municipal politics are wonderful, but increasingly dated.

Chapter 2

1. This phrase takes off from the classic study of elites, William V. D'Antonio and William H. Form, *Influentials in Two Border Cities: A Study in*

Community Decision-Making (Notre Dame, Ind.: University of Notre Dame Press, 1965).

2. Kathy Ferguson, *The Feminist Case Against Bureaucracy* (Philadelphia: Temple University Press, 1984), with an excellent discussion of the double meaning of the word *discipline,* is a pioneering attempt to bring Foucault to public administration.

A state can be defined in Weberian fashion, that is, as an entity exercising legitimate authority over territorial space. But as James Scott cautioned me long ago in graduate school: who says it's legitimate? State declarations do not imply acceptance on the part of residents.

3. Theodore Lowi, "The State in Political Science: How We Become What We Study," *American Political Science Review* 82 (1992), 3.

4. Lourdes Benería, "Accounting for Women's Work: The Progress of Two Decades," *World Development* 20 (1992). Also see Ruth Dixon-Mueller, *Women's Work in Third World Agriculture* (Geneva: International Labour Organization, 1985), on the incredibly different figures given for women agricultural workers over time in single countries and within regions. Official definitions, and the ideologies buried therein, make all the difference in the world for the selection of indicators and measurements. On people's wariness of the state, see Kathleen Staudt, *Managing Development: State, Society, and International Contexts* (Newbury Park, Calif.: Sage, 1991), chap. 2.

5. R. W. Cox, "Gramsci, Hegemony, and International Relations: An Essay in Method," *Millennium* 12 (1983), 162–75; Stephen R. Gill and David Law, "Global Hegemony and the Structural Power of Capital," *International Studies Quarterly* 33 (1989), 475–500; Stephen R. Gill, ed., *Gramsci, Historical Materialism and International Relations* (Cambridge: Cambridge University Press, 1993). We all draw insights from Antonio Gramsci, *Selections from the Prison Notebooks* (New York: International Publishers, 1971).

6. James Caporaso, "Global Political Economy," in *Political Science: The State of the Discipline II,* ed. Ada W. Finifter (Washington, D.C.: American Political Science Association, 1993).

7. Anthony Giddens, *The Consequences of Modernity* (Stanford, Calif.: Stanford University Press 1990), 57. Max Weber's famous iron cage phrase is found in *The Protestant Ethic and the Spirit of Capitalism.* The dangers of bureaucratic domination are threaded through various chapters of Ted R. Vaugh, Gideon Sjoberg, and Larry T. Reynolds, eds., *A Critique of Contemporary Sociology* (Dix Hills, N.Y.: General Hall, 1993). Also see Ferguson, *Feminist Case.*

8. Giddens, *Consequences of Modernity,* 58.

9. Oren Yiftachel, "The Dark Side of Modernism: Planning as Control of an Ethnic Minority," in *Postmodern Cities and Spaces.* ed. Sophie Watson

and Katherine Gibson, (Cambridge: Blackwell, 1995), 216; David Harvey, *The Condition of Postmodernity: An Enquiry into the Origins of Cultural Change* (London: Blackwell, 1989), chap. 4. On Latin America, see James Holston, *The Modernist City: An Anthropological Critique of Brasilia* (Chicago: University of Chicago Press, 1989); Richard M. Morse, "Cities as People," in *Rethinking the Latin American City,* ed. Richard M. Morse and Jorge Hardoy (Baltimore: Johns Hopkins University Press, 1992).

10. Sidney Plotkin, *Keep Out: The Struggle for Land Use Control* (Berkeley: University of California Press, 1987), 76, 83, 110. Also see Henri Lefebre's work, discussed in Mark Gottdeiner, *The Social Production of Urban Space* (Austin: University of Texas Press, 1985).

11. For the definitive treatment of these complex identities, see Pablo Vila, *Everyday Life, Culture and Identity on the Mexican-American Border: The Ciudad Juárez–El Paso Case* (Ph.D. diss., University of Texas at Austin, 1994; Austin: University of Texas Press, forthcoming). On the differences between "foreign-" and "native-born" people of Mexican origin in the United States, see Rodolfo de la Garza et al., "Mexican Immigrants, Mexican-Americans, and American Political Culture," in *Immigration and Ethnicity* (Washington, D.C.: Urban Affairs Institute, 1993), 227–50, where strikingly high support for English-language assimilation is noted.

12. Alejandro Portes is discussed in James D. Smith, "Measuring the Informal Economy," in a useful special issue on informal economies edited by Louis A. Ferman et al., *Annals of the American Academy of Political and Social Science* 493 (1987), 217.

13. Harvey, *Condition of Postmodernity,* 45.

14. James Scott, *Domination and the Arts of Resistance: Hidden Transcripts* (New Haven: Yale University Press, 1990), 45. My study in no way implies that resistance is to be uniformly celebrated. After all, its practitioners run the gamut from noble anarchists to sweatshop owners cutting costs with unsafe working conditions.

15. See for example Joel Midgal, Atul Kohli, and Vivienne Shue, eds., *State Power and Social Forces: Domination and Transformation in the Third World* (New York: Cambridge University Press, 1994), and Sue Ellen Charlton, Jana Everett, and Kathleen Staudt, eds., *Women, the State, and Development* (Albany: SUNY Albany Press, 1989). These books react to and elevate the analysis of *Bringing the State Back in,* ed. Peter B. Evans, Dietrich Rueschemeyer, and Theda Skocpol (New York: Cambridge University Press, 1985).

16. Kathleen Thelen and Sven Steinmo, "Historical Institutionalism in Comparative Politics," in *Structuring Politics: Historical Institutionalism in Comparative Analysis,* ed. Sven Steinmo et al. (New York: Cambridge University Press, 1992), 2. See also various writings of Anthony Giddens, including *Consequences of Modernity.*

17. Michael Lipsky, *Street-Level Bureaucracy* (New York: Russell Sage, 1980).

18. Scott, *Domination*, 5, 88.

19. Murray Edelman, *Constructing the Political Spectacle* (Chicago: University of Chicago Press, 1988).

20. Anne B. Shlay, "Shaping Place: Institutions and Metropolitan Development Patterns," *Journal of Urban Affairs* 15 (1993), 368.

21. Ibid., 400.

22. Saskia Sassen, *Cities in a World Economy* (Thousand Oaks: Pine Forge Press of Sage, 1995). See also Chapters 3–4 of this book.

23. Oscar Martínez, *Border People* (Tucson: University of Arizona Press, 1994), distinguishes between types of borders. One type is *interdependent*, a characterization of the U.S.–Mexico border supported in this book.

24. Michel Foucault, "Of Other Spaces," *Diacritics* 16 (Spring 1986), 24.

25. Sanford Schram, *Words of Welfare: The Poverty of Social Science and the Social Science of Poverty* (Minneapolis: University of Minnesota Press, 1995), 5, citing Foucault on "governmentality."

26. Ibid.

27. Bryan Roberts has pursued pathbreaking studies in Mexico and elsewhere. See the special issue of the *International Journal of Urban and Regional Research* 18 (1994), which Roberts edited and for which he wrote an introductory article: "Informal Economy and Family Strategies." See also Cathy A. Rakowski, *Contrapunto: The Informal Sector Debate in Latin America* (Albany: SUNY Albany Press, 1994).

28. Mayra Buvinic and Marguerite Berger, eds., *Women's Ventures: Assistance to the Informal Sector in Latin America* (West Hartford, Conn.: Kumarian Press, 1989); Hernando de Soto, *The Other Path* (New York: Harper & Row, 1989), 60, citing Lima's 54 percent female majority among informals.

29. Gayle Rubin was the first to name the diverse yet "monotonous" subordination of women worldwide in "The Traffic in Women: Notes on the 'Political Economy' of Sex," in Rayna R. Reiter, *Toward an Anthropology of Women* (New York: Monthly Review Press, 1975), 160; Allison MacEwen Scott, "Informal Sector or Female Sector?: Gender Bias in Urban Labour Market Models," in *Male Bias in the Development Process*, ed. Diane Elson (Manchester: Manchester University Press, 1991), 105–32. For the latest statistics on ubiquitous gender inequality, see United Nations Development Programme (UNDP), *Human Development Report* (New York: Oxford University Press, 1995).

30. Alan Gilbert, ed., *Housing and Land in Urban Mexico* (La Jolla, Calif.: Center for U.S.–Mexico Studies, University of California at San Diego, no. 31, 1989).

31. International Labour Organization (ILO), *Employment, Incomes, and Inequality* (Geneva: ILO, 1972); Keith Hart, "Informal Income Oppor-

tunities and Urban Employment in Ghana," *Journal of Modern African Studies* 11 (1973), 61–89.

32. Lourdes Benería, "Conceptualizing the Labor Force: The Underestimation of Women's Economic Activities," in *African Women in the Development Process*, ed. Nici Nelson (London: Frank Cass, 1981); see Jan Monk's case study "What Counts?" in Staudt, *Managing Development*, 93–94.

33. In 1985, Alejandro Portes documented shrinkage in "Latin American Class Structures: Their Composition and Change During the Last Decades," *Latin American Research Review* 20, no. 3 (1985), pp. 7–39, but in 1989 he co-edited *The Informal Economy: Studies in Advanced and Less Developed Countries* with Manuel Castells and Lauren Benton (Baltimore: Johns Hopkins University Press, 1989), which conceptualized rise with structural adjustment. Also see Harvey, *Condition of Postmodernity*, 187, and Michael Peter Smith, *City, State, and Market: The Political Economy of Urban Society* (London: Basil Blackwell, 1988), 217–20.

34. Good overviews are provided in Rakowski, *Contrapunto*. Also see Caroline Moser, "Informal Sector or Petty Commodity Production: Dualism or Dependence in Urban Development?" *World Development* 6 (1978), 1041–64.

35. Lisa Peattie, "An Idea in Good Currency and How It Grew: The Informal Sector," *World Development* 15 (1987), 851–60; Roberts urges the continued use of the terminology anyway: "Informal Economy."

36. Edward Soja, *PostModern Geographies: The Reassertion of Space in Critical Social Theory* (London: Verso, 1989); Edward Soja, "Heterotopologies: A Reinvention of Other Spaces in the Citadel—Los Angeles," in Watson and Gibson, *Postmodern Cities and Spaces*.

37. Roberts, "Informal Economy," 13.

38. Ray Bromley critiques the exclusion of politics in "Small May Be Beautiful, but It Takes More Than Beauty to Ensure Success," in *Planning for Small Enterprises in Third World Cities*, ed. Ray Bromley (Oxford and New York: Pergamon Press, 1985), 321–41, esp. 337–39. The exceptions include literature on Peru: Sheldon Annis and Jeffrey Franks, "Is the Idea of the Informal Sector Beginning to Change How Both the Left and the Right Think About Economic Policy?" *Grassroots Development* 13 (1989), 8–22, and the somewhat polemical, antistatist *Other Path*, by de Soto; and publications from the ILO's regional affiliate in Santiago, Chile, especially work by Victor Tokman: see for example "Policies for a Heterogeneous Informal Sector in Latin America," *World Development* 17 (1989), 1067–76. Also see Inter-American Development Bank (IDB), *Economic and Social Progress in Latin America* (Washington, D.C.: IDB, 1990). On municipal government complicity in Mexico, see Raúl Monge and Fernando Ortega, "El Comercio Informal, Explosivo: En 1990 creció tres veces más que el Establecido," *Proceso* no. 739 (December 31, 1990), 12–17.

39. On structural adjustment, see Staudt, *Managing Development,* chap. 8.

40. Secretaría de Programación y Presupuesto (SPP), *La Ocupación Informal en Areas Urbanas* (Mexico City: SPP, 1976).

41. Secretaría del Trabajo y Previsión Social de México, (STPS) and U.S. Department of Labor (USDL), *The Informal Sector in Mexico,* Occasional Paper no. 1 (Mexico City and Washington, D.C.: STPS and USDL, 1992).

42. Orlandina de Oliveira and Bryan Roberts, "The Many Roles of the Informal Sector in Development: Evidence from Urban Labor Market Research, 1940–1989," in Rakowski, *Contrapunto,* 51–71.

43. Sylvia Chant, *Women and Survival in Mexican Cities: Perspectives on Gender, Labour Markets and Low-Income Households* (Manchester: Manchester University Press, 1991).

44. Lourdes Benería and Martha Roldán, *The Crossroads of Class and Gender* (New York: Monthly Review Press, 1987); Faranak Miraftab, "Space, Gender, and Work: Home-Based Workers in Mexico," in *Homeworkers in Global Perspective: Invisible No More,* ed. Eileen Boris and Elisabeth Prugl (New York and London: Routledge, 1996), 63–80.

45. Henry Selby, A. D. Murphy, and S. A. Lorensen, *The Mexican Urban Household: Organizing for Self-Defense* (Austin: University of Texas Press, 1990), chap. 6; my own street vendor respondents also report higher than minimum wages in Kathleen Staudt, "Struggles in Urban Space: Street Vendors in El Paso and Ciudad Juárez," *Urban Affairs Review* 31 (1996), 435–54.

46. Bryan Roberts, "Enterprise and Labor Markets: The Border and the Metropolitan Areas," *Frontera Norte* 5 (1993), 33–66.

47. Nestor Elizondo, "La Ilegalidad en el Sector Informal Urbano de la Ciudad de México," cited in Victor Tokman, "The Informal Sector in Latin America: From Underground to Legality," in *Towards Social Adjustment?: Labor Market Issues in South America,* ed. Guy Standing and Victor Tokman (Geneva: ILO, 1991), 69; translated in "Illegality in the Urban Informal Sector of Mexico," in *Beyond Regulation: The Informal Economy of Latin America,* ed. Victor Tokman (Boulder: Lynne Rienner, 1992), 55–83.

48. U.S. Department of Labor, *The Underground Economy in the United States* (Washington, D.C.: USDL, 1992); Edgar L. Feige, *The Underground Economies: Tax Evasion and Information Distortion* (Cambridge: Cambridge University Press, 1989). Note the striking chapter titles of a recent collection on the United States, Susan Pozo, ed., *Exploring the Underground Economy: Studies of Illegal and Unreported Economic Activity* (Kalamazoo, Mich.: W. E. Upjohn Institute, 1996): "The Mismeasurement of Illegal Drug Markets," "The Supply of Youths to Crime," and "Explaining Tax Compliance." The major exception is Steve Balkin, *Self-Employment for Low-Income People* (New York: Praeger, 1989); I take up this topic in Chapter 7 below.

49. Bryan T. Johnson and Thomas P. Sheehy, *1996 Index of Economic Freedom* (Washington, D.C.: Heritage Foundation, 1996).

50. Bruce Wiegand, *Off the Books: A Theory and Critique of the Underground Economy* (Dix Hills, N.Y.: General Hall, 1992).

51. Ibid. 85, 99.

52. Eugene Becker, "Self-Employed Workers: An Update to 1983," *Monthly Labor Review,* July 1984, pp. 14–15.

53. Harriet B. Presser and Elizabeth Bamberger, "American Women Who Work at Home for Pay: Distinctions and Determinants," *Social Science Quarterly* 74 (1993), 823 24.

54. Cheryl Howard, personal communication, 1994.

55. See discussion of Ivan Light and others in Chapter 4.

56. M. Patricia Fernández-Kelly and Anna M. García, "Economic Restructuring in the United States: Hispanic Women in the Garment and Electronics Industries," in *Women and Work: An Annual Review,* vol. 3, ed. Barbara Gutek et al. (Beverly Hills: Sage, 1988), 49–65. The U.S. General Accounting Office (GAO) has produced several monographs on sweatshops. In 1994 the *Yale Law Journal* produced a special issue on the subject, some articles of which are cited in subsequent chapters.

57. Joan Moore and Raquel Pinderhughes, eds., *In the Barrios: Latinos and the Underclass Debate* (New York: Russell Sage, 1993), xxvii. Several chapters in their collection contain anecdotal information on informals like street vendors. See Chapter 4 for more systematically collected data on these informals.

58. Elsa M. Chaney and Mary García Castro, eds., *Muchachas No More: Household Workers in Latin America and the Caribbean* (Philadelphia: Temple University Press, 1989); Vicki Ruíz, "By the Day or the Week: Mexicana Domestic Workers in El Paso," in *Women on the U.S.-Mexico Border,* ed. Vicki Ruíz and Susan Tiano (Boston: Allen Unwin, 1987), 61–76; Mary Romero, *Maid in the U.S.A.* (London: Routledge, 1992).

59. Jaime Mezzera, "Excess Labor Supply and the Urban Informal Sector: An Analytical Framework," in Buvinic and Berger, *Women's Ventures,* 45–64.

60. Jacqueline Maria Hagan, *Deciding to be Legal: A Mayan Community in Houston* (Philadelphia: Temple University Press, 1994), 159.

61. See Chapter 4. Alejandro Portes calls this "social capital" in his opening essay in *Economic Sociology and the Sociology of Immigration* (New York:Russell Sage, 1995), 12.

62. With state downsizing since 1980, the international development literature has turned to facilitating scaled-up microenterprises. For representative examples, see Charles Mann et al. *Seeking Solutions: Framework and Cases for Small Enterprise Development Programs* (Hartford, Conn.: Kumarian Press, 1989); Maria Otero and Elisabeth Rhyne, eds., *The New*

World of Microenterprise Finance: Building Healthy Financial Institutions for the Poor (Hartford, Conn.: Kumarian Press, 1994); and UNDP, Human Development Report (New York: Oxford University Press, 1993), on "people-friendly markets." International development specialists like myself have begun to gaze at northern countries with these lenses.

63. Sidney Verba, "The Citizen as Respondent: Sample Surveys and American Democracy," American Political Science Review 90 (1996), 1.

64. Steve Barracca, "Session Three: Summary," in Memoria of the Bi-National Conference: Mexico's Electoral Aftermath and Political Future, ed. Peter M. Ward et al. (Austin: Mexican Center of ILAS, University of Texas at Austin, 1994), pp. 62–64.

65. Gabriel Almond and Sidney Verba, The Civic Culture (Boston: Little, Brown, 1963).

66. For a critique see Ann L. Craig and Wayne A. Cornelius, "Political Culture in Mexico: Continuities and Revisionist Interpretations," in The Civic Culture Revisited, ed. Gabriel Almond and Sidney Verba (Boston: Little, Brown, 1980). On Mexican clientelism, see subsequent chapters, esp. Chapters 5–7.

67. Robert Putnam, "Bowling Alone: America's Declining Social Capital," Journal of Democracy 6 (1995), 65–78; also see Robert Bellah et.al. Habits of the Heart (Berkeley: University of California Press, 1987), and Robert Bellah et al., The Good Society (New York: Vintage, 1992).

68. Putnam defines social capital in "Bowling Alone Revisited," in Responsive Community, Spring 1995, p. 20. This marketlike discourse is popular with both political scientists and sociologists (see Portes, Economic Sociology). Still, one of the best critiques of Putnam's ideas about social capital can be found in Alejandro Portes and Patricia Landolt, "The Downside of Social Capital," American Prospect 26 (1996), 18–21, 94. No one has yet considered how all the applications of social capital seem to stop at, rather than transcend, national borders.

69. For anthropological treatment in the United States, see Carol Stack, "Sex Roles and Survival Strategies in an Urban Black Community," in Women, Culture, and Society, ed. Michelle Rosaldo and Louise Lamphere (Stanford, Calif.: Stanford University Press, 1974), 113–28; Carlos Vélez-Ibáñez, "Networks of Exchange Among Mexicans in the U.S. and Mexico: Local Level Mediating Responses to National and International Transformations," Urban Anthropology 17 (1988), 27–53; and the studies of the power elite launched by C. Wright Mills. The documentation of social networks is found in Mexican studies such as Larissa Lomnitz, "Mechanisms of Articulation Between Shantytown Settlers and the Urban System," Urban Anthropology 7 (1978), 185–205; Carlos Vélez-Ibáñez, Rituals of Marginality (Berkeley: University of California Press, 1983). Many Mexicanists seem to be fascinated with the self-contained, indigenous, and/or

peasant communities that no longer represent Mexico—a nation with an urban majority.

70. Renato Rosaldo, *Culture and Truth* (Boston: Beacon Press, 1989), 198.

71. Kathleen Staudt and William Weaver, *Feminisms and Political Science: Integration or Transformation?* (New York: Twayne/Macmillan, 1997), critique this neglect.

72. Ayşe Güneş-Ayata, "Clientelism: Premodern, Modern, Postmodern," in *Democracy, Clientelism, and Civil Society* ed. Luis Roniger and Ayşe Güneş-Ayata (Boulder: Lynne Rienner, 1994), 21. Several chapters in this collection show that clientelism is alive and well in the United States. For a thorough collection of earlier treatments, see Steffen W. Schmidt, James C. Scott, Carl Lande, and Laura Guasti, eds., *Friends, Followers, and Factions* (Berkeley: University of California Press, 1977).

73. Alberto Aziz Nassif, "De Agosto de 1994: Volver a Pensar la Transición," and Jacqueline Peschard, "What Happened to Multipartism in Mexico City?" in Ward, *Memoria*, 7, 13.

74. Judith Hellman, "Mexican Popular Movements, Clientelism, and the Process of Democratization," *Latin American Perspectives* 21 (1994), 125.

75. Silvia Gómez Tagle, "Electoral Reform and the Party System, 1977–90," in *Mexico: Dilemmas of Transition*, ed. Neil Harvey (London: Institute of Latin American Studies, University of London and British Academic Press, 1993), 64–90.

76. Kathleen Staudt, "Political Representation: Engendering Democracy," *Background Papers: Human Development Report 1995* (New York: UNDP, 1996), 21–70; bicameral legislatures are averaged for 1994. After Mexico's 1994 elections, its national female representation rates exceeded those in the United States by several percentage points. Local rates are quite low (3 percent), compared with an average of 20 percent in the United States. Also see Kathleen Staudt, "Women in Politics: Global Perspective" in *Memoria of the Bi-National Conference: Women in Contemporary Mexican Politics*, ed. V. E. Rodríguez et al. (Austin: Mexican Center of ILAS, University of Texas at Austin, 1995), 16–19.

77. Massolo is cited in Nicci Craske, "Women's Political Participation in *Colonias Populares* in Guadalajara, Mexico," in *Viva: Women and Popular Protest in Latin America*, ed. Sarah Radcliffe and Sallie Westwood (London and New York: Routledge, 1993), 134. Also see Lilia Venegas, "Political Culture and Women of the Popular Sector in Ciudad Juárez, 1983–1986," in *Opposition Government in Mexico*, ed. Victoria Rodríguez and Peter M. Ward (Albuquerque: University of New Mexico Press, 1995); Vivienne Bennett, "Gender, Class, and Water: Women and the Politics of Water Services in Monterrey, Mexico," *Latin American Perspectives* 22 (1995).

78. Massolo is quoted in Bennett, "Gender, Class, and Water," 79.

Kathleen Staudt and Carlota Aguilar discuss the feminine sectors' limited payoffs but also their potential for redistributing household power relations in "Political Parties, Women Activists' Agendas, and Class: Elections on Mexico's Northern Frontier," *Mexican Studies/Estudios Mexicanos* 8 (1992), 87–106.

79. Harry Triandis, "Cross-Cultural Industrial and Organizational Psychology," in *Handbook of Industrial and Organizational Psychology*, vol. 4, ed. Harry Triandis et al. (Palo Alto, Calif.: Consulting Psychologists, 1994), 103.

80. Judith Shklar, *American Citizenship: The Quest for Inclusion* (Cambridge: Harvard University Press, 1991), 10, 63, 67. I inserted feminine pronouns periodically, consistent with the content of Shklar's other writings.

81. Barbara Nelson, "Women's Poverty and Women's Citizenship," *Signs* 9 (1984), 209–29. Also see James Holston, ed. "Cities and Citizenship," special issue of *Public Culture* 19 (1996).

82. Lawrence Fuchs, *The American Kaleidoscope: Race, Ethnicity, and the Civic Culture* (Hanover: University Press of New England, 1990), 3.

83. U.S. Commission on Immigrarion Reform (CIR), *U.S. Immigration Policy: Restoring Credibility* (Washington, D.C.: CIR, 1994).

84. According to CIR, 2.0 million out of 2.7 million amnesties went to Mexican immigrants: ibid., 52, 217.

85. Alex Stepick and Guillermo Grenier, "Cubans in Miami," in Moore and Pinderhughes, *In the Barrios*, 86.

86. Alejandro Portes and Rubén G. Rumbaut, *Immigrant America: A Portrait* (Berkeley: University of California Press, 1990), 124.

87. Jorge Castañeda, "Tolerance and Dedemocratization," in *The California–Mexico Connection*, ed. Abraham Lowenthal (Princeton: Princeton University Press, 1993), 41.

88. Victoria Rodríguez and Peter M. Ward, *Policymaking, Politics, and Urban Governance in Chihuahua* (Austin: University of Texas, U.S. Mexican Policy Report no. 3, 1992).

89. Cited in Hellman, *Mexican Popular Movements*, 133. Also see Vélez-Ibañez, *Rituals*.

Chapter 3

1. Saskia Sassen, *Cities in a World Economy* (Thousand Oaks: Pine Forge Press of Sage, 1995), 154 (definition).

2. Ibid., 106.

3. Mario García, *Desert Immigrants: The Mexicans of El Paso, 1880–1920* (New Haven: Yale University Press, 1981), 77.

4. Gordon H. Frost, *The Gentlemen's Club: The Story of Prostitution in El Paso* (El Paso: Mangan, 1983). Prostitution, regulated in Juárez, continues to provide revenue for the municipal government. See Carlota Aguilar,

"Mexico's Social Policy: Levels of Marginality of Female Prostitutes in Ciudad Juárez" (M.A. thesis, University of Texas at El Paso, 1985), and Chapter 7 in this volume.

5. In Mexico, the federal government publishes textbooks that are distributed free to public school students. This heading is from a Grade 6 text, *Historia y Civismo,* by Amelia Monroy Guttiérrez (Mexico City: Comisión Nacional de los Libros de Texto Gratuito, 1966), 160. Thanks to Dennis Bixler-Márquez, director of the Chicano Studies Program, University of Texas at El Paso, for sharing his collection with me.

6. According to Lawrence H. Fuchs, *The American Kaleidoscope: Race, Ethnicity, and the Civic Culture* (Hanover: University Press of New England, 1990), 110, and chap. 6 generally: "Mexicans who chose to remain for one year in what was now U.S. territory were granted American citizenship." Of course, second-class, discriminatory treatment was part of those citizens' subsequent experiences. See David Montejano, *Anglos and Mexicans in the Making of Texas 1836–1980* (Austin: University of Texas Press, 1987).

7. Zuezhong Zhao, "Chinese Immigrants and American Business Interests" (M.A. thesis, University of Texas at El Paso, 1995), 43–47.

8. Congress supported a larger Border Patrol staff during the mid 1990s, the subject of many newspaper headlines in El Paso. The Border Patrol works with sophisticated surveillance technology: see Chapter 5. On overall increases in staff and high-tech equipment, see Timothy J. Dunn's masterpiece, *The Militarization of the U.S.–Mexico Border, 1978–1992: Low-Intensity Conflict Doctrine Comes Home* (Austin: Center for Mexican American Studies, University of Texas, 1996).

9. García, *Desert Immigrants,* 4.

10. David Weber, *Foreigners in Their Native Land* (Albuquerque: University of New Mexico Press 1973), 46.

11. Oscar Martínez, *Border Boom Town: Ciudad Juárez Since 1848* (Austin: University of Texas Press, 1978), 35; García, *Desert Immigrants,* 34–35.

12. García, *Desert Immigrants,* p. 35–36.

13. Dunn, *Militaritization,* 11–13; James Cockroft, *Outlaws in the Promised Land: Mexican Immigrant Workers and the American Future* (New York: Grove Press, 1986).

14. Martínez, *Border Boom Town,* pp. 15–18, 23–27.

15. García, *Desert Immigrants,* 35.

16. C. Richard Bath and Roberto Villarreal, "Politics in El Paso del Norte" (manuscript, 1993), 11.

17. Ibid., 35–40. Also see Benjamin Márquez, *Power and Politics in a Chicano Barrio: A Study of Mobilization Efforts and Community Power in El Paso* (Lanham, Md.: University Press of America, 1985), 30–43.

18. U.S. Census Bureau; these and other census citations are from the City of El Paso Department of Planning, Research, and Development packet, 1992. Also see Tomás Rivera Center, *Latinos in Texas: A Socio-Demographic Profile* (Claremont: Tomás Rivera Center, 1995), 85.

19. George William Towers, *Colonia Formation and Economic Restructuring in El Paso, Texas* (Ph.D. diss., University of Arizona, 1991) 57–73. Towers uses Census Bureau data, which I have reconstructed from tables. On El Paso restructuring as dependent on Juárez, see Tom Barry, with Harry Browne and Beth Sims, *Crossing the Line: Immigration, Economic Integration, and Drug Enforcement on the U.S.–Mexico Border* (Albuquerque: Research Center Resources, 1994), chap. 7.

20. Juanita Fernández, "Hispanic Garment Workers Challenging the Urban Underclass Model" (M.A. thesis, University of Texas at El Paso, 1995), chap. 4. Fernández narrowly defines long-term residence as five or more years. Towers, *Colonia Formation*, cites higher figures (30–45 percent) from earlier studies of women living in Juárez.

21. Benjamin Márquez, "Organizing Mexican-American Women in the Garment Industry: La Mujer Obrera," *Women & Politics* 15 (1995), 65–87. Also listen to the three-part Common Ground series, "Women on the U.S.–Mexico Border" (Muscatine, Iowa: Stanley Foundation, 1994). During the early 1990s, the El Paso Chamber of Commerce information packets for prospective businesses cited a 6 percent unionization rate.

22. In "Economic Sociology and the Sociology of Immigration," Alejandro Portes cites his studies (with Robert L. Bach) of 822 Mexican migrant men who "obtained legal residence through family and employer connections in the United States." Seventy percent had "lived in the North, mostly as unauthorized immigrants. They had been able to secure their legal papers primarily through family and work ties established during this period." The rest made use of family reunification provisions. In *The Economic Sociology of Immigration: Essays on Networks, Ethnicity, and Entrepreneurship*, ed. Alejandro Portes (New York: Russell Sage Foundation, 1995), 22–23.

In 1987, the Texas legislature authorized in-state university tuition rates for northern Mexican residents who could demonstrate need. Although not shining exemplars of internationalism, Texas political leaders know the commercial value of good relations with Mexico.

23. The crossing rates are staggering: 52.4 million northbound crossings (1995), second only to San Diego's 71.7 million. Enrique Suárez y Toriello and Octavio E. Chávez, *Profile of the United States-Mexico Border* (Juárez: FEMAP for the Inter-American Foundation, 1996), 96. The U.S. Customs Department keeps track of legal crossings.

24. Debbie Nathan, "The Eyes of Texas Are Upon You," in *Women and Other Aliens: Essays from the U.S.–Mexico Border* (El Paso: Cinco Puntos Press, 1987).

25. CIR reports 2,500 random investigations yearly, showing a high rate of 89 percent compliance in 1992, but only 40 percent for "lead-driven investigations" (i.e., invesigations based on phoned-in leads). *U.S. Immigration Policy: Restoring Credibility* (Washington, D.C.: CIR, 1994), 98–99.

26. Frank Bean et al., *Illegal Mexican Migration and the United States/ Mexico Border: The Effects of Operation Hold the Line on El Paso/Juárez* report prepared for CIR, July 15, 1994, pp. 12–16. Also see David Spener, "The Mexican Border Crossing Card and US Border Patrol Policy," paper prepared for the 1995 Meeting of the American Sociological Association. CIR reports that "INS issued 173,533 BCCs [Border Crossing Cards] in 1992 and 165,349 in 1993"; 9 of 10 of them went to Mexicans rather than Canadians. *U.S. Immigration Policy,* pp. 24–25.

27. Martínez, *Border Boom Town,* 101; Márquez, *Power and Politics,* 27, 28, says the U.S. Department of Labor called El Paso a "labor surplus area." Tito Alegría's later figures are cited in Bean et al., *Illegal Mexican Migration,* 30. Alicia Castellanos Gerrero, *Ciudad Juárez: La Vida Fronteriza* (Mexico City: Editorial Nuestro Tiempo, 1980), 137, 187, shows the continual movement back and forth across the border for work, visiting, and shopping in her sizable survey sample. Many Juárez workers have U.S. laborforce experience in their work histories.

28. Institute for Manufacturing and Materials Management, *Paso del Norte Regional Economy: Socioeconomic Profile 1993* (El Paso: University of Texas at El Paso, 1993), 3–1.

29. Martínez, *Border Boom Town,* 70, 86, 98. Also see Dale Beck Furnish, "Border Laws and Other Artificial Constraints," in *Rules of the Game and Games Without Rules in Border Life,* ed. Mario Miranda Pacheco and James W. Wilkie (Mexico: Asociación Nacional de Universidades Institutos de Enseñanza Superior, 1985). This is a theme in Castellanos, *Ciudad Juárez,* as well. Mexican businesses continue to treat northward shopping as something akin to treason; see below and Chapter 4.

30. Augusta Dwyer, *On the Line: Life on the US–Mexican Border* (New York: Monthly Review, 1994), 15–16. Also see Gay Young, ed., *The Social Ecology and Economic Development of Ciudad Juárez* (Boulder: Westview, 1986). Also see Alan Weisman, *La Frontera: The United States Border with Mexico* (New York: Harcourt Brace Jovanovich, 1986), 87–88, on René Mascareñas, another industrialist who served as municipal president. Leslie Sklair has done the definitive analysis on maquilas: *Assembling for Development: The Maquila Industry in Mexico and the United States* (La Jolla: Center for Mexican Studies, University of California at San Diego, 1993), esp. chap. 5. Chihuahua is maquila territory, Victor Orozco says in stark language; its capitalist groups have become auxiliaries for foreign investors. See "Chihuahua," in *La República Mexicana: Modernización y Democrácia de Aguascaliente a Zacatecas,* ed. Pablo González Casanova and Jorge

Cadena Roa (Mexico City: CIIH, Universidad Nacional Autónoma de México, 1994), 191–223; observation about auxiliaries on p. 204.

31. Suárez and Chávez, *Profile of the United States–Mexico Border*, 102. Maquilas have spawned a huge literature beginning with María Patricia Fernández-Kelly, *For We Are Sold, I and My People: Women and Industry in Mexico's Frontier* (Albany: SUNY Albany Press, 1983); and including Ellwyn Stoddard, *Maquila* (El Paso: Texas Western Press, 1987); Susan Tiano, *Patriarchy on the Line: Labor, Gender, and Ideology in the Mexican Maquiladora Industry* (Philadelphia: Temple University Press, 1993); Sklair, *Assembling for Development*; and Young, *Social Ecology and Economic Development*. Once, 80 percent of assembly workers were female, the figure has diminished somewhat, to 60 percent, according to Sklair and others, using figures from the industry.

32. José María Fernández, a municipal planner in Juárez, is cited in *Housing Production and Infrastructure in the Colonias of Texas and Mexico: A Cross Border Dialogue*, ed. Peter Ward, Synthesis/Memoria of the Bi-National Conference held May 5–6, 1995 (Austin: Mexican Center of ILAS, 1995), 40. The contested migration-maquila literature is taken up in subsequent chapters.

33. Priscilla Connolly, "The Politics of the Informal Sector: A Critique," in *Beyond Employment: Household, Gender, and Subsistence*, ed. Nanneke Redcliff and Enzo Mingione (London: Blackwell, 1985), 55–91.

34. Sanford Schram, *Words of Welfare: The Poverty of Social Science and the Social Science of Poverty* (Minneapolis: University of Minnesota Press, 1995). On the U.S. poverty line and its conceptual distortions over time, see Joel A. Devine and James D. Wright, *The Greatest of All Evils: Urban Poverty and the American Underclass* (New York: Aldine de Gruyter, 1993). Mexico's poverty line is measured in terms of ability "to purchase a minimum food basket of basic foodstuffs"; in 1992, 43.8 percent of the population lived in poverty, and 16.1 percent in extreme poverty. See Wayne Cornelius, "Designing Social Policy for Mexico's Liberalized Economy: From Social Services and Infrastructure to Job Creation," in *The Challenge of Institutional Reform in Mexico*, ed. Riordan Roett (Boulder: Lynne Rienner, 1995), 142.

35. Hector Venegas, Texas Workforce Commission, interview with the author, 1994. This figure is used in the *El Paso Times* as well. City planner Jesse Acosta puts the percentage earning the minimum wage in the low 30s. On a Mexican minimum standard, see Suárez and Chávez, *Profile of the United States–Mexico Border*, 70.

36. See note on Oscar Martínez in Jane E. Larson, "Free Markets Deep in the Heart of Texas," *Georgetown Law Review*, 84 (1995), 215. In an interview Beatriz Vera conducted for this research with a *regidor* in Juárez in April 1993, the undercount was connected to Mexico City's desire to keep vote counts low in this PANista territory.

37. Márquez, *Politics and Power*, 22.

38. Jeffery Brannon, "The Border Colonias," in *Memoria del Congreso Internacional sobre Fronteras en Iberoamérica Ayer y Hoy*, vol. 2, ed. Alfredo Félix Buenvostro Caballos (Mexicali: Universidad Autónoma de Baja California, 1990), 75–85; Towers, *Colonia Formation*.

39. David Garza, ethnographic journal, 1992.

40. Irma Carrillo, ethnographic journal, 1992.

41. Victoria Rodríguez and Peter M. Ward, *Policymaking, Politics, and Urban Governance in Chihuahua*, U.S. Mexican Policy Report no. 3 (Austin: University of Texas, Mexican Policy Studies Program, 1992). Also see Kathleen Staudt and Carlota Aguilar, "Political Parties, Women Activists' Agendas, and Class: Elections on Mexico's Northern Frontier," *Mexican Studies/Estudios Mexicanos* 8 (1992), 87–106, on the 1986 gubernatorial elections.

42. Suárez and Chávez, *Profile of the United States–Mexico Border*, 102; City of El Paso, Texas, Adopted Budget 1994–95. This does not include county and school budgets on the U.S. side.

43. Carol Zabin, "Building Community and Improving Quality of Life in the Mexican Border Region: An Analysis of NGOs and Grass Roots Organizations" (Rosslyn, Va: Inter-American Foundation, 1994), 5.

44. Bertha Caraveo Camarena, "El Problema de la Vivienda en Ciudad Juárez: Asentamientos Humanos Irregulares" (M.A. thesis, Universidad Autónoma de Ciudad Juárez, 1993), 46–48.

45. Alonso Pelayo, "Self-Help Housing on Irregular Urban Settlements in Juárez: The Case of Lucio Cabañas Neighborhood" (manuscript, Universidad Autónoma de Ciudad Juárez, 1993).

46. Social Development official, interviewed by Sylvia Peregrino and Alberto Esquinca, June 1995. Peregrino translated the term *chavos* as "punks"—a translation suggested by the official's tone and PAN's sentiment about the anarchist-Marxists who make up some of the CDP leadership. A copy of the Straight Citizen Code, discussed below, is in the author's possession.

47. Interviews by Peregrino and Esquinca, June 1995. First names here and elsewhere are pseudonyms.

48. Furnish, "Border Laws," cites official statistics. Research assistant and daily crosser Angélica Holguín noted the obtrusive presence of Banco Nacional staff trying to estimate losses to hometown shopping in 1993.

Chapter 4

1. Rubén Villapondo, "Justifica PRI Contrabando," *Norte de Ciudad Juárez*, December 7, 1993.

2. Henry Selby, A. D. Murphy, and S. A. Lorensen, *The Mexican Urban Household: Organizing for Self-Defense* (Austin: University of Texas Press, 1990), 71.

3. Saskia Sassen, *Cities in a World Economy* (Thousand Oaks: Pine Forge Press of Sage, 1995), 106–7.

4. Ray Bromley has used the term *casual labor* in some of his work. See Ray Bromley and Chris Gerry, *Casual Work and Poverty in Third World Cities* (New York: John Wiley, 1979).

5. International agencies and nongovernmental organizations (NGOs) have jumped on the microenterprise bandwagon. Enthusiasts range from the World Bank, the Interamerican Development Bank, and the United Nations Development Programme (UNDP) to such NGOs as the Grameen Bank, Women's World Banking, and Acción Internacional. On NGOs see María Otero, "The Role of Governments and Private Institutions in Addressing the Informal Sector in Latin America," in *Contrapunto: The Informal Sector Debate in Latin America*, ed. Cathy A. Rakowski (Albany: SUNY Albany Press, 1994), 177–98.

6. Secretaría del Trabajo y Previsión Social de Mexico (STPS) and U.S. Department of Labor (USDL), *The Informal Sector in Mexico*, Occasional Paper no. 1 (Mexico City and Washington, D.C.: STPS and USDL, 1992), 37b. Also see *The Underground Economy in the United States*. Occasional Paper no. 2.

7. Global evidence of gender inequity can be found in the United Nations Development Programme, *Human Development Report* (New York: Oxford University Press, 1995). On Mexico, see Alicia Ines Martínez Fernández, *Mujeres Latinoamericanas en Cifras: México* (Mexico: FLASCO, 1993), 51; Selby et al., *Mexican Urban Household*, 123, on women's earnings as 22 percent of men's; Bryan Roberts, "Enterprise and Labor Markets: The Border and the Metropolitan Areas," *Frontera Norte* 5, no. 9 (1993), 43, on an approximate 25 percent gap. According to 1992 U.S. Department of Labor statistics, women earn 70.6 percent of men's earnings in the full-time (formal) economy. Marta Tienda et al. found significant differences between native-born and immigrant women's earnings in "Immigration, Gender and the Process of Occupational Change in the United States, 1970–80," *International Migration Review* 18 (1984), 1021–44. In an insightful analysis that documents Dominican immigrant women's lower earnings and narrower range of occupational choices in relation to a group of comparable men, Sherri Grasmuck and Patricia R. Pessar examine women's seemingly paradoxical job satisfaction and rooting activities in the United States: "The conflict over return revolves around traditional gendered privileges for middle-class and upper-working-class men, privileges that migration has challenged and many men seek to regain back home." *Between Two Islands: Dominican International Migration* (Berkeley: University of California Press, 1991), 157, and see 186–94.

8. On informal work, see Alison MacEwen Scott, "Informal Sector or Female Sector? Gender Bias in Urban Labour Market Models," in *Male Bias in the Development Process*, ed. Diane Elson (Manchester: Manchester

University Press, 1991), 105–32, and comparative studies (Philippines, Ecuador, Zambia, and Hungary) documenting that women earn half of men's earnings in Caroline O. N. Moser, *Confronting Crisis: A Comparative Study on Household Responses to Poverty and Vulnerability in Four Poor Urban Communities,* Environmental Sustainability Development Studies, no. 8 (Washington, D.C.: World Bank, 1996), 4, 17, 33.

9. STPS/USDL, *Informal Sector,* 32a–b.

10. Roberts, "Enterprise," 46; Selby et al., *Mexican Urban Households,* chap. 6. This is also confirmed in my street vendor research, discussed below in this chapter. For earnings see Kathleen Staudt, "Struggles in Urban Space: Street Vendors in El Paso and Ciudad Juárez," *Urban Affairs Review* 31 (1996), 444. Judith Adler Hellman profiled in *Mexican Lives* several street- and home-based traders (the workers I call "self-employed informals" in this study) who could not afford to work in factories that paid minimum wages (New York: New Press, 1994).

11. Larissa Lomnitz, "Informal Exchange Networks in Formal Systems: A Theoretical Model," *American Anthropologist* 90 (1988), 42–55; Bruce Wiegand, *Off the Books: A Theory and Critique of the Underground Economy* (Dix Hills, N.Y.: General Hall, 1992); Vanessa Cartaya, "Informality and Poverty: Causal Relationship or Coincidence?" in Rakowski, *Contrapunto,* 223–50; Larissa Lomnitz, "Urban Women's Work in Three Social Strata: The Informal Economy of Social Networks and Social Capital," in *Color, Class and Country: Experiences of Gender,* ed. Gay Young and Bette J. Dickerson (London: Zed, 1994), 53–70.

12. Alonso Pelayo Martínez, "El Comercio de Automóviles en Juárez: Los Espacios de la Informalidad," paper presented at the Historia Regional Comparada, Universidad Autónoma de Ciudad Juárez, October 27–29, 1993; Staudt, "Struggles."

13. The literature is voluminous. See, for example, selections in Alejandro Portes, ed., *The Economic Sociology of Immigration: Essays on Networks, Ethnicity, and Entrepreneurship,* (New York: Russell Sage Foundation, 1995), Marilyn Halter, ed., *New Migrants in the Marketplace: Boston's Ethnic Entrepreneurs* (Amherst: University of Massachusetts Press, 1995); Howard Aldrich and Robin Ward, *Immigrant Business in Industrial Societies* (Newbury Park, Calif.: Sage, 1990); Ivan Light et al., "Beyond the Ethnic Enclave Economy," *Social Problems* 41, (1994), 65–80; Ivan Light and Parminder Bhachu, *Immigration and Entrepreneurship: Cultures, Capital, and Ethnic Networks* (New Brunswick: Transaction Books, 1993); Edna Bonacich and John Modell, *The Economic Basis of Ethnic Solidarity* (Berkeley: University of California Press, 1980).

14. Frank Bean et al., *Illegal Mexican Migration and the United States/Mexico Border: The Effects of Operation Hold the Line on El Paso/Juárez,* report prepared for the CIR, July 15, 1994.

I avoid using the word *alien,* and consequently the label *resident alien,* because of the extraterrestrial images the word conjures up. Public officials and others are comfortable with this terminology: for example, Peter Brimelow, author of *Alien Nation* (New York: Random House, 1995), and Hollywood inventors of stories about outer-space landings in the United States, including one with, coincidentally, the same title as Brimelow's book.

15. Louise Lamphere, "Introduction: The Shaping of Diversity," in *Structuring Diversity: Ethnographic Perspectives on the New Immigration,* ed. Louise Lamphere (Chicago: University of Chicago Press, 1991), 4.

16. Staudt, "Struggles." *Invasion* is the politically charged word in Spanish, used for both irregular housing settlements and street vendors. My clippings file from the Juárez newspapers contains approximately 150 vendor items; Juárez media even cover El Paso street vendors. The El Paso papers lack regular coverage of street vendors on the "other side."

17. STPS/USDL, *The Underground Economy,* 18–20. Also see Wiegand, *Off the Books,* on internal IRS studies.

18. Joan Moore and Raquel Pinderhughes use the stigma terminology in their introduction to *In the Barrios: Latinos and the Underclass Debate* (New York: Russell Sage, 1993), xxvii. Regina Austin, in "'The Black Community,' Its Lawbreakers, and a Politics of Identification," *Southern California Law Review* 65 (1992), 1768–817, uses the considerable body of journalistic sources on street vendors. It is important to recognize that no good lists exist from which to draw random samples of vendors, for most members of this changing trader group do not register with the government. Consequently, most samples are small and/or purposefully drawn. Roberta Spalter-Roth analyzes seventy-five vendors in "The Sexual Political Economy of Street Vending in Washington, D.C.," in *Traders versus the State: Anthropological Approaches to Unofficial Economies,* ed. Gracia Clark (Boulder: Westview, 1988), 165–87. Yvonne V. Jones analyzes sixteen vendors in "Street Peddlers as Entrepreneurs: Economic Adaptation to an Urban Area," in *Urban Anthropology* 17 (1988), 143–70. John Gaber's research involved "hanging-out"; see "Manhattan's 14th Street Vendors' Market: Informal Street Peddlers' Complementary Relationship with New York City's Economy," *Urban Anthropology* 23 (1994), 373–408. On indirect estimates, most of which come from economists, see Philip Mattera, who calls this the "ten percent solution" in *Off the Books: The Rise of the Underground Economy* (New York: St. Martin's Press, 1985), 53. Also see Morton Paglin, "The Underground Economy: New Estimates from Household Income and Expenditure Surveys," in *Yale Law Journal* 103 (1994), 2249, whose figures for percentages of personal income and of GDP hover near 10 percent.

Interested readers can visit the open-air-markets web page, on whose informal board of directors I serve (http://www.openair.org/). It contains considerable academic citations and annotations, as well as alerts on markets under threat.

19. These and other bar-graph findings were first presented in Kathleen Staudt, "Politics of Everyday Life: Informality at the U.S.–Mexico Border," at the Southwest Political Science Association Meetings, Dallas, March 24, 1995. At the time, thirty-six questionnaires had yet to be coded. The rough proportions are not expected to vary, however, as they were spread across neighborhoods.

20. The first and second bar graphs do not have an additive value, but there is overlap in ways that would be difficult to unthread, most especially for the full-time informals like maids and Juárez street vendors.

21. Roberto Díaz Molina discusses this concession in a lengthy interview with Javier Arroyo, "Fundador del CDP, Maestro de la Vieja y Aguerrida Guardia," *Norte de Ciudad Juárez*, June 13, 1994. Although this concession from PRI is useful, Díaz says he is a *perredista* (a member of the leftist PRD, which broke away from the PRI) *"de corazón"* ("at heart").

Beatriz Vera conducted interviews and observed CDP leaders for a full day. None would admit to involvement in providing protection for informal traders and *fayuca* commerce, though this is common knowledge among former CDPistas and academics in Juárez. See Rubén Lau Rojo, "El Sector Informal y el CDP," *Noesis* 6–7 (January–December 1991), 45–52, and his "Política, Economía, y la Tenencia de la Tierra," paper presented at the University of Texas at El Paso, March 1992. An interview with attorney Jorge Ruíz, Juárez, 1993, provided much information on monetary limits at the border. The topic of monetary caps for goods borderlanders could "import" was heavily covered in the press on both sides of the border as well.

22. Andrew A. Skolnick, "Along US Southern Border, Pollution, Poverty, Ignorance, and Greed Threaten Nation's Health," *JAMA* 273(May 17, 1995), 1478–82; on drug-resistant tuberculosis, possibly due to use of over-the-counter medication, see p. 1480. Pharmacists warn about this brisk business, concerned not only about the health implications, but about the survival of their very businesses. See "Over-the-Border Drugs," *American Medical News*, February 19, 1996, pp. 11–12; and Gary W. Thompson, "Border Crossing: Pharmacists Fear for Patients' Health, Their Own Survival," *Pharmacy West*, June 1995, pp. 19–22. Thompson, p. 21, cites some examples: a month's supply of Zantac costs $85.00 in El Paso, $18.95 in Juárez; of Retin A, $20.00 versus $3.97. Ronald J. Vogel compares both prescription drugs and medical acute-care prices in "Crossing the Border for Health Care: An Exploratory Analysis of Consumer Choice," *Journal of Borderlands Studies* 10 (1995), 41–42: for Ventolin (an inhaler), $19.48 versus $3.76 (1992 prices); for a caesarean section, $6,926 versus $2,010 (1988 prices).

23. David Spener makes the most thorough analysis of cross-border (formal) small businesses in *Entrepreneurship and Small-Scale Enterprise*

in the Texas Border Region: A Sociocultural Perspective (Ph.D. diss., University of Texas at Austin, 1995). Also see his "Small Firms, Social Capital, and Global Commodity Chains: Some Lessons from the Tex–Mex Border in the Era of Free Trade," in *Latin America and the World Economy*, ed. Roberto Patricio Korzeniewicz and William C. Smith (Westport, Conn.: Greenwood, 1996).

24. In his official testimony before the U.S. Commission on Immigration Reform on March 17, 1994, Pete Duarte, chief executive officer of Thomason Hospital/El Paso, said that it was very difficult to determine the number of noncitizens served because law prohibits such queries. Half of El Paso's births occur at this county hospital; the total in 1993 was 7,029. The hospital's best guess of cost of care for the undocumented is 3 to 5 percent of the annual operational budget (Duarte testimony, p. 3). Figures are kept on emergency admissions and births. The Emergency Care Department transfers fewer than 100 stabilized patients to Juárez hospitals annually. Two very rough birth barometers provide other clues: 15–30 percent of women claimed false addresses (vacant lots; nonexistent homes) in one El Paso zip code studied by home health workers; when pre- Blockade (October 1992) and post-Blockade (October 1993) admissions are compared, those for emergencies went down less than 1 percent, while those for deliveries went up 6.8 percent. If the Blockade had been effective, we would expect deliveries to be down. The Blockade does not affect movement via BCCs, the crack in any immigration control strategy. As this book makes clear, the border has long been leaky for an official reason: the demand for labor and customers, as expressed both in poor immigration enforcement and the issuance of BCCs.

25. The conference and this charge were widely reported in Mexico City and regional city media. See Staudt, "Struggles."

26. Gregory Rocha analyzes these data in great detail; see "Entrepreneurship on the U.S.–Mexican Border: A Spatial Analysis of Informal Economic Businesses in El Paso and Juárez," paper presented to the Association of Borderlands Scholars, April 28, 1995, Oakland.

27. Staudt, "Struggles," 439.

28. David Garza, ethnographic journal, 1992. Some jobs continue to be excluded from minimum-wage coverage. The number of hours worked affects whether Social Security tax is supposed to be paid.

29. I am grateful to Veronica Martínez for administering these interviews. Well after the research was completed, I discovered a book by Alicia Castellanos Gerrero at the public (not university) library: *Ciudad Juárez: La Vida Fronteriza* (Mexico City: Editorial Nuestro Tiempo, 1980). In her pre-GATT (pre-1986) sample, she identified seven *fayuqueras:* one abandoned work after twelve years because of chronic problems with Mexican customs agents; three had lived and worked in the United States previously;

see pp. 189–92. Among Hellman's profiles in *Mexican Lives* are several people with *fayuca* experience.

The sample in our research found mostly mature women engaged in this work. Researchers and human rights advocates would do well to document Mexican border agents' abuses, not just those of the U.S. agents. These go beyond monetary corruption: for example, the not-fatherly labeling of young female "friends" as *amigitas* to seek favors for *soditas* (colloquial euphemisms, from anecdotal evidence 1996).

30. See Lau, "Política, Economía," 1992, on markets; Charles Mann et al., *Seeking Solutions: Framework and Cases for Small Enterprise Development Programs* (Hartford, Conn.: Kumarian Press, 1989). Also see *Grassroots Development*, an Inter-American Foundation journal.

31. Thanks to Luis Aguirre for conducting these interviews.

32. Aguirre interviewed her as well. The *lideresa* is featured in a local PRI magazine (*Revista los Principales de Chihuahua*, no. 51 [1992], 18–27), but her international business experiences go unrevealed in this sweet homage, "Quíen es Quíen en Ciudad Juárez: Perfil de una Mujer . . ."

33. NAFTA negotiations and documents were silent on used goods, with one exception: in a U.S. congressional document, "North American Free Trade Agreement—Mexico's Political and Legal Environment," a constituent testified that Mexican customs shot at and stalked relief workers, impounding 9,000 sweaters for Chiapas. Hearing before the Committee on Small Business, House of Representatives, 133rd Congress, First Session, Washington, D.C., February 25, 1993.

Joan Anderson and Martin de la Rosa, "Economic Survival Strategies of Poor Families on the Mexican Border," *Journal of Borderlands Studies* 4 (1991), 51–68, discuss the "economy of discards" in clothing, appliances, construction materials, and automobiles. On a grimmer note, Patricia Giovine interviews Juárez women who sell blood at one of three El Paso plasma centers in "Vender la Sangre . . . Para Cientos de Juarenses, la Venta de Plasma se ha Convertido en usa de sus Principales Fuentes Ingresos," *Diario de Juárez*, August 21, 1995. One of the women Hellman profiles in *Mexican Lives*, 152–59, vividly describes her *por libra* purchases.

34. The new peripheries are discussed in Chapters 6 and 7; immigration is more relevant theoretically in U.S. settings. Only one Central American family was identified in the Juárez sample.

35. In the new periphery maquila bedroom community, only four households had adults born in Juárez. Some previous studies dismiss the maquila migration connection on the basis of very narrow survey questions, such as "Did you migrate to work in maquilas?" I consider the behavior more significant than the survey response. So do Gay Young and Lucia Fort, who find that three-fourths of their maquila worker sample were born elsewhere, compared with half of comparable nonmaquila workers:

"Household Responses to Economic Change: Migration and *Maquiladora* Work in Ciudad Juárez, Mexico," *Social Science Quarterly* 75 (1994) 661.

36. These and other direct quotations come from the household interviews. "Papers" (*papeles*) is the regional colloquialism for legal immigration documents. First names here and elsewhere are all pseudonyms.

37. This study did *not* solicit information on false residence claims and Social Security numbers, fraud in seeking earned income tax credit, or use of U.S. mail drops to secure needs-based assistance. See selections on federal and state policy in the Urban Institute collection, *Immigration and Ethnicity*, esp. chap. 10: Wendy Zimmermann and Michael Fix, "Immigrant Policy in the States: A Wavering Welcome," which contrasts the miserly Texas and generous Massachusetts approaches (Washington, D.C.: Urban Institute, 1994).

38. CIR, *U.S. Immigration Policy: Restoring Credibility* (Washington, D.C.: CIR, 1994), 114. Chapter 5 in this book looks at new periphery residents addressing their housing problems through savings and self-sufficiency. See selections in Abraham Lowenthal, ed., *The California–Mexico Connection* (Princeton: Princeton University Press, 1993).

39. Grace Kao and Marta Tienda, "Optimism and Achievement: The Educational Performance of Immigrant Youth," *Social Science Quarterly* 76 (1995), 1–19; Margaret A. Gibson and John U. Ogbu, eds., *Minority Status and Schooling: A Comparative Study of Immigrant and Involuntary Minorities* (New York: Garland, 1991). The pattern of first- and second-generation achievement may be ending; William Finnegan, "The New Americans," *New Yorker*, March 25, 1996, pp. 52–71, describes an anomie among immigrant youth that "is not third world but thoroughly American" (p. 68).

40. The U.S. Department of Housing and Urban Development (HUD) decided to enforce existing rules to exclude the undocumented from housing subsidies: assistant director of the El Paso Housing Authority, interviewed by the author, May 1996. Various contributors to the Urban Institute collection, *Immigration and Ethnicity*, analyze the self-sufficiency assumptions of historic immigration policy, along with the way it discourages public ward status.

41. José Moreno, director, Migrant and Refugee Services, Catholic Archdiocese of El Paso, presentation to the author's seminar on border policy, September 1993. (Video on file with author.)

42. Barbara Nelson, "Women's Poverty and Women's Citizenship," *Signs* 9 (1984), 209–29. Also see Pierrette Hondagneu-Sotelo, *Gendered Transitions: Mexican Experiences of Immigration* (Berkeley: University of California, 1994), on twenty-six families.

43. Quotations from household interviews. Pablo Vila notes the significance of the image of the *nopal* (a cactus) to denote a thoroughly Mexican

look, along with its symbolism in Aztec heritage: *Everyday Life, Culture and Identity on the Mexican-American Border: The Ciudad Juárez–El Paso Case* (Ph.D. diss., University of Texas at Austin, 1994), 197 n. 10. A published version is forthcoming from the University of Texas at Austin Press.

44. From Kathleen Staudt, "Struggles in Urban Space: Street Vendors in El Paso and Ciudad Juárez," paper prepared for the Latin American Studies Association Conference, Atlanta, Georgia, March 1994. The conflict itself is analyzed in *Urban Affairs Review:* Staudt, "Struggles."

Chapter 5

1. Douglas S. Massey and Nancy A. Denton, *American Apartheid: Segregation and the Making of the Underclass* (Cambridge: Harvard University Press, 1993).

2. Duncan Earle offered a presentation on *colonias* and a list of definitions, some of them hyperbolic, to my International Politics graduate seminar, Summer 1995.

3. Pablo Vila, *Everyday Life, Culture and Identity on the Mexican-American Border: The Ciudad Juárez–El Paso Case* (Ph.D. diss., University of Texas at Austin, 1994; Austin: University of Texas Press, forthcoming).

4. U.S. General Accounting Office (GAO), *Rural Development: Problems and Progress of Colonia Subdivisions near Mexico Border*, RCED-91–37 (Washington, D.C.: GAO, 1990), 10, 23 (map). Jane E. Larson, "Free Markets Deep in the Heart of Texas," *Georgetown Law Journal* 84 (1995), 179–260, cites the lower figure for settlements (151), but a similar number (73,000) of residents. The point is, officials and advocates pursue the same sort of numerical guesswork as countries in the south and international development agencies. Only two years earlier, the GAO reported 15,000 in 80 El Paso *colonias: Health Care: Available in the Texas–Mexico Border Area*, HRD 89–12 (Washington, D.C.: GAO, 1989), 18. At the National Association of Attorneys General (NAAG) "Niños de las Colonias Conference," March 10–11, 1995, El Paso, Texas, documents were distributed with considerable information about *colonias* and their growth (up 22 percent since 1992 in El Paso County, according to tax records for 122 subdivisions, p. 17). The Texas State Attorney General Office and Texas Water Development Board reported on the board's data base and the AG's "Colonia Strike Force," which initiates investigations and litigation over *colonia*-relevant lawsuits (p. 8). The Louisiana comparison is found on p. 2. Since 1989, the state legislature has increased monitoring and regulation of *colonias* through a carrot and stick approach: if county commissioner courts do not adopt model subdivision rules (relating mainly to roads, bridges, and drainage), they are ineligible for Economic District Area Program (EDAP) money. See Larson, "Free Markets," on legal details. Another source, using secondary materials, is Dianne C. Betts and Daniel J. Slottje, *Crisis on the*

Rio Grande: Poverty, Unemployment, and Economic Development on the Texas–Mexico Border (Boulder: Westview Press, 1994).

5. George Towers, *Colonia Formation and Economic Restructuring in El Paso, Texas* (Ph.D. diss., University of Arizona, 1991), as discussed in Chapter 3.

6. Texas Department of Human Services (DHS), *The Colonias Factbook: A Survey of Living Conditions of Rural Areas in South and West Texas Border Counties* (Austin: DHS, 1988).

7. Oscar Martínez, *Border Boom Town: Ciudad Juárez since 1848* (Austin: University of Texas Press, 1978). This theme is threaded throughout Vila, *Everyday Life*. In a recent journalistic treatment, based on 600 interviews, Andres Oppenheimer distances the north and its relatively free press from an otherwise grim account. See *Bordering on Chaos: Guerrillas, Stockbrokers, Politicians, and Mexico's Road to Prosperity* (Boston: Little Brown, 1996).

8. Debbie Nathan, *Women and Other Aliens: Essays from the U.S.–Mexico Border* (El Paso: Cinco Puntos Press, 1987), 24.

9. Other literary examples, besides Nathan, include Ben Sáenz, *Flowers for the Broken* (Seattle: Broken Moon Press, 1993) and *Carry Me Like Water* (New York: Harper, 1995), as well as José Antonio Burciaga, *Spilling the Beans: Lotería Chicana* (Santa Barbara: Joshua Odell, 1995), with several essays that touch on this theme. For almost a century of ordinary people's poetry put to music in *corridos*, see María Herrera-Sobek, *Northward Bound: The Immigration Experience in Ballad and Song* (Bloomington: Indiana University Press, 1993).

10. Paul Strelson was the principal of the Bowie High School. Also see the documentary *The Time Has Come* (1996).

11. These and the following quotations are from the 1992 household interviews. Jessica Santascoy's ethnographic journal is cited.

12. *Phyler v. Doe*, 457 U.S. 202 (1982).

13. William Siembieda, an urban planner at the University of New Mexico who has studied land values, remarks that Juárez prices are higher than those on the New Mexico side in *BorderLines* 2 (1994): Juárez acre = $43,000–87,000 versus $6,000–12,000 in Doña Ana County at the southern border of New Mexico. Siembieda's presentation is also condensed in *Memoria of the Bi-national Conference: Housing Production and Infrastructure in the Colonias of Texas and Mexico* (Austin: Mexican Center of ILAS, University of Texas at Austin, 1995).

14. Alan Gilbert is the housing analyst who most forcefully argues for its inclusion as a category of informality in the introduction to his edited volume, *Housing and Land in Urban Mexico* (La Jolla, Calif.: Center for U.S.–Mexico Studies, University of California at San Diego, no. 31, 1989).

15. *A Mitad del Camino* (Juárez: Gobierno Municipal, 1994), 19–27.

From Rubén Lau, "Política, Economía Informal y Tenencia de la Tierra: El Caso de Ciudad Juárez" (manuscript, 1992), 15, listing 27 CDP *colonias*, and Bertha Caraveo Camarena, "El Problema de la Vivienda en Ciudad Juárez: Asentamientos Humanos Irregulares" M.A. thesis, Universidad Autónoma de Ciudad Juárez, 1993), 46–48, it is possible to construct a list of the CDP-controlled irregular settlements and match them with the PAN government's actions, as reported in their own propaganda and in the media.

16. Lawrence Herzog, *Where North Meets South: Cities, Space, and Politics on the U.S.–Mexico Border* (Austin: University of Texas Press, 1990), 85–87.

17. Henry Selby, A.D. Murphy, and S.A. Lorensen, *The Mexican Urban Household: Organizing for Self-Defense* (Austin: University of Texas Press, 1990), 12.

18. Victoria Rodríguez, "Urban Planning Policy in Mexico: The Case of Ciudad Juárez" (M.A. thesis, University of Texas at El Paso, 1981), 121, 129.

19. *A Mitad del Camino*, 40–41, projects the change; Javier de la Fuente was interviewed by the author, March 1996. Thanks also to Gordon Cook, former economic development director for the City of El Paso and currently at the university's Institute for Materials, Manufacturing, Management, for many conversations on this topic.

20. David Crowder, "From New Toilets to Fences, City Requires Permits," *El Paso Times*, May 30, 1995.

21. *A Mitad del Camino*, 44–46; the data bank was also described in detail in several interviews with Juárez officials conducted by Beatriz Vera, spring 1993.

22. World Bank, *Juárez: Urban Issues Survey* (Washington, D.C.: World Bank, 1991), 11.

23. Ibid., 4, 11.

24. Reported ibid., 8–9.

25. Selby et al., *Mexican Urban Households*, p. 21.

26. Betts and Slottje, *Crisis on the Rio Grande*, 67; Larson, "Free Markets."

Chapter 6

1. For the best analysis of water, drawing on interviews and documents from Servicios de Agua y Drenaje de Monterrey, see Vivienne Bennett, *The Politics of Water: Urban Protest, Gender, and Power in Monterrey, Mexico* (Pittsburgh: University of Pittsburgh Press, 1995).

2. Ibid.; and see Alan Gilbert, ed. *Housing and Land in Urban Mexico* (La Jolla, Calif.: Center for U.S.–Mexico Studies, University of California at San Diego, no. 31, 1989), and Joe Foweraker and Anne L. Craig, eds., *Popular Movements and Political Change in Mexico* (Boulder: Lynne Rienner, 1990); Susan Eckstein, "Poor People Versus the State and Capital: Anatomy

of a Successful Community Mobilization for Housing in Mexico City," *International Journal of Urban and Regional Research* 14 (1990), 274–96; Carlos Vélez-Ibañez, *Rituals of Marginality* (Berkeley: University of California Press, 1983).

3. Tonatiuh Guillén, "Servicios Públicos y Marginalidad en la Frontera Norte," *Frontera Norte* 2 (1990), 95–120.

4. Cited in World Bank, *Juárez: Urban Issues Survey* (Washington, D.C.: World Bank, 1991), 8–9.

5. Nancy Lowery, program coordinator, Center for Environmental Resource Management, University of Texas at El Paso, interviewed by the author, June 1995. Thanks also to C. Richard Bath, environmental policy expert at the University of Texas at El Paso, for many conversations over the years about these issues. On September 30, 1997, the Border Environment Cooperation Commission (BECC) approved support.

6. Jeffery Brannon, "The Border Colonias," in *Memoria del Congreso Internacional sobre Fronteras en Iberoamérica Ayer y Hoy,* vol. 2, ed. Alfredo Félix Buenvostro Caballos (Mexicali: Universidad Autónoma de Baja California, 1990); George William Towers, *Colonia Formation and Economic Restructuring in El Paso, Texas* (Ph.D. diss., University of Arizona, 1991). Numbers and information on current policy as implemented come from my interview with the Assistant Director of El Paso's Housing Authority, June 1996. Additionally, 3,000 households receive federal subsidies that they pay to private landlords. Federal changes in housing policy have provided incentives to transform housing "projects" into "apartments" through demolition/reconstruction and renovation. One such pilot effort is in operation in El Paso, and several are on the drawing board. Meanwhile, yearly renewal of leases in projects and enforcement of regulations that deny subsidies to noncitizens put such households under fairly strict surveillance.

7. Towers, *Colonia Formation;* Jane E. Larson, "Free Markets Deep in the Heart of Texas," *Georgetown Law Journal,* 84 (1995), 179–260. See Chapter 5.

8. Larson, "Free Markets."

9. John Peterson, *Whose History? Whose Place? A Cultural History of the Lower Rio Grande Valley of El Paso* (Ph.D. diss., University of Texas at Austin, 1993), 565.

10. National Association of Attorneys General, "Niños de las Colonias Conference," March 10–11, 1995, El Paso, Texas, p. 10. Fundraising and repayment through public bonds are subject to voters' approval, for residents are responsible for the long-term payoff, which adds to their expenses. Few turn out to vote on bonds, however. When a $14 million bond (allowing a $72 state and federal grant buy-in) went on the ballot on June 8, 1996, a majority of 1,020 of 12,000 registered voters approved the measure (*El Paso*

Times, June 9, 1996, "Lower Valley Approves Bond Issue") in an area with 40,000 residents. If we assume that roughly half the residents are adults, a tenth of the potential electorate turned out.

11. Rodolfo O. de la Garza and Louis de Sipio, eds., *Ethnic Ironies: Latino Politics in the 1992 Elections* (Boulder: Westview, 1996), 1, 5. Also see Valerie J. Martínez, "Unrealized Expectations: Latinos and the 1992 Elections in Texas," 113–30 in that collection, esp. 114, 119. See also C. Richard Bath and Roberto Villarreal, "Politics in El Paso del Norte" (manuscript, 1993).

12. Sidney Verba and Norman Nie, *Participation in America* (New York: Harper & Row, 1972).

13. Roberto Villarreal, "EPISO and Political Empowerment: Organizational Politics in a Border City," *Journal of Borderlands Studies* 3 (1988), 81–96.

14. James Q. Wilson, *Political Organizations* (New York: Basic Books, 1973; 2nd ed., Princeton: Princeton University Press, 1995).

15. See Bennett, *Politics of Water;* Gilbert, *Housing and Land;* Foweraker and Craig, *Popular Movements;* Eckstein, "Poor People"; and Vélez-Ibañez, *Rituals of Marginality.*

16. Alonso Pelayo, "Self-Help Housing on Irregular Urban Settlements in Juárez: The Case of Lucio Cabañas Neighborhood" (manuscript, Universidad Autónoma de Ciudad Juárez, 1993); Paul Haber, "Cárdenas, Salinas and the Urban Popular Movement," in *Mexico: Dilemmas of Transition,* ed. Neil Harvey (London: British Academic Press, 1993), 218–48; Bennett, *Politics of Water,* 77, also discusses the "clandestine faucets" in Monterrey.

17. Victoria Rodríguez and Peter M. Ward, *Policymaking, Politics, and Urban Governance in Chihuahua: The Experience of Recent PANista Governments* (Austin: University of Texas, U.S. Mexican Policy Report no. 3, 1992). In "National Solidarity in the Northern Borderlands: Social Participation and Community Leadership," Oscar F. Contreras and Vivienne Bennett report astonishingly high knowledge about the program (over 90 percent), but limited information about of specific organizational details. In *Transforming State–Society Relations in Mexico: The National Solidarity Strategy,* ed. Wayne A. Cornelius, Ann L. Craig, and Jonathan Fox (La Jolla, Calif.: Center for U.S.–Mexican Studies, University of California at San Diego, 1994), 287.

18. *A Mitad del Camino* (Juárez: Gobierno Municipal, 1994), 25–27. See Chapter 5 on housing and Chapter 7 on policy, and Boxes 5 and 6.

19. Thanks to Angélica Holguín for conducting these interviews, along with related interviews with Social Development Department staff, 1992–93.

20. Peter M. Ward, "Political Pressure for Urban Services: The Response of Two Mexico City Administrations," *Development and Change* 12 (1991), 379–408.

21. Rodríguez and Ward, *Policymaking.*

22. See selections in Victoria Rodríguez and Peter M. Ward, eds., *Opposition Government in Mexico* (Albuquerque: University of New Mexico Press, 1995).

23. See Chapter 7 as well. At 47,563 new pesos a month (6–7 new pesos = 1 dollar), the PAN governor earns a salary comparable to that of the U.S. president if salary and *nómina confidencial* ("confidential pay") are combined. Once this was made public in "Revela Barrio su Sueldo," *Norte de Ciudad Juárez*, January 15, 1995, and other media, he said that his compensation was comparable to that of the previous PRI governor but that he would, as a moral gesture, voluntarily give up 15 percent of the total. Compare this equivalence at the top to the 10:1, 5:1, and 2:1 ratios reported for U.S. and Mexican GNP, minimum wages, and income of border informals, reported in Chapter 4.

24. Magda Alarcón conducted these interviews, in spring 1993. Interestingly, EPISO was founded by a nun.

25. See Chapter 7 on the Texas university program.

26. The Forgotten Colonias Union is described in Peter M. Ward et al., *Memoria of the Bi-National Conference: Housing Production and Infrastructure in the Colonias of Texas and Mexico* (Austin: Mexican Center of ILAS, University of Texas at Austin, 1995), 33. In my interview with the director of the Border Association for Refugees and Colonia Advocacy (BARCA), July 1, 1996, Ninfa Ochoa Krueger discussed how South Texas *colonia* women organize themselves, as taxpayers, to have a collective voice in how money is spent at county levels.

27. In his comparative study of Los Angeles and San Antonio, *Mexican-Americans: The Ambivalent Minority*, Peter Skerry discusses the difficulties of organizing recent immigrants, who, despite employment and discrimination problems, may be relatively satisfied with housing and cities compared with what is available at home (New York: Free Press, 1993), 74. This is the same point Carlos Monsiváis makes in "Dreaming of Utopia," *NACLA Report on the Americas*, special report: "The Immigration Backlash," 29, no. 3 (1995), 39–41.

Chapter 7

1. Kathy Ferguson, *The Feminist Case Against Bureaucracy* (Philadelphia: Temple University Press, 1984), 123–24, has a three-part scheme on dominating bureaucratic interaction that comprises clients, constituents, and consumers.

2. John Logan and Harvey L. Molotch, *Urban Fortunes: The Political Economy of Place* (Berkeley: University of California Press, 1987).

3. Peter K. Eisinger, *The Rise of the Entrepreneurial State: State and Local Economic Development Policy in the United States* (Madison: University of Wisconsin Press, 1988), 36.

4. *Seeds Across the Border: Proceedings of a Women and Development Conference, October 30, 1995* (Ciudad Juárez: FEMAP, 1996), 5. I have served for three years in the Seeds Across the Border initiative, attending meetings and interacting with staff and participants. Data are being collected for women at different points of the cycle.

5. *Seeds*, 16. This single comment should not lead readers to conclude that household harmony necessarily increases with women's income earning. Some *banqueras'* husbands have felt threatened.

6. *Ibid.*, 17.

7. *Ibid.*, 23.

8. Carlota Aguilar, "Mexico's Social Policy: Levels of Marginality of Female Prostitutes in Ciudad Juárez" (M.A. thesis, University of Texas at El Paso, 1985).

9. *Seeds*, 19. The same metaphor was used in El Paso household interviews as well. The comment reveals some anguish about the lack of support among people of common heritage.

10. *Seeds*, 32. The state capital is a five-hour drive to the south. FEMAP has forty-four chapters all over Mexico.

11. "La Persecución de las Mujeres," *Diario de Juárez*, April 10, 1996. Despite his populist presentation, the municipal president refused to meet with the women, although he welcomed the opportunity to meet with the FEMAP president.

12. Dr. José Gómez de León, in *Seeds*, 15.

13. Margaret Schellenberg, "Seeds Across the Border: The FEMAP Experience with Community Banks in Cd. Juárez and El Paso" (M.A. thesis, University of Texas at El Paso, 1995). Margaret, a close colleague, has been involved with the Seeds initiative, working primarily with the FEMAP Foundation on the U.S. side.

14. Kermit Black's comments are summarized in Peter M. Ward et al., *Memoria of the Bi-National Conference: Housing Production and Infrastructure in the Colonias of Texas and Mexico* (Austin: Mexican Center of ILAS, University of Texas at Austin, 1995), 60–61.

15. FEMAP Foundation people, Helenmarie Zachritz and Kym Hemley, Guadalaharan anthropology professor Patricia Safa Barraza, and I had conversations about this paradox in January 1996. Cultural baggage may explain why U.S.-resident women with origins in south-central Mexico depart from the individualist predispositions of northern Mexicans. Also see Pablo Vila on the many ways northerners distance themselves from southerners: *Everyday Life, Culture, and Identity on the Mexican-American Border: The Ciudad Juárez–El Paso Case* (Ph.D. diss., University of Texas at Austin, 1994; Austin: University of Texas Press, forthcoming).

16. PANista *regidor* for the economy, interviewed by Beatriz Vera, April 6, 1993.

17. *Seeds,* 23.

18. Thanks to Jeannette Johnson-Licón for a semester project involving interviews, document collection, and analysis on the SBA. SBA has a microenterprise lending grant program, but changing criteria over the years made it difficult to apply: El Paso was not among those cities eligible one year; in another year, awards were expected to go only to those NGOs with track records. Meanwhile, Acción Internacional has opened several micro-enterprise lending projects in the United States, including El Paso. It draws on the leverage and tenuous good will of banks that are obliged to invest in their locality under the Community Reinvestment Act.

19. Siglo XXI is a twenty-first-century planning effort publicized in special newspaper inserts and articles. For the male-industrial visual, see "De Juárez 4 de las 500," *Diario de Juarez,* August 30, 1995.

20. The epigraph is from Jordi Borja, "Past, Present, and Future of Local Government in Latin America," in *Rethinking the Latin American City,* ed. Richard M. Morse and Jorge Hardoy (Baltimore: Johns Hopkins University Press, 1992).

21. Interview with the *Regidor* for the economy.

22. Director of municipal commerce, interviewed by Beatriz Vera, April 1, 1993.

23. CANACINTRA General Secretary discussed social security oversight in an interview conducted by Beatriz Vera, April 24, 1993.

24. Interview with the director of municipal commerce.

25. Ramón Galindo, dialogue following speech to a Spanish language section of the required introductory political science class, fall 1994.

26. Interview with the director of municipal commerce.

27. Kathleen Staudt, "Struggles in Urban Space: Street Vendors in El Paso and Juárez," *Urban Affairs Review* 31 (1996), 446. The municipal commerce director also spoke of donations in the interview.

28. Staudt, "Struggles."

29. I attended these meetings for a day and a half in November 1993.

30. Sanitary chief, Department of Health, interviewed by Beatriz Vera, March 26, 1993.

31. Municipal engineer, Public Inspection Department, interviewed by Beatriz Vera, March 25, 1993. I also thank María de la Luz Valverde, who read municipal codebooks obtained by Patricia Luna with support from the Center for Inter-American and Border Studies, 1991. Valverde found loopholes and contradictory guidelines in the codebooks. For the purposes of this research, the enforced, rather than the written, policy is of interest. To obtain government documents in Mexico is a special challenge, for libraries are not repositories for general users.

32. Director of human settlements, interviewed by Beatriz Vera, March

30, 1993. World Bank, *Juárez: Urban Issues Survey* (Washington, D.C.: World Bank, 1991), pp. v, 11, 22.

33. Interview with director of human settlements; general secretary of CANACINTRA, interviewed by Beatriz Vera, April 24, 1993.

34. Interview with director of human settlements; also in *A Mitad del Camino* (Juárez: Gobierno Municipal, 1994).

35. Director of municipal commerce, interviewed by Beatriz Vera, April 1, 1993. The director of human settlements also spoke of negotiations.

36. "Revelan Nómina Secreta," *Diario de Juárez*, January 20, 1995, reporting a monthly salary of 12,419 new pesos, when 6–7 new pesos = $1. El Paso City Council members currently receive $16,500 annually. The published budgets in Mexico are functionally based, making salaries hard to discern.

37. City of El Paso Office of Economic Development packet, 1993. On the ranking, see Lawrence J. R. Herson and John M. Bolland, *The Urban Web: Politics, Policy, and Theory* (Chicago: Nelson Hall, 1990), 322. My interview was with an El Paso city councilman, spring 1992.

38. Health personnel and director, West Texas Office of the State Comptroller, El Paso, interviewed by the author, spring 1992.

39. Mike Fujimoto and Madeline Janis, "Report of the Task Force on Street Vending in Los Angeles" (manuscript, 1990).

40. Jerome Greenberg et al., "The Itinerant Street Vendor: A Form of Nonstore Retailing," *Journal of Retailing* 56 (1980), 75. The fines collected must represent a minuscule fraction of the officers' salaries, which are also paid for the time spent in court for the usual nonappearances.

41. Thanks to Robert Dane'el for close observation and thick description, March 21, 1996. A form letter contains the information about proper decorum. Political scientists might well extend the obsession with electoral "exit polls" to polling people about their courtroom experiences.

42. Interview with home occupation officer, City of El Paso Public Inspection Department, spring 1995. I perused lists and made counts, thanks to the city's open administration. In "Local Zoning Ordinances Governing Home Occupations," JoAnn C. Butler reviews responses from 60 percent of 1,100 local planning agencies. She concludes that individual property owners' interests surpass those of home–based businesses that generate employment in residential zones. In *The New Era of Home-Based Work: Directions and Policies*, ed. Kathleen E. Christensen (Boulder: Westview, 1988), 189–200.

43. Thanks to Larry White for this independent research paper, University of Texas at El Paso, 1991.

44. Regional Social Security Office staff member, interviewed by the author, spring 1996.

45. David Crowder, "From New Toilets to Fences, City Requires Permits," *El Paso Times* May 30, 1995.

46. The following section is highly condensed from Staudt, "Struggles."

47. Interviewed by Beatriz Vera in Juárez, April 1993, he prefaced his comments with the remark that he probably should not be saying these things, so we do not even identify his position here. Actually, his point is obvious to many observers at the border.

48. James Q. Wilson, *Bureaucracy* (New York: Basic Books, 1989), 309–10.

49. Jeffery Berry, *The Rebirth of Urban Democracy* (Washington, D.C.: Brookings, 1993), analyzes fifteen cities with neighborhood organizations, many of them organized from the top down. El Paso has neither top-down nor many bottom-up organizations.

50. See various works by Steve Balkin, including *Self-Employment for Low-Income People* (New York: Praeger, 1989), and Alfonso Morales, "The Value of Benefits of a Public Street Market: The Case of Maxwell Street," *Economic Development Quarterly* 9 (1995), 304–30.

Chapter 8

1. Pierre Vilar is cited in Peter Sahlins, *Boundaries: The Making of France and Spain in the Pyrenees* (Berkeley: University of California Press, 1989), xv.

2. Frank Bean et al., *Illegal Mexican Migration and the United States/ Mexico Border: The Effects of Operation Hold the Line on El Paso/Juárez,* report prepared for CIR, July 15, 1994. Also see Pablo Vila, *Everyday Life, Culture and Identity on the Mexican-American Border: The Ciudad Juárez–El Paso Case* (Ph.D. diss., University of Texas at Austin, 1994; Austin: University of Texas Press, forthcoming), epilogue, and Cheryl Howard, Irma Carrillo, and Sylvia Peregrino, "Operation Blockade: A Tale of Two Cities," presented at the Western Social Science Association, Albuquerque, April 22, 1994. Also see American Friends Service Committee, Immigration Law Enforcement Monitoring Project, *Operation Blockade: A City Divided* (Philadelphia: AFSC, 1994).

3. I was honored to be asked to provide the academic testimony at these hearings on March 17, 1994. It was like talking to a brick wall, however, for commissioners had their own agendas, from the lone Hispanic, an opponent of immigration, to the advocate of border-crossing fees.

4. U.S. Commission on Immigration Reform, *U.S. Immigration Policy: Restoring Credibility* (Washington, D.C.: CIR, 1994), 13.

5. The post-NAFTA literature has dwindled, a striking contrast to the pre-NAFTA hype. Manuel Pastor, Jr., calls the latter a "virtual cottage industry" in "Mexican Trade Liberalization and NAFTA," *Latin American Research Review* 29 (1994), 154. Pastor says gains and losses are hard to separate from the effects of Mexico's mid-1980s trade liberalization, but concedes one "unsettling point: most economists are estimating that

NAFTA will produce only small gains in social welfare or well being even as they understate the labor adjustment and other transition issues"(p. 165). But also see the more recent *NAFTA As a Model of Development: The Benefits and Costs of Merging High- and Low-Wage Areas*, ed. Richard Belous and Jonathan Lemco (Albany: SUNY Press, 1995).

Added paperwork and staff are required under NAFTA, with its daunting "two phone-book sized volumes." See Allen Myerson, "Under the Free Trade Pact, Snarls on the Mexican Border," *New York Times*, June 21, 1994. James R. Giermanski analyzes transport and shipping snarls in "Texas to Mexico: A Border to Avoid," *Journal of Borderlands Studies* 10, no. 2 (1995), 33–52.

6. World Bank, *World Development Report* (Washington, D.C.: World Bank, 1991), 107. Also Pastor, "Mexican Trade Liberalization."

7. Timothy J. Dunn, *The Militarization of the U.S.–Mexico Border, 1978–1992: Low-Intensity Conflict Doctrine Comes Home* (Austin: Center for Mexican American Studies, University of Texas, 1996), 41.

8. Cindy Ramírez, "4,000 Swear Oath of U.S. Citizenship," *El Paso Times*, July 4, 1996. Ramírez cites the fifty-year *veterana*, but the household surveys also confirmed surprising numbers living in citizenship limbo for thirty or more years. The University of Texas at El Paso lent its Special Events Center for this ceremony.

9. Alicia Castellanos Gerrero, *Ciudad Juárez: La Vida Fronteriza* (Mexico City: Nuestro Tiempo, 1980), 191.

10. Regina Austin, "'The Black Community,' its Lawbreakers, and a Politics of Identification," *Southern California Law Review* 65 (1992), 1774.

11. Ibid., 1786.

12. Roy W. Bahl and Johannes F. Linn, *Urban Public Finance in Developing Countries* (New York: Oxford, 1992), 210, 237.

13. Ricardo Grinspun and Robert Kreklewich, "Consolidating Neoliberal Reforms: 'Free Trade' as a Conditioning Framework," *Studies in Political Economy* 43 (1994), 33–61.

14. Lora Jo Foo, in "The Vulnerable and Exploitable Immigrant Workforce and the Need for Strengthening Worker Protective Legislation," *Yale Law Journal* 103 (1994), 2184, discusses penalties and formidable potential fines for unscrupulous employers, but actual fines that are too small to deter exploitative behavior.

15. El Paso Mayor Larry Francis, perhaps taking cue from the noble and courageous stands of the late municipal president Francisco Villarreal, threatened to close international bridges in September 1996 because of the costs of inspection and maintenance. His action was widely reported in the local media on both sides of the border. Municipal President Ramón Galindo supported this move. The old adage "Private risk, public gain" often seems reversed at the border.

Index

voting, 24, 26, 27, 51, 118, 119, 120, 124, 126–27, 131, 140, 153, 166

wage gaps, 21, 31, 60, 69, 75, 78, 160–61, 163, 189n. 10 (*see also* poverty)
wages, minimum, 36, 40, 60, 61, 75, 81
Ward, Peter, 9, 38, 124
water, 46, 112–14, 127–31, 197n. 1
Weber, David, 33

Weber, Max, 13
welfare, 22, 82–84, 122, 129–30, 141
Wilson, James Q., 119
women, 19, 21, 27, 32–33, 36, 38, 74, 75–76, 77–78, 83; leaders, 27, 52, 78, 123, 125, 129, 131, 135, 136–42, 164, 165, 170, 200n. 24, 200n. 26 (*see also* FEMAP, gender)
World Bank, 106, 121, 148

Yiftachel, Oren, 13